H LITTLE INFORMATION RIGHT BEFORE AN ELECTION. IN FACT, IT'S

.".—HILLARY CLINTON, FORMER SECRETARY OF STATE ▶ "WHAT WE

VE SHOULD ALL REMIND OURSELVES THAT WHAT'S UNPRECEDENTED

E FIRST PLACE."—KELLYANNE CONWAY, TRUMP CAMPAIGN MANAGER

T IS UNPRECEDENTED FOR A SITTING FIRST LADY TO BE SO ACTIVELY

T WHAT IS ALSO TRUE IS THAT THIS IS TRULY AN UNPRECEDENTED

T LADY ▶ "REPUBLICANS ARE ACTUALLY OUTVOTING DEMOCRATS IN

NPRECEDENTED."—NEWT GINGRICH, 50TH SPEAKER OF THE UNITED

. THERE ARE SO MANY PRESIDENTIAL CANDIDATES BECAUSE THIS

PREY, NEW HAMPSHIRE REPUBLICAN NATIONAL COMMITTEEMAN

UNPRECEDENTED

★ THE ELECTION THAT CHANGED EVERYTHING ★

UNPRECEDENTED

★ THE ELECTION THAT CHANGED EVERYTHING ★

BY **THOMAS LAKE** | EDITED BY **JODI ENDA**

WITH A FOREWORD BY **JAKE TAPPER** AND AN

INTRODUCTION BY **DOUGLAS BRINKLEY**

Produced and published by

 **MELCHER
MEDIA**

124 West 13th Street
New York, NY 10011
www.melcher.com

10 9 8 7 6 5 4 3 2

Printed in the United States of America

LC# or CIP Data

ISBN 978-1-59591-096-7

First Edition

"We will make America strong again.
We will make America proud again.
We will make America safe again.
And we will make America great again."

TABLE OF CONTENTS

FOREW

I t was within the first few minutes of the second Republican debate in September 2015 that I knew Donald Trump would be the nominee.

He had already been rising in the polls, an ascension built on a solid foundation of populist positioning: first and foremost, the notion that Washington is broken and out of touch with the voters the government is supposed to be serving. On that premise, he built his pitches that politicians are pushing trade deals sending American jobs abroad, insufficiently protecting our borders and not doing enough to keep terrorism out of the U.S.

The potential problem for Trump seemed that his campaign was wrapped in language and behavior that was nativist, bombastic and offensive to too many voters. At first, however, it was mostly all upside for him. Trump had entered the race in June 2015, and by August had shot to the top of the polls. His temperament was an obvious potential weakness—he seemed to have no filter at all, whether he was attacking Mexican immigrants or seeming to suggest that a female TV anchor was tough on him because she was menstruating. His fans loved it; those sensitive to bigotry and misogyny, not so much.

On September 16, 2015, at a CNN debate in the Ronald Reagan Presidential Library and Center for Public Affairs in Simi Valley, California, the very first question I asked his GOP rival, Carly Fiorina, was whether she would "feel comfortable with Donald Trump's finger on the nuclear codes."

Fiorina would later say that Trump "horrified" her. But for some reason at this moment, in the second-most-viewed primary debate, she dodged, saying only that "one of the benefits of a presidential campaign is the character and capability, judgment and temperament of every single one of us is revealed over time and under pressure. All of us will be revealed over time and under pressure."

You didn't answer my question, I noted, repeating it.

"That's not for me to answer; it is for the voters of this country to answer, and I have a lot of faith in the common sense and good judgment of the voters of the United States of America," she said.

Fiorina, the only woman among the eleven GOP nominees onstage, finished her statement. The audience, comprised of well-heeled GOP donors, was more subdued than the one at the raucous Fox News debate held a month earlier in the same arena where the Cleveland Cavaliers

ORD

BY JAKE TAPPER

Anchor, CNN's "The Lead With Jake Tapper" & "State of the Union," and Chief Washington Correspondent

play basketball. I turned to Mr. Trump to offer him a chance to respond.

"Well, first of all, Rand Paul shouldn't even be on this stage," Trump said. "He's number eleven, he's got 1 percent in the polls, and how he got up here, there's far too many people anyway."

It was an undisciplined way to start, characteristically, as well as being inaccurate. (New Jersey Gov. Chris Christie was actually the last of these eleven in the polls and would have been the first cut from the main debate stage. Four lower-polling candidates participated in a separate debate.)

I then threw the same question about Trump's temperament to former Florida Gov. Jeb Bush. He, too, whiffed.

If they're not willing to take him on in any serious way, I thought to myself, they don't understand what they're dealing with here. From that moment on, I was confident none of Trump's rivals was willing or able to stop him. Whether they were afraid to criticize his vulnerabilities in an effective and robust way, or had made the strategic determination that someone else would need to take him out, it was clear that none of his GOP rivals was willing to go there until it was too late.

Hillary Clinton, in fact, was the very first candidate in either party to go after Trump after he descended the escalator in Trump Tower and announced his candidacy. But as the election continued and Trump struggled with his share of problems, the also-unpopular Clinton faced issues that turned out to be more troubling to her voters in battleground states than his issues were to those who eventually boarded the Trump Train.

> **If they're not willing to take him on in any serious way, I thought to myself, they don't understand what they're dealing with here. From that moment on, I was confident none of Trump's rivals was willing or able to stop him.**

Most campaigns are spent with rivals trying to define the other in the least flattering light. Clinton came pre-caricatured: the consummate Washington insider who thought the rules didn't apply to her. The March 2, 2015, New York Times story revealing her use of a private email server while secretary of state surprised even Clinton's top advisers, the ones who had devoted their lives to electing the first woman president.

The private email server and issues surrounding it were known to Clinton's inner circle of longtime loyalists, people such as her former State Department chief of staff Cheryl Mills and her top aide Huma Abedin.

It was not known to the extent it needed to be to her campaign chairman, John Podesta, and her campaign manager, Robby Mook. We learned how little those campaign leaders knew in the closing weeks of the campaign, when WikiLeaks released a bevy of internal emails that U.S. intelligence services said were stolen by Russian hackers, a sort of in-kind contribution to the Trump campaign from Vladimir Putin.

"Did you have any idea of the depth of this story?" Podesta emailed Mook in March 2015.

"Nope," responded Mook. "We brought up the existence of emails in research this summer but were told that everything was taken care of."

CNN's Jake Tapper interviews Donald Trump on June 3, 2016. Trump doubled down on his criticism of Hillary Clinton and the judge presiding over the Trump University case.

It wasn't. Clinton's server skirted record retention rules set by the Federal Records Act. Moreover, Thomas S. Blanton, the director of the National Security Archive, told the Times, "personal emails are not secure. Senior officials should not be using them."

Clinton would later claim she kept her pre-State Department email address and server out of convenience, but others thought Clinton—burned by the many 1990s Clinton White House scandals—likely wanted control over her records.

The damage to her campaign was incalculable. But her top advisers knew it was a problem.

"Speaking of transparency," Podesta wrote to longtime Clinton adviser Neera Tanden, "our friends Kendall, Cheryl and Philippe sure weren't forthcoming on the facts here." Podesta was clearly frustrated that the Clintons' attorney David Kendall, Mills and longtime aide Phillipe Reines hadn't shared with them all the information they needed to best prepare for the presidential campaign.

"This is a cheryl special," Tanden replied. "Know you love her, but this stuff is like her Achilles heal. Or kryptonite. she just can't say no to this shit."

And then, ascribing to the first rule of political scandal —get it all out on your own terms as soon as possible— Tanden asked: "Why didn't they get this stuff out like 18 months ago? So crazy."

"Unbelievable," agreed Podesta.

"i guess I know the answer," Tanden said. "they wanted to get away with it."

By July 2015, the inspectors general of the Office of the Director of National Intelligence and the U.S. State Department asked the Department of Justice to probe what information was transmitted on her unclassified server. A sample of forty emails from Clinton's private server should "never have been transmitted via an unclassified personal system," they wrote, given that they "contained classified information."

The inspectors general noted that "none of the emails we reviewed had classification or dissemination markings," but regardless, some "should have been handled as classified, appropriately marked, and transmitted via a secure network."

Tanden asked Podesta: "Do we actually know who told Hillary she could use a private email? And has that person been drawn and quartered? Like whole thing is fucking insane."

Indeed.

Clinton's Democratic primary rivals were loathe to prosecute Clinton when it came to the private server. Indeed, at the CNN Democratic debate in October 2015, more than a year before the election, Clinton's chief primary rival, Sen. Bernie Sanders of Vermont, said that "the American people are sick and tired of hearing about your damn emails." Clinton loved it, the Democratic crowd ate it up and from then on the only ones bringing up the issue with Clinton during the primaries were journalists.

In March, on CNN's "State of the Union," I asked Clinton if she had been interviewed yet by the FBI. It seemed a fairly innocuous question at the time, but her starkly terse one-word answer—"No"—and the angry response from her campaign afterward suggested that there was little understanding about how important transparency on this issue would be if she wanted to put it behind her. Indeed, she and her campaign pursued a line of falsehoods and obfuscation that kept the issue alive.

In July, FBI Director James Comey cleared Clinton of any wrongdoing that he thought could credibly merit a criminal charge, though he made a strong case that Clinton and her team had been "extremely careless" in their handling of classified information. Trump talked about the issue quite a bit, calling his opponent "Crooked Hillary." But with so many voters worried about Trump's temperament and qualifications, the FBI's conclusion seemed to place the issue firmly alongside so many previous Clinton scandals: ugly, but not criminal.

Privately, Democrats inside and outside her campaign fretted about issues that might have been behind the personal email server. If in 2001, when then–Sen. Hillary Clinton began her career in elected office, the Clintons had known she might pursue a presidential campaign, why had they simultaneously sought to enrich themselves by hundreds of millions of dollars? Why had they violated their pledge to not take donations from certain foreign countries for the Clinton Foundation while she was secretary of state or to maintain a rigid and strong enough firewall between the foundation and her State Department? But there was an election to win and issues greater than these, they thought, so they tried to stay focused and fight the good fight. Trump was waging a campaign that nakedly appealed to white supremacists, one that made Muslims, *Lie!*

> ## The angry response from her campaign afterward suggested that there was little understanding about how important transparency on this issue would be if she wanted to put it behind her.

Latinos and the disabled feel like second-class citizens; surely her email server was nothing compared to this hatred he was fomenting.

In early October, The Washington Post's David Farenthold broke the news of a 2005 conversation Trump had with an "Access Hollywood" anchor in which he seemed to be boasting of the various ways he could grab women by their private parts and get away with it because he was a star. His poll numbers began to tank, and by the end of the month Trump seemed to be imploding, starting with a speech at Gettysburg in which he threatened to sue the dozen or so women who had surfaced to accuse him of sexual assault or misconduct. Clinton seemed to be in such a commanding position in the polls that her campaign was discussing investments in traditionally red states such as Missouri, Georgia and Arizona. Trump's weakness with Mormon voters was even putting Utah in play. Many voters were excited about the glass ceiling Clinton was about to shatter. Her favorability ratings grew.

Then came Anthony Weiner.

The disgraced former congressman was married to Clinton's top aide, Huma Abedin, though she had left him just two months before. His time in Congress ended in 2011 after he accidentally sent an explicit photograph of his penis to the world via Twitter. More evidence of nasty extramarital social media interactions followed, as did his resignation from Congress after seven terms. A comeback New York City mayoral bid in 2013, chronicled in a documentary entitled "Weiner," ended when a soon-to-be

> **Too many of her voters in states that mattered were sufficiently uninspired, so they didn't vote. And in those same states, his voters— motivated, excited, sick of the elites—showed that those densely packed rallies mattered. They were inspired. They turned out.**

porn actress named Sydney Leathers came forward with evidence that Weiner had continued his escapades using the nom de guerre Carlos Danger. Abedin stuck with him through it all, and more, until August 2016, when the Daily Mail reported that he'd been sending inappropriate messages to a 15-year-old girl.

Russian playwright Anton Chekhov noted that one shouldn't introduce a gun in the first act unless one intends to have it go off by the third. By October 28, 2016, we were in Act III. And Carlos Danger was Chekhov's gun.

While investigating Weiner for the allegations surrounding the underage girl, FBI agents discovered thousands of Abedin's State Department emails on his laptop. Suddenly Comey's sworn testimony to Congress that the FBI had completed its review of all the evidence in the Clinton email case was no longer true. "In connection with an unrelated case, the FBI has learned of the existence of emails that appear to be pertinent to the investigation," he wrote congressional leaders just eleven days before the election. "Although the FBI cannot yet assess whether or not this material may be significant, and I cannot predict how long it will take us to complete this additional work, I believe it is important to update you."

It was as if Comey had thrown a lifeline to a drowning Trump and an anvil to Clinton. Trump had always been the candidate of change, but both he and Clinton had done their darnedest to make him seem like a scary kind of change. Now, amazingly, enough voters had a change of heart.

On the Sunday before the election, Comey announced that the newly discovered emails had been reviewed and the July conclusion stood. Clinton was in the clear.

Two days later, voters elected a candidate that exit polls showed was overwhelmingly considered untrustworthy and unqualified.

Elections are rarely about one specific event. The outcomes don't usually have a single explanation—indeed, as of this writing, Clinton seemed destined to win the popular vote but lose the electoral vote. And with Trump failing to win many more votes than did Mitt Romney in 2012 or John McCain in 2008, this election seemed more her failure in battleground states than anything else. But that said, these are the rules, and Trump convinced wide swaths of white working-class America that he got it, that he heard them, that he would be their champion. Preliminary exit polls suggested that he ended up winning white working-class voters by a wider margin than even Ronald Reagan. He carried white working-class women by a two-to-one margin. Clinton, for whatever her strengths, was never a particularly inspiring politician and failed to bring the Obama coalition to the polls. She was the status quo in an election in which voters wanted change.

To a plurality of voters nationwide, her flaws were nothing compared with Trump's. But too many of her voters in states that mattered were sufficiently uninspired, so they didn't vote. And in those same states, his voters— motivated, excited, sick of the elites—showed that those densely packed rallies mattered. They were inspired. They turned out.

As the results started coming in the night of November 8, it was hard not to conclude that enough voters in the right states, faced with the choice of someone who was *of* Washington in every possible way, including the bad ones, and someone of wild temperament who was promising to take a flamethrower to it, opted to burn it all down.

INTRODU

As I sat atop the High Roller Ferris wheel and looked down at the blinking expanse of casino-driven Las Vegas, the 2016 presidential election, for the first time, made sense to me. It was just past dusk, shortly after Hillary Clinton and Donald Trump finished debating, and a wave of clarity swept over me: Las Vegas was the new Washington. The fake Eiffel Tower was the new Washington Monument; Cirque du Soleil had replaced the Kennedy Center for Performing Arts as a premier entertainment showcase. No longer did the U.S. celebrate war heroes like Theodore Roosevelt or Dwight Eisenhower, but we had made a national fetish of celebrities for celebrity's sake. If Andy Warhol had been alive in the 1990s, he would have made pop art portraits of Clinton and Trump.

The main game in the 2016 presidential sweepstakes was to not let your cherished brand get tarnished more than that of your opponent. Character demolition was the modus operandi of both the Clinton and Trump camps. With blazing lights, bling, whistles and razzmatazz, the square-off was indeed the Greatest Show on Earth. Central casting had a P. T. Barnumesque lead figure in Trump and an avenging Joan of Arc in Clinton. In a country where elaborately choreographed Super Bowl halftime shows have become the new moon shot, where Ivy League excellence has been run roughshod over by Jerry Springerism and where facts are less important than drama, the comingling of Las Vegas and official Washington was inevitable. The race to the White House, in fact, played out in the garish manner of a Vegas extravaganza rather than the wonkfest of the 1960 Kennedy-Nixon debate. In 2016, voters were offered a ceaseless wasteland of unfiltered WikiLeaks, 3 a.m. tweets and a behind-the-scenes "Access Hollywood" video. Every waking second of the candidates' campaign was a hot microphone moment ad nauseum. The Trump-Clinton match wasn't a heavyweight championship fight. It was an overproduced race to the gutter. The main fascination of the election was monitoring how low the performer and the avenger could go—and who would end up as the villain.

Throughout the 2016 race, I kept reminding myself that other U.S. presidential elections had been equally contentious. In 1860, Republican Abraham Lincoln, a

Opposite: **Debate signage adorns the facade of the Venetian Hotel in Las Vegas, the site of the fifth Republican debate, which was hosted by CNN on December 15, 2015.**

CTION

BY DOUGLAS BRINKLEY
CNN Presidential Historian

> **It was just past dusk, shortly after Hillary Clinton and Donald Trump finished debating, and a wave of clarity swept over me: Las Vegas was the new Washington.**

die-hard opponent of slavery, wasn't even on the ballot in many Southern states. Talk about not having a clear mandate—Lincoln won that election with only 40 percent of the popular vote. Shortly after he was inaugurated, South Carolina voted to secede. Other Southern states followed suit and the Civil War ensued.

More recently, the 2000 election was a crazy humdinger that ended up being decided by a 5–4 decision in the U.S. Supreme Court. In a hard-fought race between Democrat Al Gore and Republican George W. Bush, it all boiled down to Florida. Bush was declared the winner more than a month after Election Day, following a blaze of lawsuits and recounts. But the damage was done. It took many Democrats years to accept Bush as the legitimate president.

The 2016 circus actually started in late 2014, almost as soon as the confetti was swept up from that year's midterm election. With the GOP suddenly in control of the Senate and the House, the jockeying for the White House began. At the Bush family's Thanksgiving dinner table, Topic A was "the future of our nation," according to Jeb Bush, the latest member of the Republican clan to express a desire to represent that future. His father, George H.W. Bush, and his brother George W. Bush had been the 41st and 43rd presidents, respectively. Aiming to be the 45th, "Jeb!" became the first person to announce his ambitions to the public, on December 17, 2014. The former Florida governor already had been quietly contacting and corralling big-time donors in an effort to lock up the wealthy Republicans who supported Mitt Romney in 2012 and stave off potential challengers.

With a bankroll in the tens of millions, a galaxy of establishment Republicans on his side and name recognition in the stratosphere, Bush hoped to knock off rumored rivals such as New Jersey Gov. Chris Christie, former Texas Gov. Rick Perry and Sen. Rand Paul of Tennessee.

Only one person in either party could match Bush in donor power, party support and name recognition. Hillary Clinton had been a partner to her husband, Bill, on many issues when he was in the White House. After serving as a senator from New York, she was primed for a presidential run in 2008, only to lose the Democratic nomination to Barack Obama, the high-profile senator from Illinois. When she lost, Clinton's political future was uncertain until President Obama named her as his secretary of state—a move that tacitly cleared the way for her to take a shot at succeeding him. And after she retired from the State Department at the beginning of 2013, Clinton was understood to be laying the groundwork for a second run for the presidency.

A Bush-Clinton match in 2016 seemed preordained. Only one presidential race since 1980 had been without at least one of these family names. With Obama's unspoken blessing and Vice President Joe Biden's decision to forgo a run, the Democratic nomination seemed to be Clinton's for the taking. On the Republican side, however, candidates by the dozen maneuvered toward a run.

Ignoring Bush's massive campaign war chest—well on its way to an unheard of $114 million by mid-2015—twenty-one Republicans floated their names. Sixteen eventually would file papers, making for the most crowded field in modern political history. With Sens. Ted Cruz of Texas and Marco Rubio of Florida announcing their candidacies on Twitter, the campaign was well grounded in social media, at least on the Republican side. On April 12, Clinton made her own long-awaited announcement, but not in a mere 140 characters. The 900-pound gorilla of the 2016 race, she released a fully produced video on her website and other platforms, underscoring her point that she was ready to lead the country. If she were to win, she would be the first woman president. Aside from placing her roles as a mother and grandmother among her credentials, she neither ran from that prospect, as she had in 2008, nor traded on it.

The pitfall in the Clinton candidacy was the uncertainty surrounding a private email system that she had gone to some trouble to install during her years as secretary of state. The appearance of elitism and the possible misuse of the office infuriated those opposed to her. On an official level, her campaign was dogged by congressional and FBI investigations.

Focused on the Republicans, Clinton expected only token competition in the Democratic primaries and didn't seem at all intimidated by those who stepped up: Vermont Sen. Bernie Sanders, former Maryland Gov. Martin O'Malley, former Virginia Sen. Jim Webb and former Rhode Island Gov. Lincoln Chafee.

Meanwhile, announcements from Republican candidates came in a torrent; among them were Sens. Ted Cruz, Marco Rubio, Lindsey Graham of South Carolina and Rand Paul; former Sen. Rick Santorum; businesswoman Carly Fiorina; retired neurosurgeon Ben Carson; and a flock of governors—Wisconsin's Scott Walker, New Jersey's Chris Christie, Louisiana's Bobby Jindal and Ohio's John Kasich—and former governors, including Bush, George Pataki of New York, Rick Perry of Texas, Mike Huckabee of Arkansas and Jim Gilmore of Virginia. The one that was accorded the least weight, initially, was that of real estate developer Donald Trump, who had been in and out of myriad business ventures over the years while hovering on the sidelines of politics. At times, he had aligned himself with the Democrats, but on June 16, he announced his entry into the Republican race during a speech at New York's glitzy Trump Tower. Pundits who didn't take him seriously were expecting the outright bragging that comprised much of his announcement, but many across the nation were shocked by his comments on immigration, especially the characterization that Mexico was "sending people that have lots of problems….They're bringing drugs. They're bringing crime. They're rapists. And some, I assume, are good people." Americans just weren't used to such blunt, bigoted language from candidates for president. It was generally assumed that Trump's candidacy had fizzled at the start.

Trump's course didn't collapse, though. In fact, he gained support and rapidly rose in the polls. In July, he unleashed a head-on verbal assault on John McCain, the Arizona senator who had been the Republican standard-bearer in 2008. As a young man, McCain had served in Vietnam and he'd subsequently persevered through five-and-a-half torturous years as a prisoner of war. Trump, who had avoided the armed services, said of McCain: "He's not a war hero. He's a war hero because he was captured. I like people who weren't captured." Observers predicted that Republicans would turn on Trump en masse. Some did, but many others were drawn to his unfiltered talk, even when it was directed at the sacrifices of a veteran.

Republican candidates struggled to learn the new game of politics as practiced by Trump, in which social media barbs and bombastic talk led the way to victory. Voters quickly came to expect a daily, if not hourly, barrage of intriguing jabs. Candidates of the old school who sought to comport themselves with dignity and predictability looked dizzy as they realized that they'd misread the zeitgeist in the summer of 2015.

Clinton had her own thorny problems over the summer. Sanders' grassroots campaign caught fire, with a combination of massive rallies and the deft use of Internet fundraising, at a humble average of $27 per donation. Railing against Wall Street greed and raising the alarm against global warming, Sanders exhibited a passion for his policy issues that the former secretary of state seemed to keep under wraps. While Clinton didn't draw the high-octane "yuge" (as Trump would say) crowds of Sanders, she was dedicated to behind-the-scenes political organizing on a level unmatched by any other candidate.

As the first debates approached, the race was not only jutting into new territory, it was doing so in multidimensional ways. Many Democratic voters did not identify on the old political spectrum of liberal to conservative. Voters were looking for a candidate who would break with the status quo. In the odd realignment, Clinton, who was making the strongest bid in American history to become the

A Bush-Clinton match in 2016 seemed preordained. Only one presidential race since 1980 had been without at least one of these family names.

first female president, was perceived as old school. She was facile in Internet platforms, but she wasn't genuine the way Sanders was in his posts on Facebook and she wasn't provocative the way Trump was in mastering the Twittersphere. Clinton's legion of followers, though, gave her a 31 percent lead over Sanders in December. She was well situated, but there was a long way to go.

Republican debates were punctuated by Trump's name-calling and hectoring, as he characterized his fellow candidates and even the moderators in coarse, even prurient terms that included references to the size of male sex organs and women's menstrual cycles. It was new for a candidate in an American presidential race to act with such bullying disrespect. In the past, surrogates quite often said off-color things or spread rumors—at the behest of a candidate—but candidates themselves usually tried to stay above the fray. For the person seeking the highest office to behave that way embarrassed many, but Trump's repudiation of political correctness excited enough voters to give the New York businessman a steady lead in most opinion polls through the end of 2015.

The Democratic race, surprisingly enough, was getting close, too. Sanders surpassed Clinton in fundraising. He attacked her for having close ties with Wall Street and the 1 percent, rich people who he said kept getting richer while other Americans struggled. For her part, Clinton aligned herself with Obama, whose presidency she continually praised for reviving the economy and creating overall stability. The unemployment rate was less than half what it had been when the Democrats took over the White House. If that was the status quo, Clinton was willing to inhabit the moniker.

> ## The atmosphere in her campaign was far more akin to the GOP of old—the cloth-coat Republicans who stayed in line and reveled in their constructive dullness.

At the same time, Sanders rose above the temptation to join Republicans in calling into question her previous use of a private email server. In what amounted to a campaign gift, actually intended to reflect Sanders's interest in more pressing issues, he told her in a debate that "the American people are sick and tired of hearing about your damn emails." Sanders positioned himself as a revolutionary—the defender of working people—and drew millions of followers with his own, low-grade version of the New Deal to extend prosperity to all parts of the economy.

If the Democratic race rumbled with discontent, the Republican contest exploded with it, almost continually. False charges abounded, as many of the candidates scrapped for attention in airtime and headlines. As the first caucus approached in Iowa on February 1, 2016, Ted Cruz found the need to defend himself against Trump's insinuations that he was not eligible to be president because he was born in Canada. (His mother was American, making his campaign legitimate.) On the offensive, Cruz accused Trump of representing "New York values." A wave of publicity, combined with a solid ground organization, brought Cruz first prize with a victory in Iowa. Clinton beat Sanders by a narrow margin. Nationally, Sanders had turned the race into a statistical dead heat. Both he and Trump won in New Hampshire. When Trump went on to win South Carolina, a number of Republican candidates fell away—including the onetime favorite of the establishment, Jeb Bush.

As the primary season continued, Cruz and Rubio tried actively to block Trump's path; oddly enough, in doing so, they gave him a path to victory. Splitting much of the anti-Trump vote, they allowed him to win state after state with barely more than a third of the votes. Establishment Republicans practically pulled their hair out; in horror, they disavowed him, none more staunchly than 2012 standard-bearer Mitt Romney.

A lot had happened to the Republican Party since its founding just before the Civil War, including a shift in the early twentieth century from the generally more liberal of the two major parties to the more conservative, states-rights one. That change and more subtle realignments were decades in the making. With the ascendancy of Trump, though, the future of the Grand Old Party was changing in the span of mere months. The chasm was wide on many issues, but nowhere was it more dramatic than on foreign

policy. Trump advocated a harsh look at relations with longtime European allies, even entertaining the idea of dissolving NATO and allowing Japan to have nuclear weapons. At the same time, he suggested a softer approach to longtime adversary Russia and its leader, Vladimir Putin. That stance alone indicated a clean break with the party of Ronald Reagan. Romney called the campaign "a contest between Trumpism and Republicanism."

For the moment, Trumpism won. With primary wins in early May, Donald Trump's remaining rivals bowed out. Nonetheless, in a campaign like no other, Republicans who were still in shock actively probed ways to deny him the nomination. By June, Clinton was also alone in her race; Sanders dropped out while urging his followers to stay together in the newly organized progressive group, Our Revolution. The fear in the Clinton camp was that Sanders might then support a third-party candidate. After weeks of harried negotiation, Sanders elicited guarantees

that Clinton would fight for aspects of his liberal agenda. With that, he threw his support to the presumptive nominee. On the same day, July 12, the Clinton campaign had another piece of good news in FBI Director James Comey's announcement that he would not recommend the Justice Department prosecute Clinton for using a private email server.

Both Trump and Clinton were controversial as personalities. In previous elections, issues and party loyalties were the prime drivers of voter preference. For those not swayed by those criteria, candidates themselves usually offered the final pull—in a positive sense. A voter, in the end, chose the person he or she liked. In 2016, voters didn't like either candidate all that much. In polls, both elicited far more negative response than positive. Voters sometimes based their decisions on which candidate they loathed, almost voting for his or her opponent by default. That scenario invited the potential for third-party

candidates, but the two who came to the fore lacked the needed charisma and name recognition to gain steam. Former New Mexico Gov. Gary Johnson, running on the Libertarian line, stumbled badly in his grasp of foreign affairs, while Jill Stein, a retired Massachusetts physician who ran on the Green Party ticket, was uncompromising in her stands, limiting her to only the most liberal support.

One major area of suspense was which Republican elected officials would back Trump as their party's nominee. In stark contrast to previous elections, many disavowed him. Such a thing would have been political suicide in any typical scenario, but in 2016 nothing was typical. Other officials felt their way along an uncomfortable middle path. House Majority Leader Paul Ryan said he would vote for Trump, but acknowledged that the nominee had made statements that were racist. Former President George H.W. Bush was reported to be voting for

Clinton, and there was speculation that George W. Bush would as well. Former Secretary of State Colin Powell, along with California GOP stalwart Meg Whitman and a host of the party's elder statesmen openly endorsed the Democrat. Trump was unconcerned. Turning back centuries of American politics, he relished his role as a loose cannon who included the Republican Party on his list of what was wrong with America.

Clinton had the opposite attitude, planting herself unshakably in the midst of party regulars. Person by person, precinct captain by committee chair, she had turned the Democrats into a coordinated force. She built upon those centuries of old-fashioned political loyalty, just as she built upon Obama's record during the previous eight years and her husband's during the prosperous 1990s. The atmosphere in her campaign was far more akin to the GOP of old—the cloth-coat Republicans who stayed in line and reveled in their constructive dullness. Trump, on the other hand, presided over a chaotic Republican Party that, in its own way, was reminiscent of Will Rogers' famous remark, "I don't belong to any organized political party—I'm a Democrat." Under Trump, the Republican Party was not just disheveled, it appeared to be on the verge of dismantling itself.

By summer, the expectation was that Trump, with the nomination in hand, would "pivot" to a more traditional campaign. In fact, "pivot" was one of the most overused words of 2016. According to party graybeards, Trump was supposed to transform himself overnight from a loose, brazen orator to something more in keeping with political standards. He was to present a "presidential" bearing, calmly discussing issues and leaving petty controversies behind. The pivot never occurred. Trump clung to the style that won him the nomination. By early autumn, Ryan and other party leaders refused to appear with him. Perhaps that suited his one-man-against-the-world political strategy. Clinton stayed the course. A more predictable speaker, to be sure, she frequently was assisted by her party's heavyweights, including the president, vice president, Sanders and the popular first lady, Michelle Obama.

In the last month of the campaign, Clinton's support swelled to the point that she and her surrogates had the luxury of focusing on a second goal: winning a majority in the Senate. At the same time, Trump hit a new low with the release of a 2005 video in which he boasted of forcing himself on women and claimed that his celebrity empowered him to do so. His attitude toward women had been an issue throughout his campaign, with frequent evidence that, in at least some respects, he was still the playboy of his younger years who couldn't stop himself from objectifying them.

Clinton also was haunted late in the campaign, with the release on October 27 of a new letter from FBI Director Comey announcing that the bureau was investigating a new trove of emails related to Clinton's years in the State Department. Her supporters—along with some former FBI and Justice Department officials—accused the director, a registered Republican, of violating the Justice Department's standard policy of withholding potentially influential announcements late in campaign seasons. Even George W. Bush's attorney general, Alberto Gonzales, said

> **Once the 2016 presidential campaign was over, America would struggle in 2017 to recover from the anger and distrust the race engendered. Just as the casinos never close, the story of Clinton vs. Trump will live on for years to come.**

that Comey made "an error in judgment." Clinton detractors, on the other hand, felt that word of the renewed probe had come in the nick of time. Then, two days before the election, Comey said the investigation had turned up nothing new.

On November 8, the wild ride was over. Donald Trump won. It was time to move on. But that would not be easy. Many questioned whether the long, contentious campaign was good for the nation, charging that it only deepened the gaps among the populous. Inarguably, the election of 2016 reflected American society at large. The new president was, of course, a product of twenty-first-century America's hypersaturated media culture as well as the influx of billions of dollars into candidates' war chests.

What I realized from my Ferris wheel perspective was that once the 2016 presidential campaign was over, America would struggle in 2017 to recover from the anger and distrust the race engendered. Just as the casinos never close, the story of Clinton vs. Trump will live on for years to come. Even in the nation known for the longest political campaigns in the world, America's 2016 presidential race was a whopper—nearly two years of drama and eye-popping surprises.

The battle scars are too deep to heal quickly. But after the inauguration of Trump, we'll carry on with dented pride, knowing deep in our hearts that even messy American democracy is better than no democracy at all.

1

**TWO ANGRY
MEN AND
THEIR
DISENCHANTED
ARMIES**

The essential sound of the Republican primary season was a collective roar in three syllables, a battle cry giving way to an incantation. You never knew when it might arise, just as you never knew what Donald Trump would say next, but it sometimes corresponded with violence. Trump's army made this sound in Las Vegas, when he envisioned smacking the hell out of an Iranian leader; and in Miami, when a barrel-chested vigilante hauled a protester down by the collar. Trump heard this primal chant, saw its gathering force. He leaned toward the microphone and joined in. *U-S-A! U-S-A! U-S-A!* It was loud enough to raise the dead.

The meaning of that sound had changed dramatically in fifteen years. And the story of its evolution said a lot about the political fracturing that made way for the most unorthodox major presidential candidate in modern American history.

On September 14, 2001, President George W. Bush stood on a crumpled fire truck in the wreckage of the World Trade Center, addressing rescue workers through a bullhorn.

"We can't hear you," someone yelled. The firefighters were exhausted. They'd been inhaling toxic dust all day. They had lost 343 comrades when the twin towers fell, including the driver of the truck on which the president stood, and they were losing hope that anyone else would be found alive.

"I can hear *you*," Bush said. "I can hear you, the rest of the world hears you, and the people—and the people who knocked these buildings down will hear *all* of us soon."

This would prove to be the high point of Bush's presidency. In his autobiography, "Decision Points," a picture of him in the wreckage with the bullhorn would appear just after the title page. Bush 43 had found his voice, and his cause, which boiled down to killing the bad guys before they could kill any more Americans. Now the rescuers could hear him, and they loved what they heard. They chanted: *U-S-A! U-S-A! U-S-A!*

The whole nation might as well have been chanting with them. Bush's approval rating soared to 90 percent, the highest Gallup had ever measured for any president. For a moment it all felt clear and simple, the way it had after Pearl Harbor: a war of good versus evil, with good destined to prevail. As Bush also said that day: "This nation is peaceful, but fierce when stirred to anger. This conflict was begun on the timing and terms of others. It will end in a way, and at an hour, of our choosing."

Years went by, and that hour did not arrive. Not in the caves of Tora Bora. Not with the conquest of Baghdad. Not on the aircraft carrier where Bush stood under a banner that said *MISSION ACCOMPLISHED* and declared the end of major combat operations. That hour did not arrive with rendition, or waterboarding, or secret prisons, or the atrocities of Abu Ghraib, or the deaths of many Americans whose families never knew what their blood had purchased. The conflict went on and on, and what ended instead was the moral certainty behind it, the unassailable justice of the cause. What replaced *U-S-A* was Green Day's "American Idiot," an album of protest and ridicule; and "Team America: World Police," a film that used animated puppets to lampoon Bush's military overreach. His approval rating fell steadily from 2001 to 2008, hitting 25 percent just after the economy collapsed. *U-S-A* became the sound of a colossal missed opportunity.

It came back seven years later as the sound of anger and defiance, the rebel yell of a new nationalist faction. When Trump promised to make America great again, he was not just talking about highways and factories. He was talking about the *idea* of America, the gossamer *U-S-A* that existed in the weeks after 9/11. First things first, though. It was time to tear down the House of Bush.

The Great Republican Revolt of 2015 did not really begin until mid-July, when a man who had never served in the military found he could trash a Republican war hero and suffer no political consequence.

The Great Republican Revolt of 2015 did not really begin until mid-July, when a man who had never served in the military found he could trash a Republican war hero and suffer no political consequence. But a harbinger appeared in January, when the same man walked onstage at a theater in Des Moines to inform voters at the Iowa Freedom Summit that he just might run for president. Donald Trump was still getting his act together, testing his material, frequently consulting the notes he pulled from his jacket. He got mild applause for disparaging Obamacare, moderate cheers for his promise to build a fence on the Mexican border. (In his imagination, it had yet to become a wall.) Toward the middle,

Jeb Bush was the Republican Party's early front-runner and most effective fundraiser.

when he railed against currency manipulation and collapsing bridges, the audience barely responded. Then he started talking politics, specifically who else might seek the Republican nomination, and suddenly he had their attention again.

"We have some good people," he said. "It can't be Mitt, because Mitt ran and failed. He failed."

At this pronouncement, some in the audience whooped and howled with agreement. Former Massachusetts Gov. Mitt Romney had won twenty-four states and nearly 60 million votes in 2012, and he was seriously considering another run. But six days after Trump's speech in Des Moines, Romney would say he'd reached the same conclusion: It was time to step aside and let someone else take on the Democrats.

"So you can't have Romney—he choked," Trump said. "You can't have Bush."

Here Trump had to pause for ten seconds as wild applause filled the theater. This was a conservative audience, and former Florida Gov. Jeb Bush was the party's early front-runner and most effective fundraiser. Nevertheless, "you can't have Bush" would prove to be the single most popular line of Trump's twenty-four-minute speech.

"He's very, very weak on immigration," Trump said. "Don't forget—remember his statement, 'They come for love.' Say what? They come for *love*? You've got these people coming, half of 'em are criminals. I mean, they're coming for *love*? They're coming for a lot of other reasons. And it's not love. And when he runs, you gotta remember, his brother really gave us Obama. I was never a big fan. But his brother gave us Obama, 'cause Abraham Lincoln coming back from the dead couldn't've won the election, 'cause it was going so badly, and the economy was just absolutely in shambles, that last couple of months. And *then*, he appointed Justice

Roberts. And *Jeb* wanted Justice Roberts. And Justice Roberts basically approved Obamacare, in a shocking decision that nobody believes. So you can't have Jeb Bush, and he's gonna lose, aside from that, he's not gonna win."

No one from the political establishment had reason to believe Trump. None of the experts thought he would run. But in 2015, the experts were wrong about almost everything. They thought Bush's $160 million fundraising machine would help him destroy his sixteen Republican competitors. They thought political experience was a useful selling point. They thought you couldn't be a serious candidate without a super PAC or a detailed list of policy proposals. They thought a man running for president had to treat others with a semblance of respect. Trump rewrote all the rules. In the same way that people watched Superman to imagine how it would feel to save the world, people watched Trump to imagine how it would feel to say whatever you wanted and get away with it.

A unified party could have driven him out. But Trump saw the fault lines and drove them wider. Later, Jeb Bush's allies would look back wistfully on June 15, 2015, the first official day of his candidacy, the last day party leaders had any control over the party's message. They had done the math. They knew the white vote alone could not put them back in the White House. For all his miscalculations, their last actual president had taken this to heart. George W. Bush advocated a path to citizenship for undocumented workers. He said, "Family values don't stop at the Rio Grande River." He won re-election in 2004 with as much as 44 percent of the Hispanic vote. After that number fell to 31 percent for Sen. John McCain of Arizona in 2008 and 27 percent for Romney in 2012, the Republicans knew they had to widen their tent.

And it seemed possible, at least in theory. Jeb Bush had moderate views on immigration and a Latina wife of forty-one years whom he'd met on a high-school trip to Mexico. He was revered by Florida Republicans, especially the Cubans of South Florida who could help him build a general-election coalition. "I intend to let everyone hear my message, including the many who can express their love of country in a different language," he said, and then switched to Spanish for a few words about the noble cause of the United States.

But this primary wouldn't be about welcoming Hispanic-Americans or any other minorities. It would be about the blunt force of Trump's personality. It would be about the issues he raised the next day at his own campaign kickoff, when he complained about drug dealers and rapists pouring across the Mexican border. It would come down to primal fear and raw self-interest, about voters like Patricia Messinger of Las Vegas, about the stories she told herself and others, especially the one about the restaurant job she lost and the reason she lost it, "because I'm white and 55," as she put it, and about the woman who took her job: young, Latina, undocumented, a woman Messinger did not know she was training to become her own low-cost replacement. The Patricia Messingers of America would never consider Jeb Bush. They were just too angry.

It is possible to read Trump's popularity as a kind of retribution for George W. Bush's failures. But it came with a narrower vision of *U-S-A*, one that restored simplicity at the expense of size. In his signature moments, Bush 43 united Americans from both parties. Trump's *U-S-A* was a fraction of a fraction, a group whose vigor depended on shrinking the tent.

For these voters, Trump made things fun and easy. You could go see him in Iowa in late July and get a free hot dog or hamburger and do the wave and listen to country music until he showed up and told you exactly what you wanted to hear: We were the good guys and they were the bad guys and we were going to win and they were going to lose. If we voted for Trump, everything would be fine. Sure, we had problems, mostly involving the Mexicans, the Chinese, the Iranians, the Syrians, and the Russians, but President Trump would fix them all. It used to be simple in America, and it could be simple again. Think of Sgt. Bowe Bergdahl, who deserted the Army in Afghanistan. Nuance? Complexity? Mitigating factors? Nah. Trump knew all he needed to know. "In the old days, you'd shoot him," Trump said. "Quickly."

Some white working-class voters had begun to feel like native-born foreigners, and they were thrilled to see a candidate personify the old American superpower. He talked like a man who got his way, right away, every time, whether or not he said please. Most people had to watch what they said these days, now that iPhone cameras were everywhere and a single tweet or Facebook post could ruin your career. When Trump spoke his mind, he rose so high in the polls that he held the Republican Party in a double bind. *Don't touch me*, he warned them, *or I'll run as a third-party candidate and hand the election to the Democrats.*

The more Trump horrified the party regulars, the more he delighted his supporters. In 2015, a man could hold a press conference and toss off a series of inflammatory comments about Mexican immigrants and rile up the Democrats and the big corporations and the mainstream media, thus dominating the news cycle, thus drawing more attention to his message, thus connecting with quite a few people who'd been saying those same things on their front porches after a few beers. Boom. And enough with these namby-pamby apologies. Those were for normal politicians, otherwise known as losers. An apology implied that *they*—the liars in the press, the low-energy members of the Republican establishment, the false gods of political correctness—were fit to judge *you*, a really smart and rich guy whose various towers and aircraft stood as monuments to your achievement. Which would soon include a wall on the Mexican border.

Former Trump adviser Sam Nunberg summed up the campaign strategy in two words.

"Common sense," he said. "The Republican primary voter will want it. And Washington will immediately tell you, 'You can't do that.' That's the elite class telling you, 'We're smarter than you and you don't know what's good for you.'... Further infuriating the voter, and making the voter more dedicated to Trump....

"The idea of the wall is genius too," Nunberg continued. "It touches on immigration, so it's a policy issue. Two, it touches on Trump's brand. Builder. Developer. Three, it fits the rationale and appeal of his candidacy. The wall. Subliminally, you're saying it's time to take care of America's problems....

"So then you have the wall between the Trump people and the establishment people.... And every single time you mentioned the word *wall wall wall Trump Trump Trump* on TV, the prospective primary voter is going to think, 'Trump. He's our protective wall. To protect *us.*'"

Trump had been mentally simplifying the nation's problems for at least twenty-eight years. In 1987, when Ronald Reagan was

Top: **Trump poses with fairgoers before taking some children on a helicopter ride at the Iowa State Fair.** *Opposite:* **Iowa fairgoers "vote" by dropping kernels of corn in jars bearing the candidates' names.**

president, Trump spent nearly $95,000 to place full-page ads in three newspapers calling on the U.S. to charge Japan and Saudi Arabia for American military protection. Trump had an old friend named Roger Stone, a Nixonian political operative who arranged for Trump to give a speech in New Hampshire during the primary season when then–Vice President George H.W. Bush led the race for the Republican nomination. The crowd gave Trump standing ovations before and after his address, during which he said, "Whatever Japan wants, do the opposite," and called Iran a "horrible, horrible country," and wondered aloud, "Why couldn't we go in and take over some of their oil?" A local man formed a committee to draft Trump for president.

At the time, he was too busy running his real-estate empire to run for office. But when his three older children grew up and learned the business, he thought he could put it in their hands. Right after Mitt Romney lost the 2012 election, he and Stone began talking about 2016. A few days later, Trump applied to trademark the phrase *MAKE AMERICA GREAT AGAIN*.

Trump had some rough moments in June 2015. His advisers say he never regretted the comments about Mexican rapists, because he never seems to regret anything, but his corporate brand suffered real damage. At least

a dozen companies severed ties with him, including NBCUniversal, which had broadcast Trump's reality show, "The Apprentice," and his beauty pageant, Miss Universe.

Late in the afternoon of July 1, a young woman and her father were taking a walk on Pier 14 in San Francisco when he heard a loud popping sound and saw her collapse. "Dad, help me, help me," Kate Steinle said. He performed CPR, and paramedics rushed her to the hospital, but she died there from a gunshot wound to the aorta. The police had a suspect: Juan Francisco Lopez-Sanchez, 45, an undocumented Mexican immigrant who had previously been deported five times. Two days later, Trump sent out a press release saying that Steinle's death proved him right about illegal immigration. Time and again he invoked "beautiful Kate" as one more reason for building his wall. On July 14, her brother, Brad Steinle, appeared on CNN to say, "Donald Trump talks about Kate Steinle like he knows her. I've never heard a word from his campaign manager, never heard a word from him."

That day a national poll from Suffolk University and USA Today showed a new hierarchy among the Republican presidential candidates. Trump would never trail Jeb Bush again.

In the same way that people watched Superman to imagine how it would feel to save the world, people watched Trump to imagine how it would feel to say whatever you wanted and get away with it.

The more Trump horrified the party regulars, the more he delighted his supporters.

But when Sanders said, "We can overcome a corrupt political system that allows billionaires to buy elections," he did not intend to let anyone buy him. He would run for president without a super PAC, without the soft-money support that had become the industry standard.

★ ★ ★

By 2015 in America, outrage had become a competitive sport. Nearly everyone was aggrieved about *something*, and if you expressed shock and anger over one particular thing you were likely to elicit shock and anger from others over the fact that you were not more shocked and angry about *something else*. Into this maelstrom walked Sen. Bernie Sanders of Vermont, an angry septuagenarian who said, in effect, "Here's something that should make us *all* angry." Which, in this climate, sounded like a message of unity and hope.

Sanders believed that We the People had lost control of our destiny, that a handful of rich people and large corporations had grabbed the steering wheel, and that maybe just maybe we could take it back. He wanted to stop the billionaires from hiding their untaxed money in offshore accounts, raise taxes on Wall Street speculators to help pay for free tuition at public colleges and universities, and tear down a campaign-finance system that he said rigged elections in favor of the donors who wrote the largest checks.

Ever since 2010, when the Supreme Court handed down its Citizens United decision, the richest Americans had been allowed to spend unlimited money in pursuit of their own political agendas. The Republicans embraced this new reality. The Democrats shrugged their shoulders and joined in. Even President Barrack Obama reluctantly abandoned his old grass-roots principles when he saw that massive outside spending could help him get reelected in 2012. But when Sanders said, "We can overcome a corrupt political system that allows billionaires to buy elections," he did not intend to let anyone buy him. He would run for president without a super PAC, without the soft-money support that had become the industry standard. In short, he would fight the billionaires on his own terms: with a campaign funded entirely by small donors.

This stunning rejection of the status quo would help Sanders raise far more money in the primary season than any of the Republicans—and nearly as much as his leading Democratic opponent, former Secretary of State Hillary Clinton. "My mother gives $35 a month out of her grocery budget for Bernie," said his New Hampshire state

Top left: **Sen. Bernie Sanders takes to the Iowa State Fair's Soapbox.** *Opposite:* **Sanders speaks to a fairgoer in the sweltering Iowa heat.**

director, Julia Barnes. And there were a lot of people like Barnes' mother. By establishing a kind of mutual dependency with his supporters, Sanders won their loyalty. At the Iowa State Fair on August 15, he said he'd received 350,000 campaign contributions worth an average of $31.20. A new poll showed he had just surged past Clinton in New Hampshire. A small army followed him down the Grand Concourse, chanting: *WHAT DO WE WANT? REVOLUTION! WHEN DO WE WANT IT? NOW!*

It seemed a lot of people wanted revolution. Something did seem wrong with a system wherein a middle-school teacher in suburban Iowa could be paying an interest rate of nearly 10 percent on a student loan whose balance stood at $70,000 and just kept going up. "I probably won't pay off my student loan before

I die," said Jessica Smith, who was voting for Sanders in the hope that he would save her from that fate.

Sanders had spent twenty-four years in the House and Senate, and had become a darling of the progressive movement in 2010 with an eight-hour filibuster against extending the Bush-era tax cuts. Over the years, his staff collected the email addresses of nearly 400,000 supporters across the country, and his chief strategist, Tad Devine, said they came in handy when Sanders decided to run for president. With help from the digital team at Revolution Messaging, the same outfit that helped build Obama's grassroots support in 2008, the Sanders campaign tried an unusual tactic. Instead of campaigning solely in the early-primary and caucus states, Sanders mapped out his supporters' locations

and held rallies where he could draw the largest crowds. The results were astonishing. In July and August alone, he drew 10,000 in Madison, Wisconsin; 12,000 in Seattle; 20,000 in Portland, Oregon; and 27,000 in Los Angeles.

Would these crowds help him win the early states? Not directly. But they forced the media to take him seriously—or at least give him a brief glance before turning away again. Sanders had little to offer in the way of scandal or personal insult. As he said in July, "In politics, it's how are the polls going, how much money is somebody raising, did somebody say something *dumb* yesterday.... They'll publish it over and over again. What *did* Donald Trump do yesterday? And they cover the food fight within the Republican Party. But all of this, all of that type of stuff, deflects attention from the real issues." Which included a higher minimum wage, free health care for everyone, paid family leave, and generally making the poor less poor and the rich less rich. Sanders had been saying

the same thing for forty years, and the nation was finally listening.

Sanders continued toward the state fair's Soapbox, a traditional campaign destination that allowed candidates to address residents of the first-caucus state. All three leading candidates responded to the opportunity in character. Clinton was tired of answering unpleasant questions about her use of a private email server; she had skipped the Soapbox and thus avoided more unpleasant questions. Trump liked to punish those who offended him, and he had skipped the Soapbox to penalize its host, The Des Moines Register, for an editorial calling on him to drop out of the race. But Sanders was a man of the people. There was no decision.

"THIS COUNTRY BELONGS TO ALL OF US," he shouted to a large and attentive crowd that featured pink hair and purple hair and ice-blue hair and one hairstyle that was half blood-red and half fire-orange, although, to be fair, most of the young revolutionaries had unremarkable hair. For his part, Sanders

Top: **Black Lives Matter activists interrupt Sanders at a Seattle rally on August 8, 2015.** *Opposite:* **A crowd watches the Seattle rally after Black Lives Matter activists take the microphone from Sanders.**

had a wispy crescent of white hair that nicely suited a man of his age, almost 74, which would make him five years older than Ronald Reagan—the oldest president in American history—on Inauguration Day. His age made some voters nervous, and a decade earlier he had collapsed in public from dehydration and the flu, but now, even in the blinding heat, he did not seem tired or frail. He seemed passionate, robust, energized by a clear sense of mission and a distance runner's heart. He spoke loudly and rarely smiled. Once in a while, he told a joke.

"There goes Donald Trump," he said as a chopper droned overhead. "I apologize. I left the helicopter at home."

Sanders the carpenter and Trump the millionaire's son had more in common than either would have liked to admit. Both delivered simple messages of economic populism. Both said the system was rigged against the American worker. Both proclaimed themselves ethically superior to the candidates who depended on super PACs. Sanders and Trump would become Clinton's most durable opponents. One reason: Each man made the case that he couldn't be bought.

After seventeen minutes of raging against the billionaire machine, Sanders left the Soapbox. He got some light heckling from a man who called him a "communist," but Sanders let it slide. He walked down the concourse, past signs for cotton candy and funnel cake, past a tent where children walked on the keys of a giant piano. One hundred and seventy days before the Iowa caucuses, a boring and predictable presidential race had now become downright strange. The nomination had always been Clinton's to lose. She had unmatched experience, command of the Democratic donor class, and a virtual lock on superdelegates—the party leaders who could help decide a close race for the nomination. And yet, aside from her potential to become the nation's first female president, she represented the status quo at a time when voters on both sides seemed to want sweeping change. When Sanders said Americans were sick of the two-party system, he had plenty of corroborating evidence. Only four candidates in either party were polling above 10 percent nationally. Both establishment leaders—Clinton and Bush—had negative favorability ratings. So did Trump. Of the two leading candidates in each party, the only one with a positive favorability rating was Sanders, a longtime independent and self-described Democratic socialist who would soon trim Clinton's 41-point lead in Iowa to the single digits.

★ ★ ★

Sanders the carpenter and Trump the millionaire's son had more in common than either would have liked to admit. Both delivered simple messages of economic populism.

Top: **A woman demonstrates as Black Lives Matter activists interrupt Sanders at the Social Security and Medicare anniversary rally in Seattle.** *Opposite:* **Sanders takes to the stage at the rally in Seattle.**

UNPRECEDENTED

If Trumpism had an emotional center, it was something like the fear of serpents in your living room. He conveyed this fear at his rallies by reading aloud the lyrics of a song called "The Snake," written by Oscar Brown in 1963. It told of a woman who found a half-frozen snake on the path by the water. She took pity on the snake, carried it home and set it down by the fire. It woke up and bit her.

> I saved you, cried that woman
> And you've bit me, even, why?
> And you know your bite is poisonous
> and now I'm gonna die
> Oh shut up, silly woman, said the
> reptile with a grin
> You knew damn well I was a snake
> before you took me in

Trump's vision of U-S-A demanded expulsion of the snakes: the one who killed Beautiful Kate, the one who took Patricia Messinger's job, the ones in Jersey City, real or imagined, who cheered when the towers fell. It falsely asserted that Obama was a Kenyan-born Muslim who had slithered into the White House, through a door left wide open by George W. Bush, so that when Jeb Bush said his brother had "kept us safe," Trump said what anyone would say in a room full of vipers: "I don't feel so safe."

As the summer wore on, more and more Republicans reached a different conclusion: Their party was the house, and Trump was the snake. After all, he had once been a Democrat, a donor to the Clintons, a golfing acquaintance of Bill, and when CNN's Don Lemon asked him in August what he and the Democratic ex-president had discussed in their phone call three months earlier, Trump's first response was, "Well, that's none of your business." Democratic opposition researchers began compiling a dossier on Trump, but they delayed its release to avoid helping Republicans they considered to be more electable. Indeed, the Democrats were *thrilled* to see the other party overrun by a reality-TV star who had once moonlighted as a professional wrestler. Neither Jeb Bush nor anyone else could prove that Trump was secretly working for the other team. But if he had been—if his real goal was to poison the Republicans the way he claimed the renegade Mexicans and Muslims were poisoning America—he could not have done it any better.

Trump hated losers almost as much as he hated snakes, and this hatred was seductive for an electorate that blamed its own leaders for recent defeats in presidential elections and the U.S. Supreme Court. By conventional standards, Trump should have been finished when he said that McCain "was a war hero because he was captured. I like people who weren't captured." McCain had spent five-and-a-half years in Vietcong prisons and refused to be released before other Americans. He had lost a nearly unwinnable election to Obama in 2008 and had pressed for bipartisan compromise on immigration. By conventional standards, he was a venerated elder of the Republican Party. But the standards had suddenly changed. In the reckoning of Trumpism, McCain was just another loser who let in more snakes.

Trump might have been finished again in August when he blamed Fox News host

Megyn Kelly's tough questions on the "blood coming out of her wherever." But no! It turned out that plenty of Republicans enjoyed seeing another paragon of the establishment get knocked around, especially if political correctness got a collateral kick in the pants. Nearly 30,000 people turned out to see Trump that month in Alabama, including a woman who claimed to represent a group called Women For Donald Trump.

The media covered Trump relentlessly, because he was accessible, newsworthy and usually good for some outrage, which drove up clicks and ratings. Even when his Republican competitors got some airtime, it was often because they'd said something about Trump. Then he had the pleasure of destroying them. Rick Perry, a former Air Force captain and

Neither Jeb Bush nor anyone else could prove that Trump was secretly working for the other team. But if he had been—if his real goal was to poison the Republicans the way he claimed the renegade Mexicans and Muslims were poisoning America— he could not have done it any better.

governor of Texas, called Trump a "cancer on conservatism." He dropped out before the second debate. Louisiana Gov. Bobby Jindal called Trump a "madman who must be stopped." He was gone before Thanksgiving. Sen. Lindsey Graham of South Carolina, a serious man with serious foreign-policy ideas, called Trump a "jackass," which provoked Trump to share Graham's cell-phone number on live television. Graham responded with a video on YouTube that showed him dropping the phone in a blender and setting it on fire. He was gone before Christmas.

The second phase of the Trump offensive began in November, when the retired neuro-surgeon Ben Carson caught him in national polls. Desperate to regain the spotlight, Trump raised his theatrics to a new level. On a surreal night in Fort Dodge, Iowa, he pledged to "bomb the shit" out of ISIS. He called Sen. Marco Rubio of Florida "weak like a baby." In a nine-minute rant about Carson, he compared the doctor to a child molester. He ridiculed Carson's famous story about trying to stab a friend during childhood—which had been called into question by a CNN investigation—by delivering a sneering reenactment that involved tugging on his belt and stabbing the air with a phantom knife.

"How stupid are the people of Iowa?" he asked, insulting the very first group whose support he was courting. "How stupid are the people of the country to believe this crap?"

The next night, a coordinated series of terrorist attacks in Paris killed 130 people and wounded more than 300. When Carson stumbled on questions about handling the jihadists, Republicans once again put their trust in the man with the phantom knife. Trump rolled on, leading the field, claiming he saw thousands of Muslims celebrating 9/11 in New Jersey, attacking the journalists who questioned the claim, mocking a reporter's disability.

All hell broke loose in December. A Muslim couple went on a terrorist rampage during a meeting of county health inspectors in California, killing fourteen and wounding twenty-one. The New York Times responded with its first front-page editorial since 1920, calling for an end to the "gun epidemic in America." The conservative commentator Erick Erickson took a copy of that newspaper and literally shot it full of holes. The day after President Obama gave a televised speech urging calm and tolerance, Fox News suspended two commentators; one for saying the president didn't "give a shit," the other for calling him a "total pussy."

Name-calling seemed to reach an all-time high. After Trump called for "a total and complete shutdown of Muslims entering the United States until our country's representatives can figure out what is going on," White House press secretary Josh Earnest denounced Trump's alleged transgressions, "from the vacuous sloganeering to the outright lies to even the fake hair…" Republican opponent Carly Fiorina called Trump "Hillary Clinton's Christmas gift." After someone threw a pig's head at a mosque in Philadelphia, outgoing Mayor Michael Nutter blamed Trump for encouraging anti-Muslim violence. "He's an asshole," Nutter said. BuzzFeed editor-in-chief Ben Smith told his staff it was now fair to call Trump a "mendacious racist."

Sanders brought the conversation back to his favorite topic. "Our people are fearful," he said at ABC's Democratic debate on December 19. "They are anxious on a number of levels. They are anxious about international terrorism and the possibility of another attack on America. We all understand that. But you know what else they're anxious about? They're anxious about the fact that they are working incredibly long hours, they're worried about their kids, and they're seeing all the new income and wealth—virtually all of it—going to the top 1 percent. And they're looking around them, and they're looking at Washington, and they're saying, 'The rich are getting much richer, I'm getting poorer, what are you going to do about it? What are you going to do for my kids?' And somebody like a Trump comes along and says, 'I know the answers. The answer is that all of the Mexicans, they're criminals and rapists, we've got to hate the Mexicans. Those are your enemies. We hate all the Muslims, because all of the Muslims are terrorists. We've got to hate the Muslims.' Meanwhile, the rich get richer."

Trump gained strength from the controversy. A CNN/ORC poll released just before Christmas found him leading the Republican field at 39 percent, more than double any of his rivals. Marco Rubio, believed by many to be the party's most electable candidate, was stuck at 10 percent. Jeb Bush walked alone through Boston's Logan Airport, holding onto hope and a blue duffel bag. In New Hampshire, site of the nation's first primary, Trump's lead seemed insurmountable. State Republican Vice Chairman Matt Mayberry recalled a recent conversation with two men at a local Walmart.

"Who you gonna vote for?" he asked them.

"Trump," they both said.

"Why?" Mayberry asked.

"He's not gonna be pushed around," the first man said.

"He's gonna make America great again," the second man said.

"How's he gonna make America great again?" Mayberry asked.

"I don't know," the man said. "He just is."

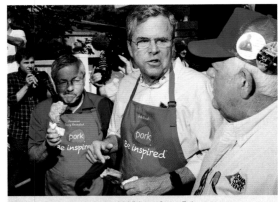
Bush enjoys a treat at the 2015 Iowa State Fair.

Brian Bolton, of Creston, Iowa, participates in a shooting competition at the 2015 Iowa State Fair.

"...The prospective primary voter is going to think, 'Trump. He's our protective wall. To protect us.'"

—Former Trump adviser Sam Nunberg

"He's gonna make America great again."

—New Hampshire Trump supporter in conversation with state Republican Vice Chairman Matt Mayberry

Ron Carnegie dresses up as George Washington at the 2015 Iowa State Fair.

"My mother gives $35 a month out of her grocery budget for Bernie."

—Julia Barnes, Sanders' New Hampshire state director

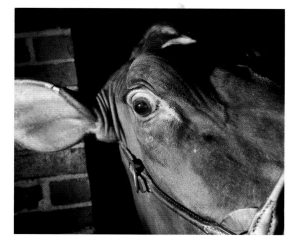

People watch Trump's helicopter take off at the 2015 Iowa State Fair.

Redman, 28 and a farmer from Leon, Iowa, was undecided about the presidential race during the 2015 Iowa State Fair.

"I probably won't pay off my student loan before I die."

—Jessica Smith, Sanders supporter

Shelby Heston, 16, gets prepped for the Cowgirl Queen competition at the 2015 Iowa State Fair.

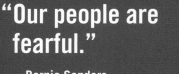

"Our people are fearful."

—Bernie Sanders

Two security guards wait for Trump's helicopter to land at the 2015 Iowa State Fair.

Fairgoer Matter Strong from Delta, Iowa, and her horse, Ghost.

DAVID AXELROD

CNN Senior
Political Commentator and
Former Senior Adviser
to President Obama

WHY I WAS WRONG ABOUT DONALD TRUMP

I could not have been more smugly self-assured.

Donald Trump had just made the most unorthodox and calamitous announcement for president, and I assured a TV audience that his would be a short-lived campaign.

"Donald Trump will not be the Republican nominee," I proclaimed, dismissing the suggestion as preposterous.

Even through the summer of 2015, as Trump became a ubiquitous call-in presence on TV and his raucous rallies became favored cable programming, I stubbornly predicted his demise.

With his unbridled, audacious style, long on edge and short on substance, I was certain that Trump would falter.

"In a parlance Trump would appreciate," I told Maureen Dowd of The New York Times in the summer of 2015, so sure was I that by winter, when the voting began, Trump would be a footnote, "we're still in the swimsuit competition. It gets harder in the talent rounds."

But he didn't fade. As the actual contests approached, I made calls to journalists and Republican operatives I knew in Iowa and New Hampshire. Those are the conversations I will most remember from the campaign of 2016.

Chip Griffin, the publisher of the Primary Digest website that catalogs the New Hampshire campaign, was the first to send up a flare in a call we had as the race ramped up.

"I'm hearing a lot of Trump out here," said Griffin, one of the most knowledgeable and reliable observers of politics in the Granite State. "I'm surprised how many folks I talk to say they're going to vote for him. They're just kind of fed up with the same old, same old. Trump seems like a shock to the system."

I heard something similar from Matt Strawn, a former Republican Party chair from Iowa, who said he was seeing more energy on Trump's behalf than he had anticipated.

"He's not going to win Iowa,"—and he didn't—"but he has supporters," Strawn said.

These old hands were surprised. I was shocked. And though I was far from the only one, I should have known better.

Eight years earlier, I had laid out for Barack Obama my theory that open-seat elections for the presidency are generally shaped by the outgoing incumbent.

Rarely do Americans, particularly those in the party opposite the president's, choose someone whose qualities mirror those of the incumbent they're replacing. And no one in the large

> ## With his unbridled, audacious style, long on edge and short on substance, I was certain that Trump would falter.

Republican field was as distinct in style and approach from Barack Obama than Donald Trump.

Where Obama was calm and deliberate, Trump was bombastic. Where Obama spoke of hope, Trump peddled fear. Where Obama was the living personification of a changing country, Trump set himself up as a bulwark against growing diversity and multiculturalism. Where Obama found an audience among intellectual elites, Trump, who was raised in privilege and lords over country clubs, proclaimed himself their sworn enemy.

But in an era where technology and globalization have been engines of both enormous growth and inequality, Trump's assault on trade and immigration have found an enthusiastic audience among white, non-college-educated voters who have seen good, middle-class jobs lost over decades.

The fact that I didn't see it from the start—and I was far from alone—speaks to the deep divides in our society that helped propel Trump in this race.

Americans live in different worlds—urban versus rural; racially and ethnically diverse versus homogenous; those who are winning in this new economy and those who have been left behind.

And in this unsettled country, it turned out, Americans heard the phrase "Make America Great Again" in distinctly different ways.

THE REALITY OF DONALD TRUMP

AS TOLD TO
MJ LEE
BY **JEFF ZUCKER**
*President,
CNN Worldwide*

I don't remember the first time I met Donald Trump, but I got to know him very well when I bought "The Apprentice" for NBC in 2003.

The reason that I wanted "The Apprentice" was NBC needed a reality-show hit. "Survivor" had been the big hit reality show that had been produced by Mark Burnett. So he was pitching a new show that was basically "Survivor" in a different jungle—the concrete jungle of New York, the boardroom. And he was attaching Donald Trump to it.

I think I had a unique appreciation for what Donald Trump could bring to a show like this. I had a much better understanding than most people of what a publicity magnet and PR machine Donald Trump was. I had been in New York for many years and knew that he was the tabloid king—always on the covers of the New York Post, the New York Daily News and *People* magazine. I both needed a reality-show hit and I wanted to be in business with Mark Burnett, and I knew that even if the show wasn't good, Trump would get us a tremendous amount of publicity.

So I made an offer for "The Apprentice"—and I wouldn't let Mark Burnett's business manager leave the Burbank set until we made a deal.

The Trump that I see now is different than the Trump who was an actor and businessman on "The Apprentice."

That Trump was a ham. So that's the

> **The Trump that I see now is different than the Trump who was an actor and businessman on "The Apprentice."**

same, right? He was a showman, so that's the same. He was a PR magnet; that's the same. He was a publicity hound; that's the same. But all of his political pronouncements and beliefs and all the allegations about him—I never knew anything about that. I never saw any of that. I was never aware of any of that.

People were talking about whether or not CNN should cover Trump. Initially, I said I did not think we should cover him because he had teased the world, certainly in 2012, with this idea that he was going to run for president. I didn't really believe he would do it. So I said I didn't want to waste our time and said we didn't need to cover him unless he announced his candidacy. Then he rode down the escalator and he announced. That was the first day we covered his campaign.

I don't think anybody knew exactly what was going to happen that day.

My biggest memory from that day is watching the reaction from S.E. Cupp, a CNN political commentator, who didn't believe what she just saw. I kind of thought, well, that's vintage Trump.

I don't think Donald Trump ever thought he was going to be the Republican nominee for president. I think he got into this race to burnish his brand and finish second or third. So, he was happy to get all this publicity, and I think that's what it was about.

Until he realized he could actually win. And now he is the president.

2

HILLARY CLINTON
STARES DOWN
HER ENEMIES

Strange things happen in politics. The actor who played Stuart Smalley on "Saturday Night Live" later won election to the U.S. Senate. The actor who played a homicidal cyborg in "The Terminator" served two terms as governor of California. The actor who starred alongside a chimpanzee in "Bedtime for Bonzo" went on to become the most hallowed Republican president of the last fifty years. These career evolutions are best understood through the following principle: All politicians must be performers, even when they're telling the truth.

Every good role demands a good player. A great politician finds her best self and plays that character whenever possible, on and off the stage, until her best self and her truest self become inseparable in the minds of the voters. When Hillary Clinton has done this—when she has most closely resembled the woman she wants the nation to see—she has come across as a crusader for women and children, an advocate for the poor and oppressed, a public servant driven by her long-held Methodist imperative to do all the good she can.

But in the spring and summer of 2015, at the start of her second campaign to become America's first woman president, the ideal

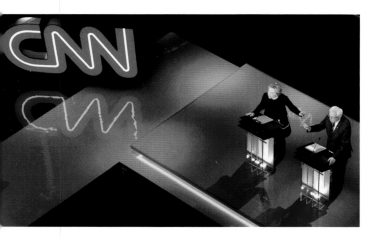

Hillary Clinton was rarely visible. What voters saw more often was a candidate caught in a cycle of skillful evasion and lawyerly dissembling, even as she went about the business of campaigning. Late in August, when Quinnipiac University polled 1,563 voters about Clinton, only 34 percent said she was honest and trustworthy. When asked for the first word that came to mind for Clinton, their most common answer was *liar*.

Through her own words and actions, Clinton had caused this crisis. But it could also be seen as the latest battle in a two-decade war with a force she sometimes called the Vast Right-Wing Conspiracy: a network of conservative politicians, media figures and activists united in pursuit of her annihilation. They imagined a Hillary Clinton presidency as something akin to nuclear winter: a disaster to be averted at all costs. They knew their enemy, understood her vulnerabilities. And for the first six months of her campaign, they watched her make the same mistakes again and again.

"It almost seems like she's being a little secretive this time," a 56-year-old Clinton supporter named VaLinda Parsons said in late July before a campaign event in Ames, Iowa. "I'm like, 'Hillary, get *out* there. Gosh! Maybe there's a reason your polling numbers are going down.'"

That reason went something like this: When the Vast Right-Wing Conspiracy unearthed one of her secrets, Hillary Clinton responded with the worst version of herself.

━━━━━━━ ☆ ☆ ☆ ━━━━━━━

On the phone with a friend before it all started, Clinton shared a thought about the campaign ahead.

"I've really come to peace with the fact that I am who I am," she told her longtime ally Hilary Rosen. "I'm just going to be

Bottom left: **Former Secretary of State Hillary Clinton and Sen. Bernie Sanders at a Democratic debate in Flint, Michigan, on March 6, 2016.**

myself. And if that's good enough, great. And if it's not, that's OK. But I think I'll be a better candidate, because I'm just going to put myself out there."

This would not be easy. Something in Clinton had changed twenty-three years earlier, during Bill Clinton's first presidential campaign, when she spoke up in defense of her law practice. "I suppose I could have stayed home and baked cookies and had teas, but what I decided to do was fulfill my profession, which I entered before my husband was in public life," she said in March 1992. The backlash, particularly from women who had made other choices, was immediate and severe. Clinton was taken aback. She had trouble grasping the notion that she had

Conversation around the "Clinton Brand" made her seem like a consumer product, a best-selling classic in need of one more redesign. First lady, senator, presidential candidate, secretary of state and now presidential candidate again. How would the latest incarnation of Hillary Clinton appeal to voters?

offended anyone. By the next day, her guard was up. And that's where it stayed.

"She herself has said she has tried to walk the line between controlling her emotions and keeping steady while not seeming 'walled off,'" her spokeswoman Kristina Schake said.

For much of 2015, Clinton was a front-runner, playing not to lose. Hacked emails released by WikiLeaks would later show it took her campaign a full day to agree on the twenty-three words of a single tweet. In April, progressives wanted her to join their quest for a $15 minimum wage. One staffer proposed a signed tweet from Clinton saying, "I stand with fast food workers in the #fight-for15." A policy adviser shot down the idea, saying, "Don't want her to come out for

$15 at this stage. Instead of standing with them, better to applaud them?" It went on like that for almost twelve hours, with input from at least nine people, before they settled on an uncontroversial message: "Every American deserves a fair shot at success. Fast food & child care workers shouldn't have to march in streets for living wages. -H"

When Clinton was cautious, she *was* being herself. In the months before she joined the race, when she had no obvious competitor for the Democratic nomination, her aides brought in marketing specialists to talk about her image. Conversation around the "Clinton Brand" made her seem like a consumer product, a best-selling classic in need of one more redesign. First lady, senator,

Top: **Clinton stands behind her lectern before the first Democratic debate, sponsored by CNN, on October 13, 2015, in Las Vegas.**

presidential candidate, secretary of state and now presidential candidate again. But when The Washington Post published a story about "Hillary 5.0" in February 2015, her chief strategist, Joel Benenson, was horrified. "But this is by far the most damaging story and most damaging type of story we can have," he wrote to campaign chairman John Podesta in an email that was later hacked and released by WikiLeaks. "…I think we need a paradigm shift in how this world operates (sic) we have to convince HRC (Hillary Clinton) and probably WJC (Bill Clinton) that her meeting with 200 people doesn't help her. Hiring corporate wizards has never been a successful strategy in campaigns."

How would the latest incarnation of Hillary Clinton appeal to voters? Her allies had a few ideas. She would campaign as a mother, a grandmother, a daughter of the Midwest. She would be warmer, funnier. As in past campaigns, she would spend time listening to everyday people, winning them over one at a time.

In April 2015, Clinton told advisers she wanted to take a road trip to Iowa. She would ride in a van nicknamed Scooby, with only a few aides and no reporters, so she could interact more naturally with people she met along the way. Her staff scheduled a departure on April 13—a Monday—but

Clinton's superstitions got in the way. She left on Sunday, April 12, instead. "She wanted to drive there and stop along the way wherever she felt like stopping, and just talk to people in rest stops and restaurants and then get to Iowa and be able to have un-herded time just listening to and connecting to people," Schake said in an interview. One of the planet's most famous people tried to go incognito—and initially succeeded. As she ordered a chicken burrito bowl at a Chipotle in Maumee, Ohio, no one seemed to recognize her.

But Clinton had already lost control of the narrative. What defined her campaign before it began was the disclosure in The New York Times on March 2 that she had used a private email server to conduct official business as secretary of state, an apparent violation of federal rules and possibly federal law. This revelation came from the Republican-controlled House Select Committee on Benghazi, whose investigators were seeking emails from the State Department about the 2012 terrorist attack that left four Americans dead. In short, Republicans trying to pierce Clinton's veil of secrecy had found even more secrets.

This predilection for secrecy had often worked against Clinton. She sometimes came across as a woman too convinced of

She sometimes came across as a woman too convinced of her own virtue to accept the public scrutiny that attended high office.

her own virtue to accept the public scrutiny that attended high office. When the first lady wanted to overhaul the nation's health-care system so that everyone would have insurance, she raised suspicion by developing her plan in secret. When she decided that free-roaming reporters might find out too much from gregarious aides, she limited their access to the press secretary's office in the West Wing. These tactics backfired, as did the Clintons' refusal to cooperate with The Washington Post on a story about their past financial dealings in Arkansas. That controversy, known as Whitewater, ultimately led to the appointment of a special prosecutor, the discovery of Bill Clinton's dalliance with an intern and his impeachment by the House.

In March 2015, Clinton had some explaining to do. According to one senior adviser, even her aides were caught off-guard by the news that she had a private email server. "Almost none of us knew about it," the adviser said. But her press conference on March 10 only raised further questions. The more reporters examined her statements, the less reliable they seemed. She said she had "fully complied with every rule," but a subsequent inspector general's report said her unconventional use of a private email server did not comply with department policy. She said she had turned over all email that "could possibly be work-related," but work-related emails from other sources contradicted that claim. Echoing her husband's classic "There is no improper relationship" quote from the 1998 Monica Lewinsky scandal, she said, "There is no classified material," which in fact there was. And when she claimed to have done the whole thing "because I thought it would be easier to carry just one device for my work," Republicans gleefully cited her recent statement to the contrary: "I'm like two steps short of a hoarder. So I have...an iPad, a Mini iPad, an iPhone and a BlackBerry."

Her aides always said she'd have to fight for the nomination, but they hadn't bargained for *this*. Where was the champion of the working class who won the 2000 Senate race in New York? The undaunted fighter who battled into June for the nomination in 2008? It seemed as if she were running against herself, and losing. A candid news conference might have slowed the drip-drip-drip of email stories. But she truly believed she'd done nothing wrong. She evaded, and then refused to talk about it, and then tried *joking* about it, with an inexplicable reference to Snapchat and the messages that "disappear all by themselves." In Nevada on August 18, when asked if she had "wiped" the email server, she said, "What, like with a cloth or something?"

If this was the new Hillary Clinton, it was time for a product recall.

★ ★ ★

First Democratic debate, Las Vegas, October 13, 2015, just before closing statements.

> **Where was the champion of the working class who won the 2000 Senate race in New York? The undaunted fighter who battled into June for the nomination in 2008? It seemed as if she were running against herself, and losing.**

ANDERSON COOPER, CNN MODERATOR:
Franklin Delano Roosevelt once said, "I ask you to judge me by the enemies I have made." You've all made a few people upset over your political careers. Which enemy are you most proud of?

CLINTON: *Well, in addition to the NRA, the health insurance companies, the drug companies, the Iranians—probably the Republicans.*

As Democrats in the audience cheered, Clinton wore a brilliant smile. This was significant. Not only did a major party's front-runner call the opposition her enemy, she was proud of it, thrilled about it, as if it felt wonderful to share a self-evident truth.

The American voter longed for a transcendent figure, a personality large enough to bridge the partisan divide. This is part of why Clinton lost in 2008. Leading by double digits in national polls less than two months before that year's Iowa caucuses, she told the Democrats at the Jefferson-Jackson Dinner in Des Moines that it was time to turn up the heat on the Republicans. She and her allies kept saying it: Turn up the heat, turn up the heat. But the speech that won the night came from a freshman senator who dreamed of a new majority, a higher purpose, a nation healed and a world repaired. "I don't want to pit Red America against Blue America," Barack Obama said. "I want to be president of the *United States* of America."

Seven years after Obama's election, it seemed fair to say that his vision of the presidency had been far less realistic than Clinton's. The pitting of Red America against Blue America had only intensified. His achievements turned up the partisan heat. Grand rhetoric gave way to frustration with a Republican Congress intent on blocking his every move. That, in turn, gave way to the unilateral exercise of power through executive orders on such issues as immigration and the environment. Innocence and idealism disappeared again. Just as Bill Clinton pledged to run the "most ethical administration in the history of the republic" before lying to the nation about his affair with Lewinsky, Obama promised unprecedented openness in government before becoming what New York Times reporter James Risen called "the

greatest enemy of press freedom in a generation." As it had with Bill Clinton, Obama's White House became a Democratic fortress under Republican siege.

Hillary Clinton had survived both sieges. She was no stranger to bipartisan compromise, especially in the Senate, but she knew the limits of playing nice. Enemy of the Republicans? With each partisan battle in Washington, that sounded more like the job description of any Democratic president. If she ever got back to the White House, Clinton could play that role to the hilt.

★ ★ ★

The late U.S. Sen. Daniel Patrick Moynihan once said, "Everyone is entitled to his own opinion, but not to his own facts." This

Bottom: **The Democratic candidates line up on stage before their first debate. Left to right: former Sen. Jim Webb, Sanders, Clinton, former Maryland Gov. Martin O'Malley and former Rhode Island Gov. Lincoln Chafee.**

quote, from the New York Democrat Hillary Clinton would succeed, made intuitive sense. It often resurfaced in partisan debates. But it did not quite account for the parallel worlds that Democrats and Republicans had come to inhabit. It was possible on either side to select the facts that pleased you most, the ones that fortified your own righteousness, and ignore or deny everything else.

When it came to Hillary Clinton, people saw what they wanted to see. This was true when she kept her family name, Rodham, during her husband's first term as Arkansas governor. It was true when the couple was investigated, but never implicated, over their role in a real estate deal known as Whitewater. And it was true in the aftermath of the terrorist attack on the American diplomatic compound in Benghazi, Libya, on September 11, 2012, when Clinton was secretary of state. The attack had killed Ambassador J. Christopher Stevens and three other Americans. It had already reverberated through one presidential election. And now it would figure into another.

Democrats appraising the House Select Committee on Benghazi in 2015 pointed out several actual facts about it, including these: No fewer than seven congressional committees had already examined the incident. A former investigator for the Republican-led committee went on CNN to allege that he'd been fired after resisting a directive to explicitly target Clinton. And Republican House Majority Leader Kevin McCarthy made a statement on Fox News that Democrats took as an accidental revelation of the truth: "Everybody thought Hillary Clinton was unbeatable, right? But we put together a Benghazi special committee. A select committee. What are her numbers today? Her numbers are dropping."

The secret email server followed her like a ball and chain. By the time Clinton apologized in September, a Quinnipiac poll showed that Sanders was drawing even with her in Iowa. Meanwhile, Washington buzzed with rumors that Joe Biden might soon join the race.

Republicans had their own facts on the matter, some regarding Clinton's evasions, some concerning Obama's lack of transparency, many pertaining to the failure of seven prior congressional committees to find some pretty interesting stuff that the House Select Committee uncovered, especially Clinton's private email server. Now the Select Committee had a few questions for Clinton. They summoned her to Capitol Hill. Late in October, with the nation watching, the Democratic front-runner would match wits with the Republicans who were trying to bring her down.

★ ★ ★

In the season premiere of "Saturday Night Live" on October 3, the actor Kate McKinnon played the role of Hillary Clinton. The real Hillary Clinton was also in the sketch, playing a bartender named Val. Clinton had seen McKinnon's impersonation of her before, and thought it was hilarious, and now she

Clinton did not have her husband's charisma or Obama's gift for soaring rhetoric. But with her sharp intellect and skillful improvisation, she could still debate anyone.

could see it up close. She had immersed herself in the "SNL" experience, rehearsing with McKinnon in the dressing room and attending the writers' meeting before the show. She met cast member Pete Davidson, whose father, a firefighter, was killed on 9/11; and Colin Jost, whose mother—Kerry Kelly, chief medical officer for the New York City Fire Department—Clinton knew from her time as a senator. Clinton may have grown up near Chicago and spent much of her adult life in Arkansas, but now she felt at home in New York.

"Hey, bartender," the fake Hillary Clinton said, slapping the bar. "Keep 'em comin'."

"Rough night?" said the real Clinton, otherwise known as Val the Bartender.

"Yeah," the fictional Clinton said, "you could say that."

All along the campaign trail, the secret email server followed her like a ball and chain. Voters wanted contrition, but the real Hillary Clinton had none to give. "At the end of the day," she told NBC's Andrea Mitchell in early September, "I am sorry that this has been confusing to people and has raised a lot of questions, but there are answers to all these questions."

Allies watched in disbelief. "I was like, 'She just called the American people

stupid!'" said Patti Solis Doyle, one of Clinton's 2008 campaign managers and a 2016 surrogate for her former boss. "What about that is good?"

Finally, around the time a Quinnipiac poll showed that Sanders was drawing even with her in Iowa, political considerations won out. "I'm sorry about that," Clinton told ABC's David Muir on September 8. "I take responsibility."

Meanwhile, Washington buzzed with rumors that Vice President Joe Biden might soon join the race. Maybe he'd run and lost twice before; maybe he often misspoke and was almost as old as Sanders, but he had compelling reasons to run again, including the dying wish of his son Beau. An election was still a popularity contest, a quest to make people *like* you, and that October it was pretty easy to like Uncle Joe.

"Oh, Val," the fictional Hillary Clinton said to the real one. "I'm just so darn bummed. All anyone wants to talk about is Donald Trump."

"Donald *Trump*?" the bartender said. "Isn't he the one who's like, 'Uhhhhh, you're all losers?'"

To recap: Here was Hillary Clinton, playing Val the Bartender, doing a middle-school impression of Donald Trump. And somehow

Top left: **Clinton and Sanders share a laugh during the first Democratic debate.** *Opposite:* **Clinton chats with her campaign staff before the Democratic debate in Flint, Michigan.**

it came across as authentic, as if playing a fictional character liberated Clinton to be herself in a way that was impossible in the guise of a presidential candidate. On a hot day in August at the Iowa State Fair, she told reporters, "I'm just havin' a good time," which seemed unlikely, given the dust and horse manure and endless questions about her email. But now she was having an *excellent* time. No one asked Val about her email or her poll numbers in New Hampshire. No one asked Val for one of those insufferable campaign selfies where you have to put on this giant smile and keep it frozen in place while someone keeps pressing the wrong button.

"I wish *you* could be president," the fake Hillary Clinton said to the real one.

"Me, too," the real one said.

It was hard to say whether a woman who had spent her adult life in mansions and private jets could still relate to the problems of women like Val the Bartender. The populist appeals of Sanders were luring some white working-class voters away from Clinton. Her millions in speaking fees from large corporations and investment banks were not helping to bring them back. In her campaign video, she said the deck was stacked in favor of those at the top. Her Democratic opponents thought the deck was stacked in favor of Clinton. They were pretty sure the Democratic National Committee had tried to help her by scheduling only six debates and putting some in obscure time slots, like Saturday nights during football games. But this theory was based on the assumption that debates would hurt Clinton. And that turned out to be incorrect.

Clinton understood that debates were a special kind of performance. She read voraciously to prepare her arguments, but she couldn't rely solely on her mastery of the issues. She had to master her emotions as well. In previous campaigns, Clinton's aides found a way to help her do that.

"In debate preps I've been involved with, she gets really angry and loses it," Patti Solis Doyle said. "But it's obviously better for her to get angry with staff in a small group of people than it is to lose it onstage, so that's how we did it. We just started and threw the worst things we could think to throw at her first and let her get through her anger and then we could focus on nuance in the answers."

Clinton was the last of five candidates to arrive at the Wynn Las Vegas for the first debate on October 13. CNN had a lectern offstage and ready for Biden, just in case, but he didn't show. A hot and dry afternoon became a cool dusk, the desert wind rolling across the parking lot, the golden windows of Trump Hotel reflecting in the distance. Clinton had ten minutes to get miked up and take her place, which she did, but something was wrong with the microphone.

"Apollo, we have a problem," she said as four sound technicians tried to fix the wiring.

"You can have my microphone," Sanders said, apparently half-kidding. "I only want to hear from you anyway."

A technician escorted her to the green room and fixed the problem just in time. "It's always something," she said, preparing to go live for her first debate in almost eight years.

"Secretary Clinton," said the moderator, Anderson Cooper, "I want to start with you. Plenty of politicians evolve on issues, but even some Democrats believe you change your positions based on political expediency. You were against same-sex marriage. Now you're for it. You defended President Obama's immigration policies. Now you say they're too harsh. You supported his trade deal dozens of times. You even called it the 'gold standard.' Now, suddenly, last week, you're against it. Will you say anything to get elected?"

Clinton did not have her husband's charisma or Obama's gift for soaring rhetoric. But Benenson, her chief strategist, said she and her advisers had developed a kind of debate playbook—a set of possible responses to almost any question imaginable—and those answers were ready when she needed them.

"Well, actually, I have been very consistent," she said without hesitation. "Over the course of my entire life, I have always fought for the same values and principles, but, like most human beings—including those

Her strongest opponent had just delivered the line of the night, a line about Clinton, and he sounded like a cranky old priest absolving his parishioner.

of us who run for office—I do absorb new information. I do look at what's happening in the world."

As the debate went on, Clinton showed easy command of domestic and foreign policy. Sanders railed against Wall Street and the billionaires. The other three men faded into the background. As expected, Cooper asked Clinton about her emails—and about the congressional testimony she would give the following week. Clinton blamed partisan politics. Cooper reminded her of the FBI investigation. Clinton said she would answer every question. Cooper gave Sanders a chance to respond.

"Let me say something that may not be great politics," Sanders said. "But I think the secretary is right, and that is that the American people are sick and tired of hearing about your damn emails."

"Thank you," Clinton said. "Me, too. Me, too."

This would become a pivotal moment in their year-long contest. Sanders could have attacked, but he held back. She took a deep breath, perhaps a sigh of relief, and reached over to shake his hand. Her strongest opponent had just delivered the line of the night, a line about Clinton, and he sounded like a cranky old priest absolving his parishioner. Clinton had regained her footing. She walked offstage and saw a friend, the Democratic strategist Donna Brazile, and they clasped hands in celebration. *This* was the campaign they'd been waiting for.

Eight days later, citing grief over the loss of his son earlier in the year, Biden announced he would not enter the race. But he had some implicit advice for Clinton.

"I believe that we have to end the divisive partisan politics that is ripping this country apart," he said. "And I think we can. It's mean-spirited, it's petty and it's gone on for much too long. I don't believe, like some do, that it's naive to talk to Republicans. I don't

think we should look at Republicans as our enemies. They are our opposition. They're not our enemies. And for the sake of the country, we have to work together."

It seemed conciliatory, even patriotic. And exactly the kind of thing you say when your last campaign is behind you.

✸ ✸ ✸

Near the end of Cormac McCarthy's novel "No Country For Old Men," the protagonist shares some advice from his father:

> My daddy always told me to just do the best you knew how and tell the truth. He said there was nothin to set a man's mind at ease like wakin up in the morning and not havin to decide who you were.

There are Republican facts and Democratic facts, and there are lies that both sides tell. But apolitical truth still exists, and telling it requires no creativity.

It is not partisan to say that Glen Doherty, one of the four Americans killed in Benghazi, loved his younger sister, Kate Quigley, and that he inspired her to be her best self, and that his talent for friendship was so immense that after he died, as many as forty people told his sister the same thing: "Glen was my best friend."

Nor would it be fair to place Kate Quigley—a political independent who would choose Biden for president if given the chance—anywhere near the so-called Vast Right-Wing Conspiracy. She felt neutral about Hillary Clinton before September 14, 2012, the day they met at Joint Base Andrews in Maryland, the same day seven Marines walked off a cargo plane carrying the flag-draped casket of Doherty, the CIA contractor and former Navy SEAL who'd been killed by mortar fire when terrorists attacked the compound in Benghazi. His sister liked Obama, who gave her children M&M's; and she liked Biden, who lightened the mood with a joke about his thinning hair; and she liked the Libyan diplomat who told her, "We're going to get the terrorists."

But Kate Quigley got a different vibe from the secretary of state. She says Clinton told her *how to feel*—that she should feel sorry for the Libyan people, because they're uneducated, and being uneducated breeds fear, and fear leads to violent protests. Looking back on it later, Quigley was convinced that Clinton used a meeting with a bereaved family member to put forth a convenient explanation that she knew to be false. She came to believe the same thing the Republicans believed: that Clinton lied about the cause of the attack on the compound because the truth—that Libya was descending into chaos—might have hurt Obama's chances for re-election.

Quigley was at work on October 22, 2015, the day Clinton testified before the House Select Committee on Benghazi, so she missed the live coverage. But she did not share the Democrats' admiration for Clinton's performance during the eleven-hour hearing.

"If she just told the truth," Quigley said, "she could have testified for twenty-five minutes."

★ ★ ★

Clinton had battled Republicans in Congress before, and not always won. In 2013, under hard questioning from Sen. Ron Johnson of Wisconsin about the cause of the Benghazi attack, she waved her hands and raised her voice and said, "With all due respect, the fact is we had four dead Americans. Was it because of a protest? Or was it because of guys out for a walk one night who decided they'd go kill some Americans? What difference, at this point, does it make?" Her supporters liked this bold show of emotion. To them, Clinton had sliced through the partisan rhetoric to make the most important

point: Four Americans were dead. But her question—*what difference, at this point, does it make?*—would appear in countless memes and videos as a kind of shorthand for what her enemies hated about her. To them, it made her look flippant, insensitive, as if she considered the inquiry a waste of her time.

Now she had another chance to face the Republicans. The warrior had flailed a little too much. This moment seemed to call for a different strategy. In between several days of preparation and mock interrogations with aides at her home in Northwest Washington, she got advice from another battle-hardened Democrat. According to two Clinton aides who recounted the conversation later, Bill Clinton told his wife not to react if the Republicans lashed out.

The Republican facts that surfaced on the day of her testimony included phone calls and an email indicating she knew that the fire at the Benghazi compound was caused by a coordinated terrorist attack—not by a spontaneous protest in response to a crude anti-Muslim video posted on the Internet by an Egyptian-born Christian living in California, as Clinton's prepared statement seemed to imply. "So if there's no evidence for a video-inspired protest, then where did the false narrative start?" asked Rep. Jim Jordan, a Republican from Ohio. "It started with you, Madam Secretary."

The Democratic facts included Clinton's steadfast denial that she misled anyone at Joint Base Andrews or anywhere else in the aftermath of the fire in Benghazi. The video was real and offensive to Muslims, some of whom scaled the walls of the U.S. Embassy in Cairo and tore down the American flag. "Congressman," Clinton told Jordan, "I believe to this day the video played a role." The Republican facts included a rare bipartisan consensus that the attack could

Bill Clinton told his wife not to react if the Republicans lashed out.

have been prevented if the compound had adequate security. But that conclusion had come from the Senate Intelligence Committee nearly two years earlier, giving credence to Democrats' assertion that the Republicans were recycling old information.

"I take responsibility for what happened in Benghazi," Clinton said, ten hours before the hearing was over.

A pattern emerged as the day went on. Certain Republican Congress members—especially Lynn Westmoreland of Georgia and Mike Pompeo of Kansas—addressed Clinton as one might address a criminal defendant on the witness stand. The optics of this were not improved by the nonpartisan fact that she was a woman and they were men. After Clinton gave a moving description of the diplomatic security officers' heroism during the attack, Pompeo resumed his interrogation.

POMPEO: *Ambassador Stevens did not have your personal email address; we've established that.*

CLINTON: *Yes, that's right.*

POMPEO: *Did he have your cell phone number?*

CLINTON: *No, but he had the twenty-four-hour number of the State Operations in the State Department that can reach me twenty-four/seven.*

POMPEO: *Yes, ma'am. Did he have your fax number?*

CLINTON: *He had the fax number of the State Department.*

POMPEO: *Did he have your home address?*

CLINTON: *No, I don't think any ambassador has ever asked me for that.*

POMPEO: *Did he ever stop by your house?*

CLINTON: *No, he did not, Congressman.*

Through Pompeo's open disdain and Westmoreland's repeated interruptions, the Republicans seemed intent on provoking Clinton into another outburst. It did not work. For much of 2015, they had succeeded in bringing out the weakest Hillary Clinton. Now they brought out the strongest. What the voters saw on television was a woman who appeared unflappable. As the provocative questions continued, she projected a mystical calm. "I would imagine I've thought more about what happened than all of you put together," she said. "I've lost more sleep than all of you put together."

She seemed defiant at times, occasionally evasive, but never angry. In the tenth hour she had a coughing fit that lasted nearly a minute. She cleared her throat, drank some water, wiped her nose and got back to work.

For much of 2015, they had succeeded in bringing out the weakest Hillary Clinton. Now they brought out the strongest. What the voters saw on television was a woman who appeared unflappable.

"I want to thank you for your patience," Gowdy told her at the end, just before the best online fundraising hour of her campaign to date. Some voters would never be convinced. Clinton had driven Kate Quigley into the arms of the Republicans. But for now, her fellow Democrats had been reassured. Multiple polls would soon show Clinton leading Sanders by more than twenty-five points.

It was a complex thing, this battle with the Republicans. Sometimes they seemed to *need* her, a physical emblem of all they stood against, and they often played the same role for her. What might have been the Vast Right-Wing Conspiracy's finest hour—catching her husband in a salacious lie and voting for his impeachment—ended with an acquittal in the Senate and a stunning loss in the court of public opinion. The inquisitors had turned the culprit into a victim. In a Gallup poll conducted December 19 and 20, 1998, the day of and the day after his impeachment, Bill Clinton's approval rating reached an all-time high of 73 percent.

Now the Republicans were attacking another Clinton. They had given her a miserable seven months. Then they gave her a gift: a chance to show her best self, a televised audition for the role she wanted most.

Top: **Clinton testifies before the House Select Committee on Benghazi on October 22, 2015.**

**TORCH IN HAND,
TED CRUZ
MARCHES ON
WASHINGTON**

3

When the sun went down in Washington and the White House glowed like a rainbow, one kind of American saw the colors and felt triumphant. This American celebrated on Facebook with a rainbow-filtered profile picture, or on the sidewalk with a kiss, or on Twitter with the hashtag #LoveWins. President Obama himself used this hashtag. He had once defined marriage as the union of one man and one woman, back when the majority of Americans felt the same way, but that was long ago, before he left what he now considered the wrong side of history. A few million people crossed over every year. Here came Hillary Clinton, and with her quite a few Republicans, and with them a new cultural momentum, so that on June 26, 2015, when the U.S. Supreme Court ruled 5-4 to legalize same-sex marriage nationwide, these triumphant Americans reveled in their victory.

Another kind of American saw the rainbows and felt uneasy, if not afraid. This American hesitated on social media, because a dissenting opinion could be construed as a stand against love itself. The silent American saw what happened that year at a pizzeria in a small Indiana town when a television reporter walked in and started

asking questions about the state's Religious Freedom Restoration Act, which permitted business owners to turn away gay customers. The proprietor could have said, "We have no comment," or perhaps, "We serve delicious pizza to everyone." Instead she said, "If a gay couple was to come in, like say, we wanted—they wanted us to provide them pizzas for a wedding, um, we would have to say no." After the story went viral online, the pizzeria's Yelp site was jammed with scathing reviews and pornographic images. A protester stood outside with a sign that said *BIGOTS*. A local high-school coach tweeted, "Who's going to Walkerton, IN to burn down #memoriespizza w me?" The restaurant closed for eight days, and its owners said they had gone into hiding.

It was too late for a truce. The people who'd been forced to stay in the closet for most of American history watched as the roles were gradually reversed. The silent American saw little choice but to play along. Which is why, when someone set up a GoFundMe page and raised more than $840,000 for Memories Pizza, every donation was anonymous. And why, after a baker in Oregon refused to bake for a lesbian wedding, some loyal customers asked for their cake in unmarked boxes. When the owners of a wedding chapel and restaurant in Iowa refused to host a gay wedding, the silent American quietly thanked them for their convictions. But the silent American stopped eating lunch there, for fear of being seen.

This is how Sen. Ted Cruz of Texas emerged from a seventeen-person field to become Donald Trump's strongest Republican challenger: He made himself the voice of the silent American. He would speak for people who felt the country—their country—had been taken away from them.

The leader of this movement would need immunity from public shaming, which Cruz certainly had. Democratic strategist James

Carville called him "the most talented and fearless Republican politician I've seen in the last thirty years." Others called him a bigot, a homophobe or worse, but Cruz had a special talent for turning insults into compliments. If he was hated equally by progressive leaders and politicians of both parties—especially his Senate colleagues—it only proved he was an enemy of the bipartisan corruption and moral decay that ran from Roe v. Wade in 1973 to Obergefell v. Hodges in 2015. And if anyone could be trusted to nominate unflinching conservatives to the U.S. Supreme Court, it was the man who boasted about needing a food-taster in the Senate dining room. Whatever side of history Cruz was on, he stood there with a megaphone and a waving flag.

This is how Sen. Ted Cruz of Texas emerged from a seventeen-person field to become Donald Trump's strongest Republican challenger: He made himself the voice of the silent American. He would speak for people who felt the country—their country—had been taken away from them.

Many would choose between Cruz and Trump, two merchants of nostalgia. One was refined and religious; the other coarse and secular. Both conjured visions of a nation gone but not forgotten: a place where straight white men didn't have to tread so lightly, and the silent American was someone else.

Cruz believed he could win by mobilizing evangelical Christians in unprecedented numbers. They already were dependable Republican voters, but Cruz's research director wrote in a campaign memo that more than 50 million had stayed home in 2012. How would Cruz draw them out? For starters, he would round up the people who had been publicly shamed for their old-fashioned religious beliefs—or their bigotry and intolerance, as those on the other side called it—and give them a public celebration.

What would Jesus have done? Not even Christians could agree. The question of same-sex marriage was dividing families, churches, entire denominations. Those on the traditional-marriage side felt increasingly isolated. In Grimes, Iowa, where Richard and Betty Odgaard shut down their wedding chapel to avoid hosting same-sex weddings, some of their children had crossed to the other side. Betty lost one friend after another. She asked if they could agree to disagree, keep the conversation going, but the chasm was just too wide.

On August 21, 2015, Cruz hosted a Rally for Religious Liberty in downtown Des Moines. Guests of honor included a florist who wouldn't provide flowers for a same-sex wedding, a fire chief who lost his job because of his writings opposing homosexuality, and an Air Force master sergeant who was reassigned after telling his lesbian commander his views on traditional marriage.

"You talked about not knowing where your friends are," Cruz told the Odgaards from the stage of a packed auditorium. "Well, let me point out there are 3,000 Iowans."

A few minutes later, the baker from Oregon told her story.

"We had lots of people that would come in," Melissa Klein said, "who were just, 'So proud of you guys! We're so glad, you know, that you're standing up for your faith.' And then they'd wanna order stuff. 'We wanna support you.' And then, I'd go to—I always put my sticker on the box. It said Sweet Cakes by Melissa, and it was a black sticker with pink writing. And, um—"

Top: **Sen. Ted Cruz poses with his wife, Heidi, and their two daughters.**

She paused to collect herself.

"—they'd ask me to not put that on the box. And so I sat there and I thought, 'If you're with me, and you're standing with me, why can't you stand yourself?'"

She paused again, this time for thunderous applause. It seemed the silent Americans were ready to make some noise.

⋆ ⋆ ⋆

But there was more than one kind of silent American, even on the political right, and this is where Cruz's path to the nomination got complicated. If one conservative voter felt silenced on issues of biblical morality, another felt silenced on race, immigration, feminism or multiculturalism. Some felt silenced about all these things. They saw themselves as victims of a new cultural orthodoxy that valued the rights and feelings of everyone but them.

The idea of a large and quiet voting bloc had come up in previous elections. Most notably, President Richard Nixon appealed to the "silent majority" for support against the antiwar counterculture in 1969. This group was understood to be mostly white, mostly conservative and slightly old-fashioned—a fair description of the voters who helped Republicans take over the South. By 2015, with the minority population growing faster than the white majority and the nation drifting leftward on social issues, these voters felt alienated. Many would choose between Cruz and Trump, two merchants of nostalgia. One was refined and religious; the other coarse and secular. Both conjured visions of a nation gone but not forgotten: a place where straight white people didn't have to tread so lightly, and the silent American was someone else.

⋆ ⋆ ⋆

Trump and Cruz both knew that conservatives viewed the mainstream media as a gear in the left-wing outrage machine, an accessory to the silencing of average conservatives. And they used this fact to their advantage. The more outrageous things Trump said, the more

the media amplified his voice. The more he excoriated the media, the more free airtime he received. Cruz also attacked the media whenever he could, like a gladiator who fires up the crowd by hurling his javelin at the referee.

"Let me say something at the outset," he said on October 28, 2015, at the CNBC debate.

"The questions that have been asked so far in this debate illustrate why the American people don't trust the media."

Republican pollster Frank Luntz was conducting a focus group that night. As Cruz went on, his scores climbed rapidly.

"This is not a cage match," Cruz said with fierce moral conviction. "And if you look at the questions: Donald Trump, are you a comic-book villain? Ben Carson, can you do math?

John Kasich, will you insult two people over here? Marco Rubio, why don't you resign? Jeb Bush, why have your numbers fallen? How about talking about the substantive issues people care about?"

This anti-media tirade reached an average score of ninety-eight. In nineteen years of focus groups, Luntz had never seen a score so close to perfect.

In hindsight, a close observer could see in that moment the qualities that would propel Cruz toward the nomination—and those that would leave him short. If it illustrated why so many Americans didn't trust the media, it also showed why some Republican voters didn't trust Ted Cruz.

Yes, he was uncompromising in his ideology, a fearless spokesman for the conservative cause. But one faction of conservatives

simply didn't believe him. When it came to the ways and means of winning, he seemed to place results above all else. The highest-scoring debate line in two decades was a complaint about a lack of substantive questions from a man who'd just been asked a substantive question.

Some of that night's questions had been needlessly provocative. But the question for Cruz was about preventing a government shutdown, an issue people *did* care about.

"Does this count?" CNBC host Carl Quintanilla tried to ask Cruz through the deafening applause. "Does this—do we get credit for this one?"

As Quintanilla grinned in disbelief, Cruz waved him off.

"And Carl, I'm not finished yet," he said. "The contrast with the Democratic debate, where every fawning question from the media was, 'Which of you is more handsome and wise?' And let me be clear—"

"So this is a question about the debt limit," Quintanilla said, "which you have thirty seconds left to answer. Should you choose to do so."

Cruz's fight against federal deficits and Obamacare led to the government shutdown of 2013 even as it solidified his national reputation. Now, given a second chance to address one of his signature issues, he instead grumbled for thirty-five more seconds about media bias and cage matches. He ran out of time, never having touched the original question, and when moderator John Harwood said, "We're moving on," Cruz's response could only be described as disingenuous:

"So you don't actually wanna hear the answer, John?"

Then again, many voters on both sides saw winning as the ultimate virtue. There once was a candidate who changed world history for the better. First he had to win the Republican nomination, which he did after

If Cruz lost the battle, it would not be for lack of weapons. And throughout the summer and fall of 2015, his most powerful weapon was Donald Trump.

his aides packed the convention hall with supporters who got in using counterfeit tickets. Did the end justify the means? If Honest Abe Lincoln had played by every rule, you might not know his name.

By 2015, Christian conservatives were sick and tired of losing. They gave Iowa to Mike Huckabee in 2008, to Rick Santorum in 2012, and both those candidates lost to other Republicans who then compounded the insult by losing to Obama. Huckabee and Santorum were men of faith. Neither had what it took to win.

Republicans had elected only two presidents in the last thirty years. Both were named Bush. The first had Lee Atwater. The second had Karl Rove.

Cruz had Jeff Roe, the merciless political operative who once produced a radio ad that mocked an opposing candidate's physical appearance and suggested he could be squashed like a bug. The ad became infamous after its target, Missouri State Auditor Tom Schweich, shot himself to death for other reasons. Now Roe was Cruz's campaign manager. His chief spokesman was Rick Tyler, who'd promoted the error-filled "documentary" on Bain Capital that helped sink Mitt Romney in 2012. One of Cruz's top surrogates in Iowa was the radio host Steve Deace, who kept on the wall of his studio a sign adapted from a line by

H.L. Mencken: "There comes a time in every man's life when he must spit on his hands, raise the black flag, and begin slitting throats."

If Cruz lost the battle, it would not be for lack of weapons. And throughout the summer and fall of 2015, his most powerful weapon was Donald Trump.

It was clear from the beginning that Trump was not a lifelong social conservative. If he was a Christian, as he claimed to be, he was the rare variety who said he never asked God's forgiveness. He had once supported both Hillary Clinton and late-term abortion rights, two of social conservatives' worst nightmares. But Cruz made a basic wartime calculation, and it went something like this: *The enemy of my fifteen other enemies could be a useful friend.*

As Trump demolished one mutual foe after another, along with the notion of political decorum, Cruz stood by and softly encouraged him. In September, at a joint rally in Washington against the nuclear deal with Iran, Cruz put his arms around Trump. He later said there might be a role for Trump in a Cruz administration. He said President Cruz might hire Citizen Trump to build a wall on the Mexican border. On December 11, four days after Trump's call for a temporary ban on Muslim immigration, Cruz posted this message on Twitter:

The Establishment's only hope: Trump & me in a cage match. Sorry to disappoint -- @realDonaldTrump is terrific. #DealWithIt

★ ★ ★

When the cage match finally started, around the middle of January, both Trump and Cruz understood its larger meaning. The winner would be the man who could prove to Republican voters that *he* was the real American.

In the broad outlines of his biography, Cruz embodied the complexity of the American experience. His father had fled persecution in Cuba and worked his way through the University of Texas, washing dishes for fifty cents an hour, learning English at the movies. His mother came from Irish and Italian ancestry and had split her childhood between the Mid-Atlantic and the Deep South. The two mathematicians settled in western Canada, analyzing seismic data to help oil companies find hidden reserves, and there they gave their newborn son a name that reflected his diverse heritage: Rafael Edward Cruz. For most of his childhood they called him Felito, a shortened version of "Little Rafael," but the kids in junior high thought Felito

When the cage match finally started, around the middle of January, both Trump and Cruz understood its larger meaning. The winner would be the man who could prove to Republican voters that *he* was the real American.

sounded a lot like Frito or Dorito, and he got tired of all the teasing. When his mother told him he could change his nickname, it came as a revelation. He could be anyone he wanted: Rafael, Edward, Raph, Ralph, Ed, Eddie or even Ted, a name his conservative father hated because of its connection to the Kennedy. Well, too bad. Felito was becoming his own man. He decided on Ted.

Who would Ted be, and where would he be *from*? Were his people the classmates from Second Baptist High in Houston, his debate partners at Princeton, his professors at Harvard Law? Was he a product of Texas or the Ivy League? Someone who aspired to the presidency might find a way to be all these things—to use every part of his story to widen his popular appeal. "Politics is about addition," he liked to say. But sometimes he couldn't help dividing or subtracting.

Most Americans who lived through 9/11 remember exactly where they were when they heard the news. Everyone changed somehow. Cruz was a 30-year-old attorney working for the Federal Trade Commission under President George W. Bush. Later, in an interview on "CBS This Morning," he would reveal one of that day's surprising effects.

"I grew up listening to classic rock," he said, "and I'll tell you sort of an odd story. My music tastes changed on 9/11. And it's a very strange—I actually, intellectually, find this very curious. But on 9/11, I didn't like how rock music responded. And country music

collectively, the way they responded, it reso-
nated with me....I had an emotional reaction
that says, 'These are my people.'"

The story is oddly relevant to what transpired between Cruz and Trump in the weeks
before the 2016 Iowa caucuses. *These are
my people*? Even if Cruz's story was true, it
represented the politics of division. Liking
country music did not require forsaking rock
'n' roll. Yes, the country singers Toby Keith
and Alan Jackson lit up the sky after 9/11.
So did a lot of non-country singers, including
Tom Petty, Wyclef Jean and Paul Simon, all of
whom played a telethon ten days after 9/11
that helped raise nearly $150 million for the
victims and their families.

In January 2016, when Trump got nervous
about Cruz's rising poll numbers and broke

their nonaggression pact, he used the same
charge he had used against Obama: *This man
is a counterfeit American*. Most constitutional
experts said Cruz was eligible to be president, despite his Canadian birth, because his
mother was an American citizen at the time.
Trump didn't care. He amplified the charge
with rock 'n' roll, to which he held an unwaver-
ing allegiance, by adding Bruce Springsteen's
"Born in the U.S.A." to his pre-rally playlist.

It was high time for Cruz to tell Iowa voters
how he really felt about Trump. He could
have stuck to the issues, focusing on Trump's
many heresies against conservatism. Instead,
when the radio host Howie Carr asked him
about Trump playing the Springsteen song,
Cruz said, "Well, look, I think he may shift in
his new rallies to play 'New York, New York,'

because Donald comes from New York and he embodies New York values."

With that, the Iowa race became a competition of xenophobias, a civil war of the silent Americans. Trump warned the voters against a "Canadian anchor baby," connecting suspicion of Cruz with antipathy for illegal immigrants. And Cruz cast Trump as a pro-choice *cultural* foreigner from the host city of the hated mainstream media—the same city where America's gay liberation movement began.

But for Cruz, it was another case of needless subtraction. When the planes hit the towers in 2001, he had a boss in the White House who liked country music and brush-clearing and guns and religion and all those red-state things you expect from a Texas Republican. In October, Bush put on a jacket that said FDNY and walked to the mound at Yankee Stadium and threw out a first pitch that got those blue-state Yankees chanting *U-S-A*. Philosophical disagreements aside, the last Republican president knew how to play nice with New York.

When Cruz repeated the phrase "New York values" at the debate on the Fox Business Network on January 14, it gave Trump his best debate moment of the primary season.

"New York is a great place," Trump said, his voice going unusually soft. "It's got great people, it's got loving people, wonderful people. When the World Trade Center came down, I saw something that no place on Earth could have handled more beautifully, more humanely than New York....You had two 110-story buildings come crashing down. I saw them come down. Thousands of people killed, and the cleanup started the next day, and it was the most horrific cleanup, probably in the history of doing this, and in construction. I was down there, and I've never seen anything like it. And the people in New York fought and fought and fought, and we saw more death, and even the smell of death—nobody understood it. And it was with us for months,

the smell, the air. And we rebuilt downtown Manhattan, and everybody in the world watched, and everybody in the world loved New York and loved New Yorkers."

It took a lot of doing for a Republican to get on the wrong side of Bush 43 with the bullhorn in the rubble, but Cruz had found a way. On the front of the next day's New York Daily News, the Statue of Liberty gave him the finger. Even in the polarized climate of 2016, a candidate would eventually need more friends than enemies. Of his fifty-three Republican colleagues in the Senate, none had endorsed Cruz. Iowa's Republican governor took the extraordinary step of calling for Cruz's defeat. Meanwhile, Huckabee's super PAC called him a fake Christian because of his admitted failure to tithe. The New York Times called him a fake populist firebrand because of an undisclosed campaign loan from Goldman Sachs. Iowa's Republican secretary of state reprimanded him for deceptive mailers that tried to frighten voters to the polls by raising the specter of a nonexistent civil infraction called a "voting violation."

In spite of all this, Cruz still had a plausible route to the nomination. At least two of his top advisers believe he would have won if not for the choice his top lieutenants made in the last hours of the Iowa campaign.

Even in the polarized climate of 2016, a candidate would eventually need more friends than enemies. Of his fifty-three Republican colleagues in the Senate, none had endorsed Cruz.

Any explanation of how Cruz won Iowa must acknowledge the fact that he ran a more technologically advanced campaign than any other Republican.

★ ★ ★

Any explanation of how Cruz won Iowa must acknowledge the fact that he ran a more technologically advanced campaign than any other Republican. Shortly after the congressional election of 2014, Cruz sat down with a renowned data scientist named Chris Wilson and told him what it would take to be his director of research and analytics.

"Senator Cruz would not accept an operation that was inferior to anybody else in the field, Republican or Democrat," Wilson said in an interview. "And that if I was going to accept this job, it was incumbent on me to ensure that was the case. And that any time he ever felt we were falling behind another campaign in our use of data and analytics and just overall, every aspect of it, from machine learning and artificial intelligence, technology and everything, that I'd be replaced. He wasn't rude about it. He just was very clear and matter-of-fact that he expected us to have a superior operation, not just on the Republican side but in the general election as well."

With occasional advice from Cruz's 80-year-old mother, Wilson and five other data scientists built a voter-turnout machine of unusual sophistication. They identified

seventy-seven separate issues that mattered to Iowa voters. They built psychological profiles on each voter and determined through frequent door-to-door and telephone surveys the statistical likelihood that any given voter would vote for any given candidate on any given day. Their message to gun-loving rural Iowans focused on hunting, and their message to gun-loving urban Iowans focused on crime. Their message to Rubio leaners differed from their message to Trump leaners, which differed from their message to Carson leaners, 3,185 of whom they considered persuadable in the week before the caucuses.

One prolific volunteer, Bill Charlier, a 38-year-old auto mechanic from Des Moines, frequently included the following sentence in his conversations with other voters:

"Here's why I chose Cruz over Carson."

For evangelical voters who wanted nothing to do with politics as usual, Carson emerged in the summer and fall of 2015 as the gentle alternative to Donald Trump. He took a slim lead in national polls in late October, sending Trump to a new level of onstage histrionics. But Carson fell apart on close inspection. It turned out that a patriotic and religious neurosurgeon did not necessarily make a credible presidential candidate. That left voters looking for

Top left: **Cruz campaign staff at a rally in Miami in March 2016.**
Opposite: **Cruz speaks at the Faith & Freedom Coalition conference in June 2015 in Washington, D.C.**

an alternative to the alternative, a maverick who actually knew policy, and many of them defected to Cruz. By January, Carson's campaign had splintered and his support in Iowa had plummeted. Three days before the caucuses, Roe told reporters the argument his volunteers were making to the Carson voters:

"Any vote that's not for us is probably a wasted vote."

He had a point, both in Iowa and beyond. Though not one vote had been cast, polls indicated that only three candidates—Trump, Cruz and Rubio—had any real chance to win the nomination. But one-quarter of Iowa Republican voters would divide their support among nine other candidates who had already passed from the realm of viability. Throughout the primary season, that segmentation would

favor Trump. So would the misstep that turned Cruz's first victory into something resembling a moral defeat.

⁗⁗⁗⁗⁗⁗⁗⁗⁗⁗⁗ ★ ★ ★ ⁗⁗⁗⁗⁗⁗⁗⁗⁗⁗⁗

On the night of February 1, seventeen minutes before the caucuses began, CNN senior digital correspondent Chris Moody shared some news about the Carson campaign in two posts on Twitter:

> Carson won't go to NH/SC, but instead will head home to Florida for some R&R. He'll be in DC Thursday for the National Prayer Breakfast.
>
> Ben Carson's campaign tells me he plans to stay in the race beyond Iowa no matter what the results are tonight.

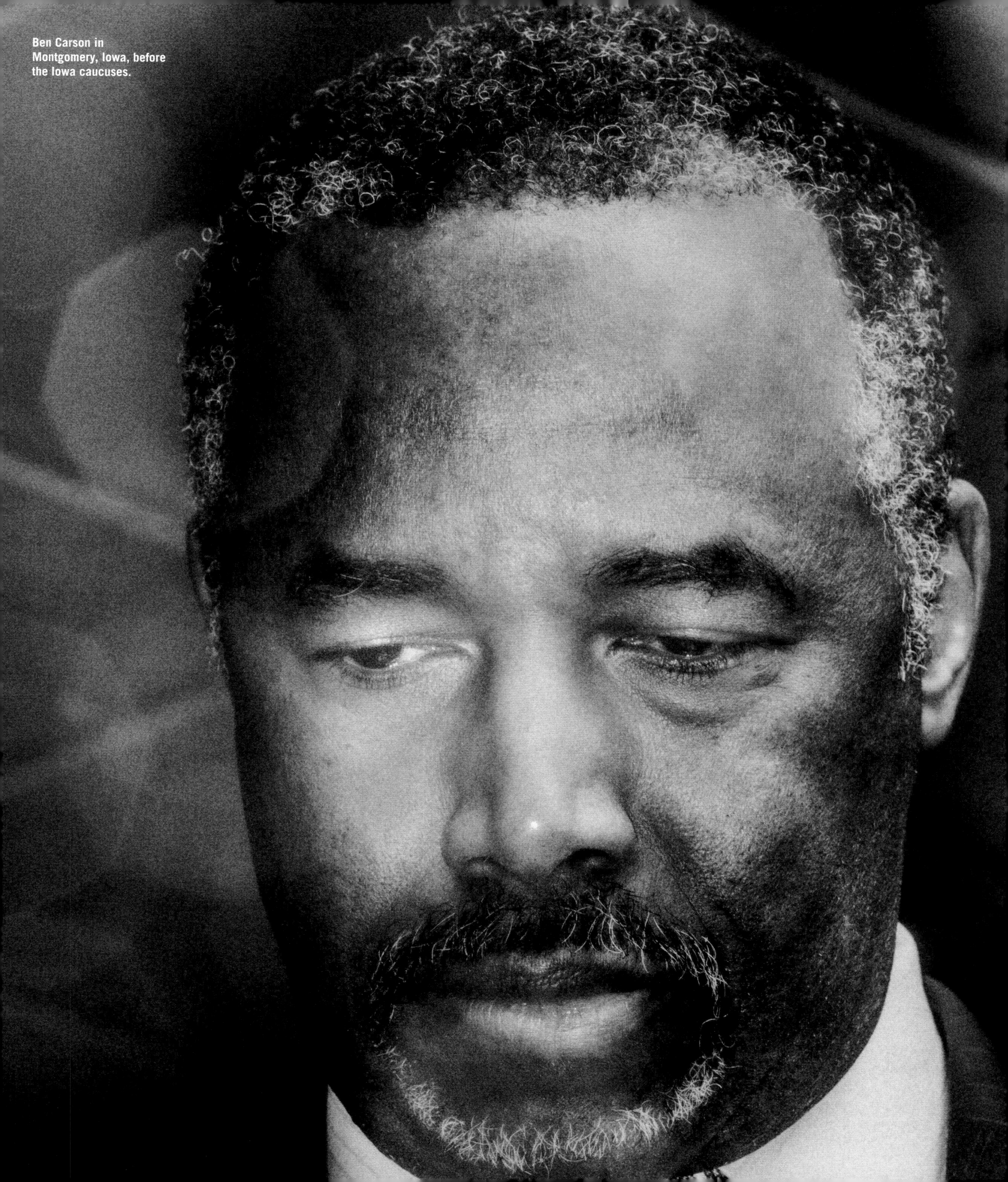

Ben Carson in Montgomery, Iowa, before the Iowa caucuses.

The news aired on CNN television two minutes later.

DANA BASH, CHIEF POLITICAL CORRESPONDENT: *He's going to go for several days. And then afterwards, he's not going to go to South Carolina. He's not going to go to New Hampshire. He's going to come to Washington, D.C., and he's going to do that because the National Prayer Breakfast is on Thursday. And people who have been following Ben Carson's career know that that's really where he got himself on the political map, attending that prayer breakfast and really giving it to President Obama at the time. He became a hero among conservatives, among evangelicals especially.*

JAKE TAPPER, CHIEF WASHINGTON CORRESPONDENT: *That's very unusual—*

BASH: *Very unusual.*

Watching CNN in the lobby of the Marriott hotel in downtown Des Moines, Chris Wilson thought the same thing. He says he believed Carson might leave the race soon, and he wanted Carson's supporters to know right away.

Around 6:50, as Carson and a spokesman, Jason Osborne, pulled up to a caucus site, their smartphones buzzed with new messages. The news about Carson's trip to Florida was taking on a life of its own. On Twitter at 6:53, Osborne tried to clarify:

> *@RealBenCarson will be going to Florida to get fresh clothes b4 heading back out on the campaign trail. Not standing down.*

But in the fog of war, three of Cruz's top aides—Wilson, Roe and senior communications adviser Jason Miller—made a quick decision. According to Wilson, Cruz was in transit and was not consulted. Wilson took an iPhone picture of the TV screen. It showed a banner that said, *CAMPAIGN: CARSON TO TAKE A BREAK AFTER IOWA.* This picture

At 7:29 p.m., a Cruz precinct captain from the small town of Arion in western Iowa received a voice mail that said, "Hello, this is the Cruz campaign with breaking news: Dr. Ben Carson will be . . . suspending campaigning following tonight's caucuses."

accompanied a notification that went out to volunteers on the Ted Cruz mobile app at 7 p.m.—the precise time the caucuses were starting. The message said:

> *CNN is reporting that Ben Carson will stop campaigning after Iowa. Make sure to tell all of your peers at the caucus supporting Carson that they should coalesce around the true conservative who will be in the race for the long haul: TED CRUZ!*

The game of telephone had begun, with the message gradually becoming less favorable to Carson and more favorable to Cruz. *CARSON TO TAKE A BREAK* became *Carson will stop campaigning.* In another notification to precinct captains, deputy state director Spence Rogers wrote, *Breaking News. The press is reporting that Dr. Ben Carson is taking time off from the campaign trail after Iowa and making a big announcement next week. Please inform any Carson caucus goers of this news and urge them to caucus for Cruz.*

It is not clear what the "big announcement" was supposed to be. Nor is it always obvious when semantic drift becomes an outright lie. At 7:29 p.m., a Cruz precinct captain from the small town of Arion in western Iowa received a voice mail that said, "Hello, this is the Cruz campaign with breaking news: Dr. Ben Carson will be…suspending campaigning following tonight's caucuses."

Big announcement. Stop campaigning. Suspending campaigning. Were these fair representations of *CARSON TO TAKE A BREAK*? The precinct captain, Nancy Bliesman, said in an interview that she still believed in Cruz, still hoped and prayed he would be the next president. She did not even hear the voice mail until after the caucus. But this was her reaction: "Well, I wasn't happy, because I don't like it when people cheat."

How did Cruz overcome a polling deficit to win Iowa by three points over Trump? There are many possible answers. He had a superior data operation. He visited all ninety-nine counties and held as many as seven events per day. His silent Americans—the religious ones—felt an unprecedented threat to their liberty and turned out in record numbers, just as he thought they would. A cattle farmer named David Taylor stopped on his way to the Fremont Community Center and picked up two more Cruz voters, both in their eighties, who would caucus for the first time in their lives.

Months later, Cruz's national co-chair, U.S. Rep. Steve King of Iowa, said not a single voter had come forward to report changing a vote from Carson to Cruz because of confusion over the status of Carson's campaign. Iowa Republican Party Chairman Jeff Kaufmann said he did not believe the messages about Carson played an important role in the final results. Carson took fourth place with about 9 percent of the vote, a point ahead of his final polling average. "I was reasonably happy today," he told supporters before he left Iowa that night, "until I, you know, discovered the dirty tricks that were going on."

Tears came to Betty Odgaard's eyes during Cruz's victory speech in Des Moines. She had stood up for her faith, and Cruz had stood up for her, and more than 51,000 Iowans had stood up for Cruz, giving him the highest Republican vote total in the forty years since the Iowa GOP started keeping count. Newly emboldened, Cruz reached for the mantle of President Ronald Reagan.

"To the Reagan Democrats: Your party has left you," he said. "And the Republican Party wants you. We welcome you back. Because together this year, Republicans and the Reagan Democrats can send an unmistakable message: the message of a Reagan-like landslide that once and for all will drive the liberal elites and the Washington Cartel into the Potomac and out to sea, never to be seen again."

He was trying to unite all the silent Americans. But the Reagan Democrats were not Cruz Democrats. They were breaking for Trump. So were a surprising number of the evangelicals Cruz hoped to consolidate. Also problematic: Rubio had made a late surge, nearly overtaking Trump for second place in Iowa, and now Carson seemed intent on staying in the race, further splintering the evangelical vote.

Why did Cruz win Iowa? What mattered most in political terms was the explanation that *voters believed*, and the way it might influence upcoming primaries. "Ted Cruz didn't win Iowa, he stole it," Trump said on Twitter two days later. With a bully's genius for exploiting weakness, he would make sure the Iowa incident followed Cruz for the rest of the campaign. He would make it simple, the way Trump usually did, with a nickname straight out of fourth grade. "Low-energy" Jeb Bush had already been severely damaged by such name-calling. "Little Marco" Rubio and "Crooked Hillary" Clinton would face the bully soon enough. Now it was Cruz's turn. Every time Trump said his name, the words would reverberate across the media landscape. Rafael? Edward? Felito? No. Trump would go with "Lyin' Ted."

Cruz speaks at a tea party event before the New Hampshire primary.

4

**THE REPUBLICANS
ENTER THE
TWILIGHT ZONE**

Here is the story of thirty-eight days in early 2016 that saw the party of Lincoln and Reagan become the party of Donald Trump. He had not won anything before this stretch began, and by the end he'd won so much that he seemed almost bored with winning. There is no way to know whether anyone could have stopped him in these days—whether a better strategy by one or more opponents might have altered the course of history—but the story of those efforts is one of blunders and miscalculations, of desperate gambles that did not pay. Time and again his rivals stumbled on themselves and each other while Trump ran on, untouched. "Hostility works for some people; it doesn't work for everyone," he said on March 8, acknowledging the strange asymmetry that allowed him to say what others could not say, in a tone others could not use, while turning a victory speech into an infomercial for the water and wine that bore his name.

In fairness to the last three men who stood between Trump and the nomination, these thirty-eight days seemed to widen the very contours of reality. They did not know a modern American candidate could gain strength by encouraging violence. They were unprepared for an opponent who would be heralded by the white-nationalist fringe. They were unaware that a Republican could win a landslide victory in South Carolina the day after telling a century-old fictional story about an American general executing forty-nine Muslim terror suspects with bullets dipped in the blood of pigs.

But if the Grand Old Party crossed a cosmic boundary somewhere between early February and the Ides of March, it had spent many years drifting toward the line. The party had survived for 161 years. It had produced eighteen presidents. And by 2015, it was not quite sure what it wanted to be. Its growing faction of low-income voters had few common interests with its corporate financiers, who were battling the social conservatives while also fighting the populists. If this was the party of struggling white people, it had chosen an awkward standard-bearer in Mitt Romney the last time around: a man who said corporations were people, casually mentioned that his wife drove a couple of Cadillacs, and railed against the 47 percent of low-income Americans who paid no taxes even as he lowered his own taxes by parking millions in the Cayman Islands.

Trump never pretended to be Joe Six-Pack. That would have been implausible, and a little too ordinary. Instead he won over working-class Republicans by playing the master of men like Romney—by playing a golden colossus who would gladly strike down all that displeased the "real" Americans. *Let the market govern big corporations?* No. The golden colossus would bend corporations to the people's will. Punish Ford and Carrier for outsourcing American jobs. Punch China in the *face*. And if all those other Republicans were really on your side, why did they go around asking billionaires for money? Why did Jeb Bush, Marco Rubio and Ted Cruz all go hat in hand to the industrialists who planned to spend nearly $900 million on the upcoming election? On the weekend of the Koch Brothers' famous retreat in August 2015,

> There is no way to know whether anyone could have stopped him in these days...but the story of those efforts is one of blunders and miscalculations, of desperate gambles that did not pay. Time and again his rivals stumbled on themselves and each other while Trump ran on, untouched.

Trump taunted them on Twitter: "I wish good luck to all of the Republican candidates that traveled to California to beg for money etc. from the Koch Brothers. Puppets?"

Given Trump's disruptive power, only a superlative candidate could have beaten him. On February 6, as the decisive 38-day stretch began, many Republicans thought Rubio could be that candidate. He routinely beat Hillary Clinton in head-to-head polling. He'd finished only a point behind Trump in Iowa, and that week another candidate's tracking poll showed him almost neck and neck with Trump in New Hampshire. Five months younger than Cruz at age 44, Rubio was the youngest candidate in the race and perhaps the most charismatic, with a personal story about hard work and American gratitude that played well almost everywhere. Although he'd never led in the polls, he was surging at the right time.

But first he had to finish the New Hampshire campaign, which meant taking the stage at that night's debate, which meant one last showdown with his antagonist: New Jersey Gov. Chris Christie.

"If he beat out Bush, Christie and Kasich in New Hampshire, Rubio was probably going to be the nominee of the party," Matt Mowers, Christie's New Hampshire state director, said later. "You had to stop him in New Hampshire, or he wasn't going to be stopped."

Rubio would be stopped: partly by the collision that night, and partly by forces that had been gathering within the party for a long

One school of thought says the whole thing was Rubio's fault. It says he never should have been in the race. In the Republican Party, candidates *knew how to wait their turn.* And it was not Rubio's turn.

time. At one inflection point after another in February and March, these forces conspired against everyone but Trump.

✯ ✯ ✯

As Republican-on-Republican rhetorical violence escalated in early January, one of the party's best political brawlers did something unusual: He called for peace. Christie's poll numbers were falling, thanks in part to negative ads from a pro-Rubio super PAC, and his response was a somber warning.

"Do not be fooled," Christie said in a campaign ad. "Any significant division within the Republican Party leads to the same awful result: Hillary Rodham Clinton, in January of 2017, taking the oath of office as president of the United States. This country cannot afford that outcome. And thus, we Republicans have a duty—I believe, a profound *moral* duty—to work together."

This is how seriously Christie took his profound moral duty: He went on the radio on January 7 and said that if Rubio ran against Clinton, she would "pat him on the head and then cut his heart out."

As it turned out, Christie would do that job himself—with help from the other Republican

candidates. One Republican operative recalled being approached by Christie's staff: "The first thing they said was, 'We're going to go after Rubio—destroy him.'"

Why did they gang up on Rubio instead of on Trump? On someone who generally shared their values instead of someone who didn't? One school of thought says the whole thing was Rubio's fault. It says he never should have been in the race. In the Republican Party, candidates *knew how to wait their turn.* And it was not Rubio's turn.

But Rubio would not wait. Even though his list of accomplishments was short. Even though he was the third-most popular Republican presidential candidate *in his own state.* Even though his destruction of Jeb Bush called to mind a Burmese python invading the Everglades: Maybe he swallows the alligator, but both of them perish in the fight.

"In hindsight," said Al Cardenas, former chair of the Florida Republican Party, "Marco's entry into this race was predictably fatal for both he and Jeb."

Another theory says it was Bush's fault. It says he was always too weak to play the favorite. It says the donors who put nearly $122 million in his super PAC should have

used that money to kindle a bonfire, because at least that way it couldn't have done the work of Donald Trump. It wouldn't have clogged Facebook feeds in Iowa with a video mocking Rubio's boots, filled New Hampshire mailboxes with nasty literature about Ohio Gov. John Kasich or bombarded voters in South Carolina with costly three-dimensional mailers that turned Rubio into a weather vane blowing in the wind.

Rubio made plenty of his own mistakes. Many of the things Christie did right—taking scores of questions at his town halls, staying afterward until the last hand was shaken, texting local politicians to remind them he cared—were things Rubio neglected. He showed up late and left early. His wall of handlers made him inaccessible. One Republican leader in New Hampshire wanted Rubio to sign a card for a girl who'd lost her home in a fire. He gave it to someone on Rubio's staff and never saw it again.

A CNN/WMUR poll released four days before the New Hampshire primary showed Rubio firmly in second place, behind Trump,

with 18 percent. Christie was tied for sixth place, with just 4 percent. That made him an especially dangerous creature: the kind with very little to lose.

Besides that, he and Trump had been friends for years. Trump told Christie in 2015 that he didn't expect to make it past October—at which point he would endorse Christie, according to a Christie adviser who asked not to be named in order to speak about behind-the-scenes maneuvers. "I think they always had an understanding that the first one out would probably endorse the other," the adviser said.

Rubio's disaster at St. Anselm College in New Hampshire began when he pivoted from a question about his own experience to a talking point about another first-term senator who had run for president: "And let's dispel once and for all with this fiction that Barack Obama doesn't know what he's doing. He knows exactly what he's doing. Barack Obama is undertaking a systematic effort to change this country, to make America more like the rest of the world."

Opposite: **Former President George H.W. Bush and former First Lady Barbara Bush at the Houston Republican debate hosted by CNN on February 25, 2016.**

the Obama line for a fourth time, Christie delivered the final blow: "It gets very unruly when he gets off his talking points."

When Rubio walked into the holding room after the debate, he didn't know the extent of the damage. According to a campaign official who was there, he tentatively asked his staff: "How was that?"

Christie had been out of contention for weeks. His attack on Rubio that night would not help him win New Hampshire. But it did help his old friend from across the Hudson River, the man he would endorse in twenty days.

During the first commercial break, Trump grabbed Christie's arm.

"Wow," he said, according to a source familiar with the exchange. "That was tremendous."

☆ ☆ ☆

The Hillary Nutcracker, which retails on Amazon for $30, is a crude figurine of Hillary Clinton that does, in fact, crack nuts.

A moment later, Rubio repeated himself, almost word for word. "Let's dispel with this fiction that Barack Obama doesn't know what he's doing. He knows exactly what he's doing."

Christie pounced. "I want the people at home to think about this," he said. "That's what Washington, D.C., does. The drive-by shot at the beginning with incorrect and incomplete information and then the memorized twenty-five-second speech that is exactly what his advisers gave him."

The Christie loyalists cheered. No one had to check the record. Live on national television, Rubio had just supplied evidence for Christie's most persistent and damaging claim. Christie turned to look at Rubio. "When you're president of the United States," he said, "when you're a governor of a state, the memorized thirty-second speech where you talk about how great America is at the end of it doesn't solve one problem for one person."

It got worse from there. In short order, Rubio repeated himself yet again. In a nearby holding room, his aides watched in horror. As one adviser recalled, "He said it once. He said it twice. And then the third time, everybody was like, 'My God, he said it a third time!'"

But Rubio wasn't done. When he repeated

Another theory says it was Bush's fault. It says he was always too weak to play the favorite. It says the donors who put $122 million in his super PAC should have used that money to kindle a bonfire, because at least that way it couldn't have done the work of Donald Trump.

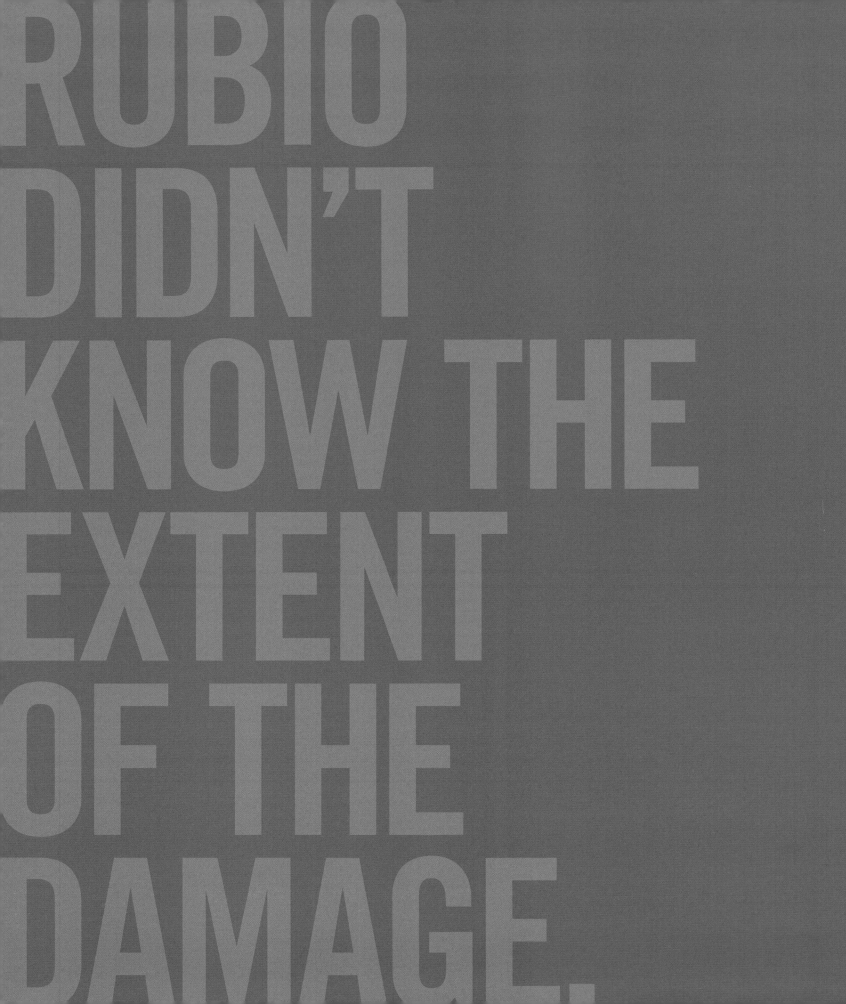

RUBIO DIDN'T KNOW THE EXTENT OF THE DAMAGE.

This product appeals to a certain kind of Republican, and occasionally turns up at campaign events. Rubio autographed one at his Super Bowl party less than twenty-four hours after his calamitous debate. The nutcracker also appeared at a popular lunch spot in Manchester, New Hampshire called the Puritan Backroom. Its bearer was Glenn Fiscus, age 80, who had already gotten the box signed by Christie, Carly Fiorina and three-time presidential candidate Pat Buchanan. Now, hoping for one more autograph, Fiscus handed the box to Kasich.

"No thanks," Kasich said, handing it back. "Give me a piece of paper. I'll write you a note."

This was the ground Kasich claimed during the primaries: that of the rare Republican who gave Democrats their dignity. He tried to stay positive even as his opponents went negative. He had been known as brusque and short-tempered in Washington and Columbus, but for the most part he kept that side of himself under wraps during his presidential run.

Kasich held more than 100 town halls in New Hampshire, rarely mentioning his opponents, often sounding more like a therapist than a presidential candidate. Yes, he was a Christian, but he said little about religious liberty or the Ten Commandments.

He preferred to talk about loving your neighbor, visiting the elderly, giving people hugs. He gave a lot of hugs at those town halls, many after hearing stories of grief, and he gave one more at Clemson University two days before the South Carolina primary.

"Over a year ago, a man who was like my second dad, he killed himself," said Brett Duncan Smith, a young man in dark-rimmed glasses who had driven up from the University of Georgia. "And then a few months later, my parents got a divorce. And then a few months later, my dad lost his job. But—and I was in a really dark place for a long time. I was pretty depressed. But I found hope, and I found it in the Lord, and in my friends, and now I've found it in my presidential candidate that I support. And I'd really appreciate one of those hugs you've been talkin' about."

The image of Kasich embracing Smith was a glimmer of beauty in a mud-soaked brawl, a moment that might have changed something. But this would have required a Republican primary electorate that did not exist in 2016. Maybe it was there in the Reagan era, or the time of George H.W. Bush, but it disappeared in the years thereafter. There was no single reason. The party's devaluation of expertise and civility was gradual and relentless, like the ocean carving away the shore.

Bottom left: **Ohio Gov. John Kasich and his family sit down with CNN's Anderson Cooper for a town hall on April 11, 2016, in New York.**

Kasich spent much of his campaign stuck in an unpleasant paradox. He appealed to independents and even some Democrats who could not help him win, and turned off Republicans who could.

Here was President George W. Bush, who expressed pride in his own academic mediocrity. Here was Sen. John McCain of Arizona, whose choice of running mate claimed to read "all" the newspapers and magazines but could not name a single one. Here was that running mate, Alaska Gov. Sarah Palin, whose false alarm about government death panels helped normalize the wild conspiracy theories that would later emanate from Trump. Here was Senate Republican Leader Mitch McConnell, proclaiming in 2010 that his top goal was to ensure that Barack Obama was a one-term president.

How did Kasich become estranged from his own party? He disagreed with Democrats on most issues, but he did not hate the Democrats or the intellectual elite. To the contrary: He boasted that, as chair of the House Budget Committee, he helped President Bill Clinton balance the federal budget. He accepted Obama's expansion of Medicaid in Ohio. Kasich spent much of his campaign stuck in an unpleasant paradox.

He appealed to independents and even some Democrats who could not help him win, and turned off Republicans who could.

Kasich's surprising second-place finish in New Hampshire required a specific confluence of events: the Bridgegate scandal that Christie wore like a millstone, the ream of political obituaries that Bush could not prove wrong and the Ambush at St. Anselm, after which Rubio's voters defected to Kasich en masse. Even then he won only 15.8 percent of the vote, nearly 20 points behind Trump.

In 2016, Republican primary voters did not want a Republican who made nice with the Democrats. They preferred a man who glibly told stories of Muslim prisoners and blood-covered bullets.

★ ★ ★

To win South Carolina and become the front-runner again, Ted Cruz had one task: to carry his core demographic. This group had given him victory in Iowa. It was too small to

help him much in New Hampshire. But South Carolina appeared to be his friendliest territory yet. Nearly three-quarters of the state's Republican primary voters called themselves born-again or evangelical Christians.

On the surface, it seemed like a simple choice. Here they had a conservative Christian from a Southern state with the endorsement of James Dobson, a legendary figure on the Christian right who told people of faith that it was "time for us to rally around Sen. Ted Cruz." Who would they be rallying to defeat? A foul-mouthed New Yorker who recently said, "I could stand in the middle of Fifth Avenue and shoot somebody and I wouldn't lose voters."

Trump's astonishing victory among South Carolina evangelicals did not just foreshadow the end of Cruz's campaign. It raised serious questions about the political vitality of the Christian right. And it helped ensure that millions of the faithful would either stay home in November or choose between a Democrat and a man so confused by Christian ritual that in Iowa he mistook a communion plate for an offering plate.

Why did these voters reject a candidate who spent his whole campaign claiming to be their champion? David Woodard, a former Republican operative who teaches political science at Clemson University, said many of them looked at Cruz and reached the following conclusion:

"Well, he certainly didn't win me over by his Christian behavior."

Opposite: **Sen. Ted Cruz backstage before the Republican debate in Houston in February 25, 2016.**

The Ben Carson incident in Iowa raised ethical questions about the Cruz campaign. The South Carolina primary raised more. A fake Facebook page claimed erroneously that U.S. Rep. Trey Gowdy had switched his endorsement from Rubio to Cruz. An unsettling flier from the Cruz campaign morphed the faces of Rubio and Obama.

Cruz's campaign manager, Jeff Roe, said in an interview that Cruz's tactics were fairly tame compared to some previous South Carolina primaries. (He was right about that.) He rejected the notion that Cruz ran an unethical campaign and blamed Rubio, Carson and Trump for creating that narrative. "And it was successful" in South Carolina, he said. "But it has no bearing in reality."

On February 22, two days after finishing behind Trump and Rubio in South Carolina, Cruz fired his chief spokesman, Rick Tyler, for spreading a news item that falsely accused Rubio of disparaging the Bible. "I have made clear in this campaign that we will conduct this campaign with the very highest standards of integrity," Cruz said. "That has been how we've conducted it from Day One."

If Cruz really meant this, it is not clear why he hired Tyler in the first place. In a previous campaign, for Missouri Senate candidate Todd Akin, Tyler said of Akin's opponent, "If Claire McCaskill were a dog, she'd be a 'Bullshitsu.'"

> **Trump's astonishing victory among South Carolina evangelicals did not just foreshadow the end of Cruz's campaign. It raised serious questions about the political vitality of the Christian right.**

Was Tyler caught violating the standards of the Cruz campaign, or upholding them? Either way, it cost him his job.

Why did so many evangelicals vote for Trump? He appealed to their patriotism, their frustration with globalism and political correctness, their longing for the way things used to be. One line of reasoning came from Sen. Jeff Sessions of Alabama. A Republican operative says Sessions told him, "You don't get it—we have to do something. We're losing America. Our country is in peril. He's the only person who can bring about radical change. Sometimes God uses ungodly people to do his will."

★ ★ ★

After his disastrous debate, Rubio had another kind of defining moment. It was like opening a door to an alternate future and catching a glimpse of the Republican Party that might have been. He stood on the stage in South Carolina, giving a thumbs-up and smiling that million-dollar smile. To his left stood Sen. Tim Scott, the first African-American since Reconstruction to represent a Southern state in the Senate. Gowdy stood on Rubio's right, next to Gov. Nikki Haley, the daughter of Indian immigrants. "Take a

picture of this," Haley had said of Rubio's entourage, "because the new group of conservatives that's taking over America looks like a Benetton commercial!"

Long after Rubio's campaign ended, his communications director, Alex Conant, thought of that picture: a Hispanic man, a black man, a white man, an Indian-American woman, all of them children of the Reagan Revolution, all ready to lead the party of tomorrow. "It still pops up on my Twitter feed pretty routinely," Conant said in July, "mostly from people who are bemoaning whatever Trump's latest outdated statement is, and they say, 'To think, this is what we could have had.'"

Rubio had some momentum coming out of South Carolina. His aides expected 2,000 people at a rally outside Nashville; more than 5,000 turned out. In Nevada he beat Cruz for the second time in a row. Endorsements rolled in. The establishment coalesced behind him. But time was short. Trump had won three of the first four states; Rubio had won zero. "And so," Conant said, "there was a real expectation amongst our supporters, our donors, the media, that Marco would confront Trump at the Houston debate. We were ready to do it, but I also don't think there was any other choice."

Rubio seemed to enjoy lampooning Trump. "If he hadn't inherited $200 million," he said in Houston, "you know where Donald Trump would be right now? Selling watches in Manhattan."

But he moved in a perilous direction. The more the race resembled entertainment, the more it favored the professional entertainer. Was Trump an unserious candidate? It was easier to make this case while looking the part of a *serious* candidate. Rubio knew that. He had tried that. And it simply didn't work. Fifteen days later, comprehending both the magnitude of his errors and the imminent end of his campaign, he explained the conundrum of running against Trump. He'd been giving serious policy speeches for months, he said, and the media paid little attention.

"And the minute that I mention anything personal about Donald Trump, every network cut in live to my speeches, hoping I would say more of it."

Now Rubio tried to keep the spotlight on himself by offending Trump in new and inventive ways. "You wanna have a little fun?" Rubio asked his fans in Dallas. They cheered. He pulled a smartphone from his pocket. "All right. What does Donald Trump do when things go wrong? He takes to Twitter. I have him right here. Let's read some. You'll have fun."

Rubio's grin registered somewhere between *Hollywood red carpet* and *boy with hand in cookie jar*. "He called me Mr. Meltdown," Rubio said during a riff that lasted more than ten minutes. "Let me tell you something: Last night during one of the breaks, two of the breaks, he went backstage. He was having a meltdown. First he had this little makeup thing, applying like makeup around his mustache because he had one of those sweat mustaches. Then he asked for a full-length mirror. I don't know why, because the podium goes up to here, but he wanted a full-length mirror. Maybe to make sure his pants weren't wet, I don't know."

Bottom left: **Attendees at a Marco Rubio rally in Hialeah, Florida, on March 9, 2016.**

Rubio was the talk of the nation. The networks had given Trump frequent coverage, helping him drown out the other candidates. Now he had an apprentice. In Georgia on February 27, Rubio said Trump should sue the person who gave him the nation's worst spray tan. In Virginia a day later, he said Trump would make America orange. Then he jumped all the way into the gutter. "He's always calling me Little Marco," Rubio said. "…He's taller than me—he's like six-two. Which is why I don't understand why his hands are the size of someone who's *five-two*." He held up his right hand, curling the fingers to make them short. "Have you seen his hands? They're like *this*. And you know what they say about men with small hands—"

"And you know what they say about men with small hands—"

— Sen. Marco Rubio

The audience gasped in amusement and surprise, with a dash of what might have been horror.

"—you can't trust 'em," said the man who wished to lead the free world.

Two days before the pivotal contests of the first Super Tuesday, the Republicans stood in a startling place. A field of seventeen candidates had been narrowed to five. And combined, the four who weren't named Trump had less national support in the latest CNN/ORC poll than Trump, who on CNN's "State of the Union" with Jake Tapper that morning refused to disavow former Ku Klux Klan grand wizard David Duke or the white supremacists who evidently found his message inspiring.

Democrats watched in fascination. They couldn't have scripted the Republican primaries better if they had tried. According to Clinton ally (and former nemesis) David Brock, founder of the pro-Clinton research organization Correct the Record, only four Republican candidates ever worried them: Bush, Christie, Wisconsin Gov. Scott Walker and Rubio. Whenever Democratic researchers found dirt on those four, they publicized it right away. Now three of those candidates were gone, and the fourth was rapidly fading. The Democrats had built a vast opposition file on Trump as well, but they saved that material for later. They *wanted* him to win the primaries, Brock said, because they were pretty sure they could destroy him in November.

"We got the race we wanted," Brock said, "for better or worse."

Trump won seven states on Super Tuesday. Cruz won three, just enough to stay viable. Rubio won only Minnesota. Cruz argued that he could beat Trump one-on-one if Rubio would only get out of the race. But Rubio stayed in.

In Cruzworld, another idea surfaced. Maybe they could persuade Rubio to join forces against Trump. Cruz was serious enough about the alliance that he authorized Sen. Mike Lee of Utah to go to Miami ahead of the CNN debate there on March 10 to help work out a deal.

"I think the two of them as running mates would have been unstoppable," Lee told CNN later. "They would have united the party."

Lee bought a ticket to Miami at his own expense and booked a hotel suite where he hoped Cruz and Rubio would meet. According to two sources familiar with the talks, Rubio initially seemed open to the idea. But just as Lee was about to board his flight, Rubio had a change of heart. "I don't think I can do

this. I don't think I can back out and not be a presidential candidate prior to the primary in Florida," Rubio told Lee, according to one of the sources. Lee flew to Miami anyway, but the meeting never took place.

Instead of meeting with Cruz, Rubio reached out to his onetime mentor, Jeb Bush, to ask for an endorsement. Bush still was revered in Florida Republican circles, and his stamp of approval could have helped rally the party to Rubio's side before the must-win Florida primary.

But the governor had not forgotten his protégé's disloyalty, his impatient decision to enter the race. Bush withheld his endorsement, leaving Rubio to fight Trump on his own.

✯ ✯ ✯

On the morning of March 11, four days before the Florida primary, Corey Lewandowski stood in a ballroom at Trump's Mar-a-Lago Club in Palm Beach, holding a Monster energy drink. Trump's campaign manager had a volatile relationship with the press. One moment he could joke around; the next he might threaten to have a reporter blacklisted. Now he made a joking threat with a sinister undertone.

"You ask tough questions," he said, "you get roughed up."

The reference seemed obvious, and astonishing: Earlier that week, a Breitbart reporter named Michelle Fields alleged that Lewandowski had grabbed and bruised her arm when she tried to ask Trump a question. (Prosecutors would decline to file any charges, citing their inability to prove a crime.) In a few minutes, Ben Carson would stroll inside and offer his endorsement of Trump, the man who recently compared him to a pedophile. In a few hours, former First Lady Nancy Reagan would be interred on a misty hillside in California after her death

Trump won seven states on Super Tuesday. Cruz won three, just enough to stay viable. Rubio won only Minnesota.

at age 94. This day of mourning would also be remembered for its violence, which could now be called a recurring theme for the Trump campaign.

At the front of the ballroom, still waiting for Trump, Lewandowski continued his spontaneous news conference.

"What about the candidate himself?" a reporter asked. "You know, 'I feel like punching the guy in the face,' he said at one rally. That doesn't help, does it?"

"Well, look," Lewandowski said, "I think Mr. Trump's people are very, very passionate. And they're angry, because of the way this country has been taken advantage of, from so many other countries. And so that's the frustration level that I think a lot of people in this country feel, and people express it in different ways."

Most Trump supporters were white, and they often expressed that anger against African-Americans. This happened at a Trump rally in Kentucky in March, when a white nationalist and other Trump supporters were caught on video repeatedly shoving a young black woman. It happened in Nevada in December, when officers removed an African-American protester and a Trump supporter yelled, "Light that motherfucker on fire!" It happened in North Carolina in March, when a man in a cowboy hat punched a black protester in the face and then said, "Yes, he deserved it. The next time we see him, we might have to kill him." It happened in

It is hard to run against a man who turns violence into entertainment, and entertainment into votes. His fellow Republicans had many flaws. But there is another reason they could never appeal to some voters the way Trump did: They had too much common decency. Only Trump could tell security to confiscate protesters' coats before ejecting them into a 25-degree night.

After the mayhem in St. Louis, Trump canceled a rally in Chicago, citing danger from thousands of militant protesters. Fistfights broke out in the arena. A bottle struck a police officer. Scenes of violent chaos appeared on television. And Cruz held on to conventional wisdom like a man to a sinking lifeboat. Which is to say he blamed Trump.

"When you have a campaign that affirmatively encourages violence," Cruz told reporters in Illinois, "you create an environment that only encourages that sort of nasty discourse."

But Cruz misjudged the new Republican electorate. Blame Trump? Not a chance. The protesters added to the flavor. They made it more exciting. Many were college students;

Alabama in November, when white Trump supporters punched and kicked a black protester, after which Trump used a phrase strikingly similar to the one Lewandowski uttered at Mar-a-Lago: "Maybe he *should* have been roughed up."

In other words, Trump gave them permission. And sometimes more than that. In Iowa on February 1, he said, "So if you see somebody getting ready to throw a tomato, knock the crap out of 'em, would you?" The following month, as security escorted a protester out of a Michigan rally, Trump said, "Get him out." He added, "Try not to hurt him. If you do, I'll defend you in court. Don't worry about it."

On March 11, at Trump's rally in St. Louis, more than thirty people were arrested. A black man stood by an ambulance, with tissue paper in his nostrils and bloodstains on his shirt, telling someone he'd been sucker punched. Inside the Peabody Opera House, as protesters disrupted the proceedings for more than ten minutes, Trump stumbled upon a profound and unsettling truth: "Honestly, can I be honest with you?" he said. "It adds to the flavor. It really does. Makes it more exciting. I mean, isn't this better than listening to a long, boring speech?"

> **It is hard to run against a man who turns violence into entertainment, and entertainment into votes. His fellow Republicans had many flaws. But there is another reason they could never appeal to some voters the way Trump did: They had too much common decency.**

UNPRECEDENTED

many were black and Latino. They symbolized the leftist thought police Trump had been preaching against from the beginning. This is why Cruz's top aides came to see the entire Chicago incident as a strategic play by the Trump campaign—and a brilliant one at that. Trump the perpetrator became Trump the victim. The next morning he tweeted, "The organized group of people, many of them thugs, who shut down our First Amendment rights in Chicago, have totally energized America!"

Before March 11, Cruz thought he could win Missouri and North Carolina. He lost them both, along with his best hope of overtaking Trump. Whatever the anti-Trump demonstrators meant to do, Cruz's aides

believe they delivered both states to the man they despised. Who was soul-searching after that? Not the protesters. They believed they had won by closing down Trump's rally. Not the Trump voters. This was their party now.

Barely 200 people turned out for Rubio's election-night bash in his hometown, Miami, in the only county of Florida's sixty-seven he did not lose to Trump. Some left before Rubio arrived. A few more stayed to watch him drop out of the race and disappear behind a black curtain. Some went past the curtain, looking for him, imagining some kind of after-party. Instead they found an aide wiping tears from her eyes and a security guard nudging them toward the door.

"The candidate is gone," he said.

BY
DANA BASH
*CNN Chief
Political Correspondent*

THE PLAYFUL SIDE OF JEB BUSH

Of all the countless rallies, town halls, bus trips and glad-handing I witnessed during this campaign, the events of one evening in September 2015 encapsulated most of the major dynamics of this election, including its tone and tenor.

I was covering a Jeb Bush town hall in New Hampshire. My goal was to try to figure out why the man Republicans assumed would be their nominee wasn't resonating with GOP voters. As Bush's event went on, I realized that my premise was wrong. The former Florida governor was connecting with the audience in the room. He was engaging, and they were engaged. They asked him questions about policy and politics and he answered with knowledge and self-deprecating humor. Then I realized the problem: Bush's charm did not emanate through the camera. In person, he was comfortable in his own skin. On television, he looked awkward. It was a dichotomy like I had never seen in my nearly two decades of covering politics.

Just as I came to that realization, I saw an email on my phone that Donald Trump was making a speech in which he said Bush's relationship with Marco Rubio was "bullshit." (Rubio, a fellow Floridian, had long called Bush his political mentor.) Trump had already gone after his GOP opponents with unprecedented ad hominem attacks, but by using the word *bullshit* on the stump, the reality television star went further than before with self-described non-politically-correct language.

After Bush's town hall, he held a brief press conference, as he almost always did with his traveling press corps. By the time we gathered, Bush had been briefed by his staff about what Trump had said. So when I started to ask for a response, he knew exactly what I was talking about. Initially, I tried to

ask my question without repeating the word Trump had used, but Bush wasn't having it. In front of a gaggle of reporters and cameras, he told me he wouldn't answer the question unless I said exactly what Trump had said. Bush was being playful, a moment in which he reminded me of his brother George, whom I had covered at the White House. I finally

> **Trump had already gone after his GOP opponents with unprecedented ad hominem attacks, but by using the word *bullshit* on the stump, the reality television star went further than before with self-described non-politically-correct language.**

gave up, saying aloud for the world to hear that Trump had just said the Bush-Rubio friendship was "bullshit." Bush's response wasn't particularly memorable—and it was nothing compared to the way he handled the audacity of one presidential candidate using crass language to describe competitors for the nomination.

In retrospect, the evening was littered with moments and personal characteristics that ended up defining the 2016 campaign. An insider with decades of governing experience and a genteel sense of humor was trounced by an outsider who didn't feel shackled by the boundaries of traditional political decorum. As it turns out, the former didn't stand a chance against the latter. It's just not what GOP voters were looking for in 2016.

IN THE DOGHOUSE: THE PRESS AND DONALD TRUMP

BY

JEREMY DIAMOND
CNN Politics Reporter

"Jeremy, you're a dishonest guy."

I had just finished covering another raucous Trump rally—this time in Richmond, Virginia—punctuated by especially vitriolic confrontations between protesters and Trump supporters, when my phone rang.

It was Corey Lewandowski, then Trump's campaign manager, calling to ask me why the brief news story that I had just written focused on the protesters and not the rally itself. Before Trump even left the stage, I had written 300 words to get out the news of the confrontations—which included a Trump supporter spitting on a protester—and I had just gotten back to my laptop to flesh the story out.

"Hold on," Lewandowski suddenly said.

The next thing I knew, Donald Trump was on the phone chewing me out.

"Jeremy, you're a dishonest guy. You're a very, very dishonest guy," he said, emphatically.

He chastised me for focusing on the protests, rather than on his stump speech, and he accused me of overstating the number of protesters (I counted them myself) and of lowballing the size of his crowd (I got the figure from the fire marshal).

"There were over 7,000 people! There were only nine protesters," Trump protested. "You wrote a very dishonest story."

I let him finish venting and began to explain my reporting, but—*click*—he had already hung up on me.

What's mind-boggling is that I had reported that nearly 5,000 people attended his rally—a large number compared to the crowds at his primary opponents' rallies— but a presidential candidate thought the perceived slight was worth personally calling a reporter to complain.

That call was a peek into the mind of the brash billionaire: his obsessive focus on the size of his crowds and the media's coverage of them, as well as his preoccupation with any and every story written about him. His call came less than ten minutes after he had left the rally, and clearly that time had been spent browsing his coverage.

It was also an early glimpse into Trump's contentious relationship with the media, which grew more combative over time, and the bullying tactics he and his aides would employ to try to garner more favorable coverage from the reporters covering his campaign day in and day out, like me.

In the coming year, Trump spokeswoman Hope Hicks would email me to say that Trump believed I was a "bad guy" because I disputed his crowd count at a rally. And Trump himself would tell me "nobody listens to you" after I asked him a tough, policy-oriented question during a news conference. Days after that news conference, he would introduce me to his wife, Melania, as though nothing had happened—and that's when I finally understood that his behavior toward me was just one of many tactics he employed as he sought to gain the upper hand in his battle for publicity.

> **"Hold on," Lewandowski suddenly said. The next thing I knew, Donald Trump was on the phone chewing me out.**

I would also spend weeks at a time in what the campaign coined the "doghouse," a penalty box of sorts for reporters whose stories had personally angered Trump. That treatment resulted in weeks of radio silence from his small circle of aides.

As the campaign drew to a close and the Republican nominee amped up his attacks on the media, his supporters grew increasingly hostile toward reporters. There were boos and threats. And his supporters also picked up on Trump's trademark attack: "dishonest."

BY
DOUGLAS HEYE
CNN Political Commentator and Former Spokesman for the Republican National Committee

A STAIN ON THE REPUBLICAN SOUL

On a rainy Paris December morning, I visited the Bataclan theater.

It was a month after the terror attacks of 2015. The atmosphere remained raw, emotional. The next day, in Saint-Denis, blocks away from the basilica where French royals are buried, I visited the site of the police raid and shootout that killed the ringleader of the attacks. The tributes at the Bataclan, hugging a stranger bereft in grief, while wrapped in my own, then walking on the same street where one of the terrorists was killed were grim reminders of the challenges we face. Over the holidays, I thought more and more of the gravity of our elections, eventually coming to the conclusion there was no scenario in which I could vote for Donald Trump.

There was no, "Aha! Never Trump!" moment, just a slow realization that if I believed the problems America faces are serious, voting for Trump was not an option.

And so in early January, I penned a piece for the Independent Journal Review saying just that, citing Trump's "perversion of conservatism" and his "existential danger for the party."

Eight months of Trump's lack of policy

> # Republicans must confront our demons and take concrete, sustained action if future viability, much less our now governing majority, is a long-term possibility.

knowledge and the Trump-generated outrage du jour made the decision easy. Trump validated my decision over and over.

Now that the election is over and Trump has won, I worry about the party's future—despite our congressional majorities and control of the White House. He might have won, but his racial and sexist remarks have left a stain on the GOP's soul. Women, minorities and today's young voters will be voting for decades to come and may turn away from the party forever.

It is clear—from this election and national demographics that continue to change to the GOP's detriment—that Republicans must confront our demons and take concrete, sustained action if future viability, much less our now governing majority, is a long-term possibility.

Those of us who did not support Trump identified his shortcomings, but not the pre-existing feelings and divisions within the party. Some—including those who drove the 2013 government shutdown—had a vested interest in either a hostile takeover or the party's destruction.

Many people predicted a Democratic wave of 2016 and the death of the Republican Party, just as they did in 2008 and 2012. Instead, part of the outcome of Tuesday's elections is a new Republican Party. Now we will have to roll up our sleeves and support the new president for the common good. It's every bit as important as understanding how we got here.

BY
GLORIA BORGER
*CNN Chief
Political Analyst*

A WOMAN PRESIDENT? MILLENNIALS CAN WAIT

Hillary Clinton had once been the inevitable nominee in 2008, and that did not work out so well. Back then, she ran on her "lifetime of experience" and less on her gender. This time, she was determined to do both, ready to appeal to women and expand that already-existent gender gap against the GOP. Fair enough. But I recall seeking out millennial women supporting Sanders—at one particular rally in snowy Exeter, New Hampshire, last February. And I dutifully asked, "Does the fact that Clinton is a woman matter to you as women? Does the possibility of electing the first woman president enter into your thinking?"

The responses struck me. None of these young women cared. Their explanations were strikingly similar, paraphrased here: "It doesn't matter because of course we will have a woman president in our lifetime. Just maybe not this one." So, after all these years of pushing for gender equity, it had come to this: Younger women were so convinced a woman could get the job, they disregarded gender. Success in raising young women to believe they can be president, as it turns out, was hurting Hillary Clinton. Just another twist in a campaign full of them.

And who can forget that debate moment in October 2015 when Bernie Sanders told Anderson Cooper that he didn't care about Clinton's "damn emails." Shortly after, I sat down with Team Sanders—Bernie and Jane—and he stuck to that script. (And by the way, Sanders the curmudgeon rates your questions as you ask them, as in "good question," "fair question," "excellent question" or, conversely, "Do I have to tolerate people like you?") But looking back then, Sanders very often directed his ire on the media (consumed with picking a fight) as opposed to Clinton herself. Indeed, he complained to me that he was being "really begged…to attack Hillary Clinton. They want to make this personal. I choose not to do that."

Until he did—and no one had to beg him as the race became more competitive. Sanders surged as he took on Clinton on her Wall Street speeches, campaign contributions, even her judgment. The Democrats, who liked

> **Success in raising young women to believe they can be president, as it turns out, was hurting Hillary Clinton.**

to compare their issue-laden campaign to the GOP issue-free campaign, found themselves precisely where they did not want to be: in a character contest.

It was a fight that went on longer than most of us would have predicted. Maybe I should have known earlier when Vice President Joe Biden told me last January—much to the chagrin of the Clinton camp—that Bernie has "authenticity" on the issues of income inequality and that Clinton, well, "it's relatively new for Hillary to talk about."

Oops.

5

**THE REALIST,
THE IDEALIST
AND THE
DEMOCRATIC
MACHINE**

She knew Iowa would be a dog-fight. Knew she might lose again. Knew she had to win, because she was going to lose New Hampshire, which could lead to a loss in Nevada, and nobody won the nomination by losing the first three states. This was not a coronation. Anyone who thought so was forgetting three things. Iowa had an unusual number of hard-core liberals. Iowa's hard-core liberals could not wait to caucus for Bernie Sanders. And in five of the last seven competitive primary cycles, Iowa had predicted the Democratic nominee.

It did in 2008, the last time Hillary Clinton campaigned there, when a political upstart came out of nowhere and ruined her plans. What struck her 2016 Iowa state director about Clinton was her willingness to learn from mistakes, her fierce resolve not to repeat them. Even if she had trouble admitting them in public, she was honest with herself. Matt Paul could see that when he met with her in New York in March 2015, eleven months before the caucuses. Paul knew Iowa well from past campaigns and his work in state government, and her diagnosis of 2008 sounded right to him. That campaign was too big, too impersonal, too staged. She wanted to go back to the formula that helped her win her first Senate race in New York in

2000: small events, face-to-face interaction, actually *listening* to voters. She might have to win them over one at a time.

One advantage Clinton had was the caucus system itself, and the strange and byzantine protocol by which it awarded delegates to the national convention. It would function as a check against liberal students and their visions of a President Sanders.

Like all self-perpetuating social orders, the Iowa Democratic Party knew how to keep newcomers in their place. In the early '70s, still horrified by the national convention riots of 1968, party elders made a plan to diminish the influence of young radicals. Their system rewarded longstanding voters by giving each county more "delegate equivalents" in the *current* election for higher turnout in *past* elections. In a rural county, where residents were more likely to show up for midterm elections, a caucus vote might be worth double the statewide average. In a college town it might be worth half.

If this sounds like a system that could have swayed the closest vote in caucus history, it might have done just that. And if the Iowa results of 2016 seem to fortify a host of conspiracy theories, well, Sanders always said the game was rigged.

Two candidates won the 2016 Democratic primaries, at least in the grander scheme.

Previous spread: **The final two Democratic primary candidates shake hands at the last debate of the primary season April 14, 2016, in Brooklyn, New York.** *Bottom left:* **The Brooklyn debate, sponsored by CNN.** *Opposite:* **A Bernie Sanders rally in Chicago on February 25, 2016.**

Clinton believed in playing the game as it actually was, reaching for every possible advantage. She had to beat Sanders. For the realist, there are no moral victories.

Clinton believed in playing the game as it actually was, reaching for every possible advantage. She had to beat Sanders. For the realist, there are no moral victories.

Sanders had to lose in order to be right. If the economy and the political system were rigged against the average worker, they could not be rigged in *favor* of the candidate demanding their liberation from the billionaires. And if the billionaires were as powerful and corrupt as he claimed, they would never let Sanders become president. Rein in Wall Street? Not on their watch. Single-payer health care? The drug and insurance companies would fight back. No one knew that better than Clinton did.

Sanders in 2016 resembled Clinton in 1994, when she was first lady and her health care proposal met its bitter end. Then, *she* was the idealist colliding with hard political reality. During a CBS News debate on November 14, 2015, Clinton looked at her opponent and caught a glimpse of her younger self:

SANDERS: *It will not happen tomorrow. But when millions of people stand up and are prepared to take on the insurance companies and the drug companies, it will happen, and I will lead that effort. Medicare for all, single-payer system is the way we should go.*

NANCY CORDES, CBS NEWS: *Secretary Clinton, back in 1994, you said that momentum for a single-payer system would sweep the country. That sounds Sanders-esque. But you don't feel that way anymore. Why not?*

"No. Revolution never came. I waited and I've got the scars to show for it."

CLINTON: *No. Revolution never came. I waited and I've got the scars to show for it.*

They were still waiting for revolution in Iowa City, home to the University of Iowa, the seat of a county unofficially known as the People's Republic of Johnson County. Two nights before the caucuses, at a rally on campus with the liberal philosopher Cornel West and the rock band Vampire Weekend, Sanders sang along with the anthem of American socialism: Woody Guthrie's "This Land Is Your Land."

Clinton had many celebrities on her side too, but her Iowa campaign was fairly unglamorous. No more helicopters. Not so many mega-rallies. Iowa voters wanted to get to know their candidates, and Clinton obliged. She held medium-size events in school gymnasiums and small meet-and-greets at private homes. "She dug in and *worked*," Paul said.

Clinton also had one of the best field operations in caucus history. Hikers for Clinton. Kayakers for Clinton. Quilters for Clinton. Organizers searched Twitter for people talking about Clinton, invited them for coffee and then recruited them as precinct captains, according to Marlon Marshall, Clinton's director of state campaigns and political engagement. Marshall said a good field operation could move the needle by 3–5 points in a caucus state like Iowa. And Clinton would need every last point.

Mary Hoyer, chair of the Henry County Democrats in rural southeastern Iowa, did not support Clinton. But she couldn't help noticing the campaign's systematic pursuit of voters.

"I swear," she said, "they hit every single house in town, in Mt. Pleasant, like three or four times."

On caucus night, Clinton and her aides watched the returns come in from a suite on the tenth floor of the Savery Hotel in

> **Clinton had been earning her victory for nearly fifty years, the length of her membership in the party. The caucuses did what the Democrats had intended. They kept power within the establishment, and kept the revolution outside the gates.**

downtown Des Moines. She had a concession speech written, just in case. Hours passed with the race too close to call. A blizzard was approaching. Clinton held a razor-thin lead. The party had not called the race. But she needed to leave for New Hampshire to beat the storm. "You should go out and speak," her campaign manager, Robby Mook, told her. Clinton made a decision: She would declare victory, and hope she was right.

They edited her speech in the car on the way to Drake University, but she ignored the teleprompter and spoke from the heart: "As I stand here tonight, breathing a sigh of relief—thank you, Iowa!" Someone held up a giant pair of red boxing gloves. A few supporters sang along with her anthem, "Fight Song," by Rachel Platten, but many were too shocked by the closeness of the race to do much celebrating.

On the plane to New Hampshire, she ate ice cream. She did not find out about her narrow victory until after she'd touched down.

Clinton won the vast majority of rural and exurban counties, many with more than 60 percent of the vote. These counties were crucial to her statewide victory, in part because each rural vote was worth more than each

"It will not happen tomorrow. But when millions of people stand up and are prepared to take on the insurance companies and the drug companies, it will happen, and I will lead that effort."

—Bernie Sanders

college-town vote under the state delegate equivalent system.

Meanwhile, in the People's Republic of Johnson County, turnout was even higher than it had been for Barack Obama in 2008. Liberal students and their liberal professors flooded the caucuses for Sanders, their dream candidate, helping him beat Clinton there by almost 20 points. But as caucus expert John Deeth later calculated, the average Johnson County voter counted about half as much as the average Iowa voter did.

According to the Iowa Democratic Party, 171,517 votes were cast on caucus night. At the national convention, these votes would translate into twenty-three pledged delegates for Clinton and twenty-one for Sanders. But Ben Foecke, executive director of the Iowa Democratic Party, told CNN that the party did not know how many votes were cast for each candidate, because some smaller precincts awarded delegates by voice vote.

Deeth and David Redlawsk, a Rutgers University professor who studies the Iowa caucuses, agreed on this point: If the raw numbers could be known, they might show that Sanders won the popular vote. But it didn't matter. Sanders had his chance. The experts said he might have won if he'd spent more time in rural Iowa, courting the

voters whose party loyalty gave them outsize influence. His supporters wondered about the influence of the party chairwoman, Andy McGuire, whose neutrality was called into question by a vanity license plate that said *HRC 2016*. (According to Foecke, McGuire already had the plate before she was elected chairwoman. He said she removed the plate and remained neutral during the caucuses.)

Clinton had been earning her victory for nearly fifty years, the length of her membership in the party. The caucuses did what the Democrats had intended. They kept power within the establishment, and kept the revolution outside the gates.

★ ★ ★

If there is one constant in American history, it is the rigging of the system against African-Americans. Even after slavery ended, Democrats spent most of a century excluding them from democracy by all available means: poll taxes, literacy tests, cross-burnings, murder.

Then a Democrat restructured American politics. President Lyndon Johnson had spent much of his twelve-year senatorial career voting with white supremacists for political convenience, but he came to believe

Top left: **A woman watches Sanders speak at a rally in Louisville, Kentucky, in May 2016.**

that segregation was both un-Christian and dangerous to the republic. A swaggering bully who stood six-three and weighed 210 pounds, Johnson was legendary for his persuasive ability. He needed all his power to ram through the Civil Rights Act of 1964 and the Voting Rights Act of 1965. In the Randall B. Woods biography, "LBJ: Architect of American Ambition," Johnson's aide Jack Valenti recalled the president's strong-arming of Sen. Richard Russell Jr., the segregationist from Georgia.

> "Dick, you've got to get out of my way. I'm going to run over you. I don't intend to...compromise."
>
> "You may do that," Valenti remembered Russell replying. "But, by God, it's going to cost you the South and cost you the election."
>
> So be it, Johnson responded.

The Democrats did lose the South, but they gained the loyalty of the same voters they had once persecuted. African-Americans did not just become reliable Democrats. They became an indispensable part of the Democratic establishment—the same Democratic establishment that Bernie Sanders wanted to dismantle.

This was the fatal contradiction of the Sanders campaign: He ran for president as a Democrat, but he thought he was *better* than the Democrats. And for many party loyalists, especially African-Americans, it seemed an odd time to call for revolution. Here was a white man from a white state condemning the system that had just put a black man in the White House for the first time.

Black Democrats' rejection of Sanders in 2016 is a lesson in the distance between high ideals and the facts on the ground. He'd been fighting for civil rights since he was a student at the University of Chicago in the early '60s, when he went to jail for protesting segregated schools. He stood on the National

Following spread:
Sanders prepares for the Democratic debate on March 6, 2016, in Flint, Michigan.

Mall in Washington in 1963 as Martin Luther King Jr. told the nation about his dream. Twenty-five years later, when the Rev. Jesse Jackson ran for the Democratic nomination, very few elected Democrats endorsed the man who could have been the nation's first black president. But Jackson did win the Vermont caucuses, thanks in part to support from Sanders, the independent mayor of Burlington. By his own admission, it was the first time Sanders had voted in a Democratic caucus. Some Democrats complained about his intrusion. One woman slapped him in the face.

This tension followed Sanders throughout his career as a progressive independent in the House and Senate. He usually voted with the Democrats. But he stood outside the party, a lonely prophet raving about compromise and corruption, isolated geographically from black voters and politically from black politicians. Like him or not, the man had nerve: No Democrat in his right mind would have publicly encouraged a primary challenge to Obama in 2011 for his alleged betrayal of the progressive cause.

Clinton had her own trouble with progressive activists in 2016, much of it regarding her husband's centrist policies of the 1990s. Given the party's leftward drift in recent years, his support for welfare reform and her complaint about young criminal "super-predators" made easy retroactive targets. Young Democrats of all races blamed Bill Clinton's crime bill for mass incarceration and sentencing disparities between the predominantly black users of crack cocaine and the predominantly white users of powder cocaine. But Democrats of a certain age remembered the complex reality of 1994: the rampant crime in major cities, the long list of black victims, the black mayors and pastors who supported the bill, the black legislators who gave it their votes. (Sanders voted for it, too.) The Clintons had worked alongside black Democrats for decades. And if the crime bill had a host of unintended consequences, they belonged to the entire Democratic establishment.

Given her connections to the last two Democratic administrations, Clinton *was* the establishment, for better or worse. She knew what worked and what didn't. She knew policy in granular detail. But in the winter and spring of 2016, detailed realism could be a hard sell compared to the grand promise of free college and single-payer health care. Clinton needed a way to turn Sanders's idealism into a disadvantage. She found one just in time.

In the debates, Sanders often cited Clinton's $675,000 in speaking fees from

He stood outside the party, a lonely prophet raving about compromise and corruption, isolated geographically from black voters and politically from black politicians.

Sanders had to lose in order to be right.

Goldman Sachs as evidence that she wouldn't get tough with the big banks. Clinton struggled to answer the charge. She tried invoking 9/11 and loyalty to her home state of New York to explain her connections to Wall Street, but that made no sense. She agreed to release the speech transcripts "when everybody else does," but Sanders had none to release. She finally hit on a winning response at the NBC News debate in Charleston, South Carolina, on January 17.

"He's criticized President Obama for taking donations from Wall Street, and President Obama has led our country out of the Great Recession," Clinton said. "Senator Sanders called him weak, disappointing. He even, in 2011, publicly sought someone to run in a primary against President Obama....I'm going to defend President Obama for taking on Wall Street, taking on the financial industry and getting results."

Sometimes Clinton's message got lost in the weeds. Not here. *I'm with Obama. Sanders is not.* It was clear, simple, devastating, a blunt instrument to swing whenever her challenger got too close.

Despite constant attacks by the Republicans, Obama's approval ratings increased in February and March—making the alliance even more valuable to Clinton. According to her spokesman, Brian Fallon, this was "neither a change election nor a stay-the-course election." Her message split the difference: She gave Obama credit for bringing the country out of the Great Recession, but frequently mentioned American workers' stagnant wages as a way to acknowledge there was still work to do.

For eleven fleeting days in February, Sanders held the lead. He nearly tied Clinton in Iowa. He won a landslide in New Hampshire, as expected in the state that bordered his own. And when the eleven days ended on February 20, he kept it close in Nevada, where CNN entrance polls showed he

had won the Latino vote. But her aides didn't worry. Those Nevada entrance polls held a clue to what lay ahead: Clinton won African-Americans by 54 points.

In a span of three days, from the South Carolina primary on February 27 to the Super Tuesday primaries across the South on March 1, black voters gave Clinton a lead she would never relinquish. The African-Americans of the Democratic Party did not *want* a revolution. They had real power within their party, and they were not looking for a Democratic socialist to blow it up. They knew Hillary Clinton, who went undercover to expose illegal school segregation in Alabama in the 1970s and had been working for racial justice ever since.

Exit polls from Alabama said a lot about these voters. They were not like the young Sanders voters, many of whom had never voted before, many of whom weren't even Democrats. In Alabama's Democratic primary, there were more women than men. More old than young. Thirty-seven percent were black women, and they broke for Clinton by 88 points. Nearly half called themselves moderate or conservative. Three in five attended church at least once a week. Most said the next president should continue Obama's policies, and Clinton won that group by 76 points. Nearly one-third said Sanders

> ## I'm with Obama. Sanders is not. It was clear, simple, devastating, a blunt instrument to swing whenever her challenger got too close.

was too liberal, and Clinton won that group by 90 points.

In Union Springs, Alabama, the seat of a county where Clinton won 2,451 to 178, Mayor Saint T. Thomas explained why he voted for Clinton. When black voters turn out in Union Springs, one thing they vote for is the preservation of their voting rights— the right for which Medgar Evers gave his life, the right for which John Lewis spilled his blood on the Edmund Pettus Bridge, the right Hillary Clinton spent much of her career protecting.

"The name 'Clinton' rings a bell," the mayor said. "And Sanders doesn't."

"I just don't have a *history* with him, per se."

"I have to go with what I know."

★ ★ ★

To understand why the Nevada Democratic State Convention nearly became a riot—why people screamed obscenities, why a man waved a chair like a weapon—it helps to go back nine months to a slightly more civilized gathering. On August 28, 2015, at the Democratic National Committee's summer meeting in Minneapolis, a presidential candidate accused the DNC of rigging the nomination process. This was *not* Bernie Sanders.

"Think about it," former Maryland Gov. Martin O'Malley said. "The Republicans stand before the nation. They malign our president's record of achievements. They denigrate women and immigrant families, they double down on trickle-down and they tell their false story.

And we respond? With *crickets*. Tumbleweeds. A cynical move to delay and limit our own party debates."

There was silence, then tentative applause, then a few loud cheers.

"Four debates," he said, holding up four fingers. "Four debates? Four *debates*?" He gave a look of disgust, as if tasting an expired oyster.

O'Malley did not call out Congresswoman Debbie Wasserman Schultz by name. Nor did he explicitly say the DNC's chairwoman was biased toward Clinton, whose presidential campaign Wasserman Schultz co-chaired in 2008. The DNC's charter required that Wasserman Schultz remain neutral in the nomination process. She repeatedly denied any favoritism. But speaking on condition of anonymity, a former senior DNC official voiced the suspicions of many Democrats:

"If anyone thinks Debbie Wasserman Schultz was neutral, I have land to sell you."

Here the notion of rigging gets complicated. If the DNC meant to help Clinton, the DNC may have actually *hurt* Clinton. If party leaders thought fewer debates would deprive her competitors of publicity and keep Clinton in the lead, that strategy also kept Clinton from taking back the narrative. More than two months passed between the first Republican debate and the first Democratic debate, and for those two months it seemed as if everyone but Clinton was setting the agenda. Only *after* the first debate—which, by many accounts, Clinton won—did her recovery begin.

But the narrative of a rigged system had already taken hold. Sanders made sure of that. Thus, to many of his revolutionaries,

Bottom: **Sanders greets supporters after a rally in Lexington, Kentucky, in May 2016.** *Opposite:* **Former Maryland Gov. Martin O'Malley at the first Democratic debate, sponsored by CNN, in Las Vegas on October 13, 2015.**

every loss felt like a conspiracy—even when the evidence pointed elsewhere. The events at one Nevada Democratic caucus site on February 20 signified a party that could barely perform its basic functions, much less commit grand electoral theft. Outside the William V. Wright Elementary School in southwestern Las Vegas, where voters from eleven precincts lined up beneath a clear blue sky, the Democratic machine chugged along with lurching imprecision.

Voters were told to arrive by noon. At noon, a party official walked to the end of the line and gave its last occupant a red card that said *END OF LINE*. In theory, no one arriving thereafter would be allowed inside. But by 12:18, five people stood behind the red card.

"It's the democratic process," said a man who identified himself as Joe Gordon, professional gambler. "They're not gonna shut anybody out."

Moments later, the party official returned and told the stragglers they were too late. Some left. Some did not.

"I was here—I was just in the wrong line," Gordon said with an adequate poker face. The official did not call his bluff. As he sauntered inside, guarding his candidate preference like a pocket ace, more

cars pulled into the parking lot. A Sanders supporter named Sharifa Wahab frantically called friends and relatives, imploring them to come vote for Sanders. Thirty minutes past deadline. Forty. Fifty. They kept showing up. They kept getting in. They voted in Precinct 6540, which Sanders won by eight votes. If the Democrats rigged it for Clinton, they did a horrendous job.

But the more states Clinton won, the more Berniecrats felt cheated. When Bill Clinton was seen campaigning for his wife near a polling place in Massachusetts on March 1, more than 100,000 people signed a petition calling for his arrest. When Clinton won Arizona by 18 points on March 22, Sanders supporters blamed long lines and voter-registration discrepancies. They were fighting the system now, as well as Clinton, and they were not inclined to believe those who said Sanders was too far behind to catch up.

Clinton's chief strategist, Joel Benenson, believed the race was mathematically over after March 15. He knew that more campaigning would sharpen Clinton and give her

> **If the DNC meant to help Clinton, the DNC may have actually *hurt* Clinton. If party leaders thought fewer debates would deprive her competitors of publicity and keep Clinton in the lead, that strategy also kept Clinton from taking back the narrative.**

a head start on organizing in such battle-ground states as Pennsylvania.

"But there are concerns, too," he said in an interview. "You worry about using up too many resources. You worry about getting attacked too much. You worry about unifying the party."

In late March, Sanders started winning again. He won blowouts in Idaho, Utah, Alaska, Hawaii and Washington state. He took Wisconsin and Wyoming. But Clinton kept the overall delegate lead, which increased when the pro-Clinton superdelegates—party leaders and elected officials—were taken into account. Which also displeased the Berniecrats. Nerves frayed. Tempers flared. Clinton and Sanders had spent months in a civil and restrained contest of ideas, partly because Sanders had refused to attack Clinton on the issue of her emails. But now they were sick of each other. She narrowed her eyes with contempt. He widened his with indignation. She agreed to more debates. At their ninth, in Brooklyn on April 14, one verbal clash led moderator Wolf Blitzer of CNN to interject, "If you're both screaming at each other, the viewers won't be able to hear either of you."

What did Clinton want the Democrats to hear? That she knew ten times more than Sanders did about foreign policy. That one vote against the Iraq war fourteen years earlier didn't make him an expert on the

Trump saw the Democratic chaos, and it pleased him. System rigged in Clinton's favor? He liked the sound of that.

Middle East. That she had plans not just for what she would do but for *how* she would do it. That Sanders didn't. That he talked all the time about breaking up the banks but did not appear to actually know *how*. That her many contributions from Wall Street didn't mean she couldn't get tough with Wall Street. That when she went to George Clooney's house with Jane Fonda and Ellen DeGeneres and Steven Spielberg for a fundraiser that cost as much as $353,400 per couple, it was an acceptable means to a worthy end: big money in politics could help put Clinton in the White House and thus help overturn *Citizens United* and remove big money from politics.

Clinton's decisive victories across the Northeast in the second half of April effectively ended the contest. Sanders was undeterred. He was not really a Democrat, after all, and so he ignored the Democrats who told him that his continued presence in the race would ultimately help the GOP nominee.

In Nevada, his operatives began a complex series of maneuvers that would use the county and state conventions to change the results of the caucuses and cut into Clinton's delegate lead. It was all within the rules, but it seemed to run counter to his theory of upholding the will of the people.

Clinton's operatives struck back. They checked a list of delegates against a statewide database. The party determined that fifty-eight were ineligible to represent Sanders at the Nevada state convention on May 14. Some were not registered Democrats. Some were not even registered to vote. And while this number was a tiny fraction of more than 2,000 Sanders delegates to the state convention, the disqualifications gave the Sanders camp another reason to cry foul. A Sanders ally took the stage and read a "minority report" protesting the delegate purge.

"And that was like the match on the gasoline," said Annette Magnus, a Clinton supporter who was there. "And people in the room went *nuts.*"

Whatever irregularities might have prevailed at the Nevada state convention, the net result was a 20–15 pledged delegate lead for Clinton—an accurate reflection of the popular vote.

What happened in Nevada was a microcosm of the Democratic race. Sanders ran as the candidate who best represented the average Democrat. And when average Democrats gave Clinton an overwhelming lead in the popular vote, he talked about trying to win the nomination by winning over the superdelegates, whose very existence he previously wanted to abolish. Sanders tried to work the system, and failed.

But if the DNC wanted party unity, it created the opposite. And at the Nevada Democratic State Convention, Magnus saw the consequences up close. When she told Sanders supporters they were too late to get in, they yelled obscenities in her face. Inside the convention hall, they raised middle fingers toward the stage. A man picked up a chair, as if considering its use as a projectile. Barely two months before their national convention, the Democrats were still fighting each other. Sanders would keep fighting until

Bottom: **Clinton waits to go onstage for the CNN Democratic debate in Flint, Michigan.**

mid-July, more than a month after Clinton clinched the nomination, and finally offer a reluctant endorsement even as supporters pledged to write in his name in November.

For all their turmoil, the Republicans had their presumptive nominee a month before the Democrats did. Trump saw the Democratic chaos, and it pleased him. System rigged in Clinton's favor? He liked the sound of that. Millions of people already believed it. Trump would take it from here.

★ ★ ★

Throughout the primaries, Clinton kept an eye on Trump. She was the first candidate in either party to denounce his angry rhetoric, the week after he became a candidate. She didn't mention Trump by name, but there was

no mistaking her subject when she said, at a Democratic dinner in Virginia, "Recently, a Republican candidate for president described immigrants as drug dealers, rapists and criminals. Maybe he's never met them." She ran her first ads against Trump in New York in April, before either of them clinched the nomination. And when the last of Trump's rivals dropped out in early May, Clinton and her aides looked past Sanders and hustled to prepare for her next opponent.

One day her spokeswoman Christina Reynolds was listening to two policy aides talk about the flaws in Trump's plans on taxes and the economy. It reminded her of something that happened in 2000, when she and others working at the DNC referred to a George W. Bush proposal as "Bush's risky tax scheme." And she realized that by debating Trump's

proposals, the Clinton campaign was normalizing him. "You can't do that," Reynolds said in an interview. "And we would have meetings to talk about the idea that we can't run against him as if he's Mitt Romney, because he's not. And the moment that we let him be Mitt Romney or John McCain or George Bush, then he is acceptable to a group of people who should not find him acceptable."

Trump presented an unusual challenge: There were *too many* possible angles of attack. "We saw that Republicans were so frustrated in their primary that nothing ever seemed to work," said Mook, Clinton's campaign manager. "There was sort of a food fight where they were just throwing everything they could left and right." Or, as Oren Shur, her director of paid media, put it, "It's infinite. We could run against this guy for ten years and just scrape the surface of his vulnerabilities."

They decided they needed to approach Trump in a different way entirely. The race was less about the issues than about Trump's character, his qualifications, his fitness to do the job. He was not Mitt Romney or John McCain or Bob Dole or any other Republican of elections past. He was, they thought, uniquely unqualified. They didn't just disagree with him on issues, as they might with a different Republican. They thought he was unstable, dangerous. The challenge was how to convince voters of that, to distinguish him from more typical opponents, to raise an unusual alarm.

"We said, look, let's get eventually to a place where we're calling him unfit," Mook said. "Let's start with some half-measures."

Her advisers were being cautious—something Clinton is often accused of being. But as she prepared for her first TV interview after Trump became the presumptive nominee, Clinton herself decided to raise the stakes.

In a briefing memo, her staff had advised

And so it was that in the words of the Clinton campaign, Trump became *temperamentally unfit.* This would be the core of Clinton's argument against Trump for the next five months.

her to answer questions about Trump's qualifications or fitness by saying, "You have to let the people decide," senior adviser Mandy Grunwald said in an interview. "But she said, 'No, I have to say he is unfit, he is unqualified, he shouldn't be president of the United States. I don't want to build up to that conclusion a couple of weeks from now, or months from now. I'm going to say that today because I do not think he should be president of the United States.'"

Still, Clinton's staff struggled for weeks, trying to figure out a better way to make their case. Something was missing, they thought. But they weren't sure what it was.

Finally, digital director Teddy Goff hit on it. The description of Trump as unfit needed a modifier. And so it was that in the words of the Clinton campaign, Trump became *temperamentally unfit.* This would be the core of Clinton's argument against Trump for the next five months: that someone of his mental and emotional tendencies was unequal to the task of leading a global superpower. She would press this argument at her convention, at the debates, in numerous ads and speeches. All along the campaign trail, Trump would help her make that case.

6

THE ART OF POLITICAL CARJACKING

One morning in February in 2016, Joel Searby decided that *someone* had to do *something*. He decided that someone might as well be him. And so he began searching for a third-party candidate who would be more Republican than the leading Republican.

Yes, it had come to this. Searby, a political strategist in Florida, spent his days in the winter and spring researching independent candidacies and the people who might be amenable. He kept getting the same answer. Various members of Congress: no. Radio host Dave Ramsey: no. Dwayne "The Rock" Johnson: no. Former Secretary of State Condoleezza Rice? "The answer was no, and then no again, and then ultimately 'Hell, no!'" Later, Searby joined forces with other Republican operatives and the conservative leader Bill Kristol. The recruitment continued. Retired Marine Gen. James "Mad Dog" Mattis: no. Sen. Ben Sasse of Nebraska: no. Former nominee Mitt Romney: no. No one wanted to be accused of splitting the Republican vote and thereby helping elect another President Clinton.

On May 29, Kristol gave the dwindling #NeverTrump faction a ray of hope. As he waited to board a flight to Israel, he tweeted, "Just a heads up over this holiday weekend: There will be an independent candidate—an impressive one, with a strong team and a real chance." His candidate had a Harvard Law degree, a Bronze Star for service in Iraq as a legal advocate in the Army Reserve and, as it turned out, a name that few voters had ever heard. *David French* for president? No, not even. French, a writer and attorney in Tennessee, admitted he had neither the money nor the political talent for this challenge. As he later said on MSNBC, someone made an intimidating phone call to his house. Racists on the Internet mocked the daughter he and his wife had adopted from Ethiopia. And French decided not to run.

Once again, establishment Republicans found themselves in a place they could not have imagined. They were a party without a candidate.

Ten months earlier, they had looked so strong. Their contenders included successful governors, charismatic young senators (who also happened to be Hispanic), a business executive (who also happened to be a woman) and a famous neurosurgeon (who also happened to be African-American). Republican leaders called it the party's deepest field in decades. But of the seventeen Republicans running for president, one was not like the others. He changed parties like he changed his shoes, going from Republican to Independence Party to Democrat to Republican to having no party affiliation before claiming once again to be a Republican. Who was Trump, and where was his allegiance? At the first debate on August 6, he gave an unequivocal answer. Bret Baier of Fox News asked the candidates to raise their hands if they would *not* pledge to support the eventual Republican nominee, if they would *not* rule out running as an independent. Only

Previous spread: **Fifteen candidates participated in CNN's Republican debate on September 16, 2015, at the Ronald Reagan Presidential Library in Simi Valley, California. From the longest campaign to the shortest, the fourteen Republican candidates who withdrew from the race, starting top left: John Kasich, Ted Cruz, Marco Rubio, Ben Carson, Jeb Bush, Chris Christie, Carly Fiorina, Rand Paul, Rick Santorum, Mike Huckabee, George Pataki, Lindsey Graham, Bobby Jindal and Scott Walker. At bottom, the winner of the 2016 Republican nomination for president, Donald Trump.** *Opposite:* **Trump backstage with staff members at a March 11, 2016, press conference at his Mar-a-Lago Club in Palm Beach, Florida. Trump was joined by Carson, who announced he was endorsing Trump.**

> **But of the seventeen Republicans running for president, one was not like the others. He changed parties like he changed his shoes, going from Republican to Independence Party to Democrat to Republican to having no party affiliation before claiming once again to be a Republican. Who was Trump, and where was his allegiance?**

one hand went up, and that hand belonged to Trump.

"If I'm the nominee," he said, "I will pledge I will not run as an independent. But— and I am discussing it with everybody, but I'm, you know, talking about a lot of leverage."

There was no mystery here, no attempt to hide the truth. This was a political carjacking.

The Republican front-runner had just told everyone he was using the party for his own ends. He would drive their car as long as it suited him. And then, whenever he so desired, he would jump out and send it over a cliff.

But the Republicans did not perceive this existential threat until it was too late. Even if they had tried to force him out somehow, it probably would not have worked. According to the Republican National Committee's chief strategist, Sean Spicer, criticizing Trump only increased his appeal with the disgruntled electorate. To those who said the party should have found a way to stop him, Spicer had this reply: "I think for people to say that is like

looking at a guy in the pool and saying, 'Well, if you just swam faster, you would have beat Michael Phelps.' No shit."

Anyway, Trump was talking about a lot of leverage. He *loved* talking about leverage. In his 1987 book "The Art of the Deal," he wrote, "The worst thing you can possibly do in a deal is seem desperate to make it. That makes the other guy smell blood, and then you're dead. The best thing you can do is deal from strength, and leverage is the biggest strength you can have."

Did the Republicans want him as their front-runner or as their third-party competitor? Trump had the leverage to make them choose. Donors threatened to stop giving to the RNC if a major candidate wouldn't pledge to support the eventual nominee. Other candidates wondered why they had to sign loyalty pledges in exchange for RNC voter data if Trump wasn't going to sign one. Pressure mounted on Spicer and his colleagues to get a deal done. Spicer negotiated for weeks with Trump's first campaign manager, Corey

Top: **Kasich is surrounded by journalists in the spin room following the Republican debate in September 2015.** *Opposite:* **Trump in the spin room after CNN's Republican debate on February 25, 2016, in Houston.** *Following spread:* **An Air Force One plane used by President Ronald Reagan served as a backdrop to a Republican debate at the Ronald Reagan Presidential Library.**

Lewandowski. Finally, on September 3, Spicer and RNC Chairman Reince Priebus delivered the loyalty pledge to Trump Tower. Trump signed it. Spicer and Priebus quietly left the building. Trump went down to the lobby and trumpeted the news.

"The best way for the Republicans to win is if I win the nomination and go directly against whoever (the Democrats) happen to put up," he said. "And for that reason, I have signed the pledge."

For the moment, it looked as if the Republicans had won. They'd made Trump fall in line. They thought he'd be gone by Christmas. They were wrong.

All sixteen of his competitors signed the pledge as well. Only later did the consequences become clear: In binding Trump to the party, they had bound themselves to Trump.

★ ★ ★

What gave Trump his leverage—what left the party vulnerable to hostile takeover—was an anti-establishment fury that eventually turned the Republicans against themselves. It began shortly after Barack Obama won the presidency in 2008, and continued with Sen. Mitch McConnell of Kentucky's resolution to do all in his power to make Obama a one-term president, and flared more brightly with the anti-Obama tea party movement, and began causing collateral damage shortly after that. One after another, Republicans won House and Senate seats on promises to stop Obama at all costs. They voted more than sixty times to repeal all or part of his Affordable Care Act, but these symbolic gestures only reinforced the notion that they couldn't get anything done. Pretty soon you had Republicans (such as Ted Cruz) building careers on defying other Republicans (such as McConnell) for their failure to stop Obama. They were like a team that loses five in a row and tries to fix everything with a chair-throwing brawl in the locker room.

Most Republican voters didn't like Obama any more than their party leaders did. They thought he had telegraphed his disdain for white working-class Americans in 2008 with his comment about them becoming bitter and clinging to guns and religion, and their frustration with him increased every time he went on television to preach about gun control or warn against religious intolerance. Some believed he was a Muslim. Some hated having a black president. And some were tired of hearing a former law professor talk down to them. Party leaders saw a growing coalition of voters with one thing in common.

"They made a decision to go out and

What gave Trump his leverage— what left the party vulnerable to hostile takeover—was an anti-establishment fury that eventually turned the Republicans against themselves.

In binding Trump to the party, they had bound themselves to Trump.

"The only thing that mattered was, do they hate Barack Obama? Are they anti–Democratic Party? Are they reliable votes?"

—Tony Fratto, former aide to President George W. Bush

attract voters to the party who had one redeeming characteristic, and that was a consistent anti–Democratic Party view and a hatred, in particular, a hatred of Barack Obama," said Tony Fratto, a former aide to George W. Bush. "The attraction was not whether they shared our views on trade or long-term entitlement spending or design of a health care system or views on education policy. None of that mattered at all. The only thing that mattered was, do they hate Barack Obama? Are they anti–Democratic Party? Are they reliable votes? And if they are those things, then we want them in the party."

The contempt for Obama was inescapable. There was Rep. Joe Wilson of South Carolina, yelling "You lie!" during Obama's second speech to Congress. There was Arizona Gov. Jan Brewer, pointing a finger in his face. There was Trump in 2011, demanding to see his birth certificate. There was Romney in 2012, seeking and receiving Trump's endorsement.

"Being in Donald Trump's magnificent hotel and having his endorsement is a delight," Romney said, four years before declaring him a "phony" and a "fraud" in a futile attempt to stop him from winning the nomination. That was the problem for Republicans who tried to delegitimize Trump in 2016. Some had accepted his

endorsement. Some had accepted his campaign contributions. Through words and actions, many had signaled their approval.

By August 2015, Trump already had demeaned John McCain and Megyn Kelly of Fox News and Mexican immigrants, among others. Was this beyond the pale? Did this disqualify him from bearing the Republican standard? Apparently not. Shortly after the first debate, Scott Walker said, "Any of the people on that stage where I was standing would be infinitely better than Hillary Clinton as the next president of the United States." In December, standing by Trump at another debate, Cruz said, "What I can tell you is all nine of the people here would make an infinitely better commander in chief than Barack Obama or Hillary Clinton." At yet another debate with Trump in January, Jeb Bush said, "Everybody on this stage is better than Hillary Clinton."

The party unwittingly helped Trump in other ways, too. After a bruising primary cycle in 2012, the RNC cut the number of debates from twenty-seven to twelve—thus giving Trump's challengers less time to take back the spotlight. The 2016 primary schedule and delegate-allocation rules were designed to help the front-runner lock up the nomination quickly, and they did just that for Trump.

Top left: **Trump and Christie enter the September 2015 Republican debate together. The two had been friends for years.** *Opposite:* **Waiting in his trailer for the September 2015 Republican debate to begin, Carson poses as his wife, Candy, snaps a photograph.**

As he marched through the primaries, many in the Republican establishment began working against him. "Looking back," Sen. Lindsey Graham of South Carolina told CNN's Wolf Blitzer on March 7, "We should have basically kicked him out of the party." A few days earlier, more than 120 foreign-policy and national-security experts signed an open letter declaring that Trump would "make America less safe" and "diminish our standing in the world." Romney chimed in: "His promises are as worthless as a degree from Trump University. He's playing members of the American public for suckers. He gets a free ride to the White House, and all we get is a lousy hat."

At the Fox News debate in Detroit on March 3, Brett Baier posed a gut-wrenching question to Marco Rubio, John Kasich and Ted Cruz: "Tonight, in thirty seconds, can you definitively say you will support the Republican nominee, even if that nominee is Donald J. Trump?"

Questions like this one had loomed over the entire race. Was Trump really a Republican? Did he stand for the things Republicans stood for? Did the other candidates owe him anything? Hours earlier, Trump had threatened again to run as an independent. Now his last three opponents had one more chance to disavow him.

"I'll support Donald if he's the Republican nominee," Rubio said.

"Yes," Cruz said, "because I gave my word that I would."

"Yeah," Kasich said, because a deal was a deal.

Trump forced the Republicans into a quandary. If you pledged to support someone, what would it take to negate that pledge? Which was worse? Breaking your word, or defending someone you found indefensible? There was no simple answer. It turned out Kasich would *not* support Trump. Others also would withhold endorsements. In May, after Cruz and Kasich dropped out and Trump became the presumptive nominee, Jeb Bush wrote on Facebook, "Donald Trump has not demonstrated that temperament or strength of character. He has not displayed a respect

for the Constitution. And, he is not a consistent conservative. These are all reasons why I cannot support his candidacy."

Would Trump have supported the nominee had it been someone else? No one knew. But he believed his hostile takeover had earned him some loyalty—even from the Republicans he kept insulting.

"A pledge means something," Trump said at a rally after Bush's announcement. "Jeb Bush, a very low-energy individual, signed the pledge. While he was signing it, he fell asleep, so maybe that's his excuse."

Some Republicans criticized Priebus, the RNC chairman, for declaring Trump the presumptive nominee after Cruz dropped out on May 3. (Technically, Kasich was still in the race; he would drop out the next day.) But Mike Shields, a former RNC chief of staff and a CNN contributor, defended Priebus for upholding the will of the voters.

"The chairman's job is to defend the party. It is not to pick and choose who's qualified for the voters to talk to once the nominating process starts," he said. "I can't tell you how many times people would criticize him, go after him and say, 'You've got to do something about this, fix it, just do something.'... If Trump loses, he will have lost on his own. He won't have lost because the party bosses killed him, because the party didn't help him,

because the party disrespected his voters. There's a message there for the Trump voters going forward. The Republican Party didn't say, 'We don't want anything to do with you.'"

⁕ ⁕ ⁕

By late May, the nation's highest-ranking Republican had not yet endorsed the presumptive nominee. House Speaker Paul Ryan felt pressure from both sides of the party, especially from other House Republicans who thought his ambivalence toward Trump could hurt their own chances for re-election in November. At a meeting of Republicans in Florida, Ryan pulled a confidante, Tom Davis, into a corner and asked him what he thought. "I said, 'You've got no choice,'" the former Virginia congressman recalled. "'You've got to protect your members. If you weren't speaker, you'd have more leeway. But you're the lead elected (Republican) official in the country. If you break from this, it's a deluge. You won't get reelected speaker in all likelihood. You'll get thrown under the bus. The party splits.'"

Maybe it already had. After Romney's defeat in 2012, Republicans commissioned an extensive self-study that became known as the Autopsy Report. It concluded that the party had done a bad job of appealing to women, minorities and young voters. It said

Bottom left: **Trump and Bush vie for the floor during the September 2015 Republican debate.** *Opposite:* **The remaining candidates confer at the end of the final Republican debate in Miami in March 2016.**

It sounded desperate, maybe even crazy, but to them it felt like the only way to save the party. They hoped their own candidate would lose in November. And they hoped it wouldn't be close.

Republicans should embrace comprehensive immigration reform in an attempt to win over crucial Hispanic voters. "If Hispanic Americans perceive that a GOP nominee or candidate does not want them in the United States (i.e., self-deportation), they will not pay attention to our next sentence," the report said. "It does not matter what we say about education, jobs or the economy; if Hispanics think we do not want them here, they will close their ears to our policies."

Now they had a presumptive nominee whose entire campaign was a rejection of that report. Trump's idea of comprehensive immigration reform was a border wall and a Muslim ban. What was Ryan to do?

"It's no secret that he and I have our differences," Ryan wrote in his hometown newspaper, The Janesville (Wisconsin) Gazette, on June 2. "I won't pretend otherwise. And when I feel the need to, I'll continue to speak my mind. But the reality is, on the issues that make up our agenda, we have more common ground than disagreement."

This tepid endorsement did not unify the party. A few days later at Romney's annual ideas summit in Park City, Utah, donors and executives aggressively questioned Ryan about his decision to endorse. Foreign-policy leaders despaired. Establishment figures worried that Trump would drive away women, Hispanics and younger voters for generations to come.

The cycle had begun with such promise. The Republicans had a large, talented pool of candidates vying to run against a beatable Democrat. Now some Republicans looked toward a very different best-case scenario. It sounded desperate, maybe even crazy, but to them it felt like the only way to save the party. They hoped their own candidate would lose in November. And they hoped it wouldn't be close.

BY

MJ LEE

*CNN National
Politics Reporter*

LEAVING THE TRUMP BUBBLE

In May, my editors called with unsettling news: I was being moved to a new beat.

I had been covering Donald Trump since the earliest days of his campaign, following the Republican candidate around the country through the strange twists and turns of this election. But with Hillary Clinton on the verge of clinching her party's nomination, I now had a new candidate—someone I had never covered and whose staff I barely knew.

I hit the ground running, heading west to San Diego where Clinton was campaigning ahead of the California primary.

Maybe because I was so preoccupied with my work—trying to source up quickly, poring through previous months of Clinton coverage—it took some weeks for this realization to hit me: I felt, quite literally, like a new person.

I was still exhausted and stressed, but most of all, I was happier.

I had grown so accustomed to covering Trump that I had ceased to realize how deeply his events disturbed me.

Walking into Clinton rallies, I no longer worried about being booed or yelled and cursed at by people in the crowd. This had become a regular part of Trump events, and I had no way of knowing then just how much the animosity of his supporters toward the press would intensify in the coming months.

At Clinton events, there was no threat of violence. CNN had hired private security for journalists covering Trump, to keep an eye on us just in case things ever got too rowdy. They were often ex-police officers, always kind and never in the way. As glad as I was to have them there, they were also a nagging reminder that something bad could happen.

And covering Trump, I spent months at rallies in auditoriums and gymnasiums surrounded by thousands and thousands of white faces. Though their comments rarely felt

malicious, my conversations with Trump supporters frequently led to uncomfortable questions or off-color remarks about my ethnicity.

One man said that "new Americans" were hurting the country, and said he was referring to people like me. Another man asked if I was Connie Chung, a Chinese-American journalist forty-one years my senior.

I don't think I realized just how self-conscious I felt at Trump rallies until the moment I stopped feeling it. And I don't think it was until after I left the Trump bubble that I realized how worried I had been.

> **I don't think I realized just how self-conscious I felt at Trump rallies until the moment I stopped feeling it.**

Over the last year-and-a-half, I've grappled with the question of what it means to be an American, and confronted the sentiment that some people are more authentically American than others. And I've feared that the vitriol of the campaign, and the divisions that have deepened in this election, might not be easily healed.

I became a citizen in September. In the midst of this campaign, I've thought often about a letter I keep in the living room of our home.

Former Sen. Bob Dole—whom I had admired for years for his amazing story of resilience after sustaining serious injuries in World War II, and interviewed at the Republican National Convention this summer—had written to congratulate me on my new citizenship. And he wrote this:

"Throughout my life, I have always believed in the strength and potential of our nation.

We certainly have our ups and downs. Not everyone agrees with one another, especially this year. But through it all, we have remained the greatest nation in the world for a number of good reasons—and for that I am proud."

I've reread that letter numerous times. I hope that Sen. Dole still feels that optimistic as America transitions to a new president, and still believes that the difficult campaign will turn out to have been a passing phase in our country's many ups and downs.

A MOMENT IN HISTORY

On a June night in New York, Hillary Clinton breathed a sigh of relief, savoring the boisterous applause bouncing from the walls of the crowded Brooklyn Navy Yard.

Clinton has long had a love-hate relationship with big campaign rallies.

She held them often during her first presidential run, but when the crowds for Barack Obama soon grew larger, she declared: "Enough of the big rallies." The second time around, when the Democratic nomination initially seemed hers for the taking, the crowds for Bernie Sanders eclipsed hers from the very beginning.

But on this night, at the end of a long road of primaries and caucuses, after finally vanquishing Sanders, she stood onstage and absorbed the moment like few other times during her second bid for the White House.

"Tonight caps an amazing journey," Clinton exclaimed, placing her hands over her heart in a sign of appreciation for those who stood before her. "A long, long journey."

Yet a joyful journey it rarely was.

A campaign for the history books—a quest to elect the first woman president—seldom felt historic. The chaotic twists and turns often felt far more ugly than uplifting, and all sides own a piece of the blame.

BY
JEFF ZELENY
CNN Senior Washington Correspondent

> ## The chaotic twists and turns often felt far more ugly than uplifting, and all sides own a piece of the blame.

After being stung by an early bout of confidence, Clinton's was a candidacy that oozed caution. She followed a rigorous script, right down to precise words used for a tweet sent out in her name. Her highly structured campaign stops allowed little room for the spontaneity or fun that her friends still insist she loves.

But nearly a century after women won the right to vote in the United States, for this moment at least, Clinton looked more relieved than at any other time in her campaign.

"I'm going to take a moment later tonight and the days ahead to fully absorb the history we've made here," Clinton said, accepting victory as she became her party's presumptive nominee. "But what I care about most is the history our country has yet to write. Our children and grandchildren will look back at this time, at the choices we are about to make, the goals we will strive for, the principles we will live by. And we need to make sure that they can be proud of us."

She wore white on this early June night, as she would more than a month later when she officially accepted the nomination at the Democratic convention. She also wore a look of contentment.

While Clinton likely couldn't see it, in the back of the cavernous hall a father hoisted his young daughter onto his shoulders so she could get a better glimpse of this moment in history.

CNN, AND A RACE LIKE NO OTHER

BY JEFF ZUCKER
President, CNN Worldwide

The campaign began for us when we made the decision, at the beginning of 2015, to invest heavily in political coverage, both on television and online. We wanted to "own" politics on all of our platforms. We created a whole new CNN Politics digital site, and went on a hiring spree there, and did the same thing for TV.

When Trump jumped in, CNN recognized, I believe sooner than most others, that there was something to his candidacy. I feel incredibly proud of our overall coverage with regard to Trump. People have been critical of the amount of attention we gave Trump in those early, initial months, but I think that's a testament to the fact that we understood—more than most other newsrooms in New York and Washington—that Trump had much broader appeal.

In recent years, CNN has changed its approach to covering news. When there is a big story, we go "all in" on it. There was no bigger story over the last eighteen months than the election, so we went all in.

One of the things we did throughout this cycle was to "event-ize" the major days and nights. Whether it was a debate, a town hall, a primary night or the conventions, our approach was the same. Cover them as big events to let the audience know they are important. We often refer to it as a "game day" approach to our coverage.

That added a degree of energy and excitement to our programs, while never getting in the way of our news-gathering, our analysis or our interviews. We did a tremendous amount of reporting, breaking news and news-making interviews through this entire process.

Jake Tapper had two of the most important interviews of this entire campaign cycle, both with Donald Trump. One was about David Duke and the KKK, and the other was about Judge Curiel. Those were unbelievable moments. When Anderson Cooper said to Donald Trump at a CNN town hall, "with all due respect, sir, that's the argument of a five-year-old," that was an important moment. Overall, just the sheer volume of town halls and debates that CNN did is something that stands out to me about this cycle.

Our first debate was Simi Valley at the Reagan Library. Jake Tapper asked both Marco Rubio and Jeb Bush whether they had any issues with Donald Trump's finger on the nuclear button. They both took a pass and did not say they had any issue. My point is this: The questions were asked right from the start. His competitors took a pass. How is that the fault of the media?

I also think the media became much more willing to call things out over the course of this election. Fact-checking used to be a separate discipline from reporting, and I think reporting became fact-checking in this cycle. I think that's a change for the better, frankly, and a really important change.

Our election-night panels included the Greek chorus. There were Trumpers. There were never-Trumpers. There were traditional mainstream Republicans. There were people who were for Hillary. There were people who were for Bernie. Multiple points of view. So to cover both sides of the story, you had to have at least four, if not five, points of view. On top of that, we wanted to have our own traditional analysts. So you end up with six, seven, eight people on a panel.

> When there is a big story, we go "all in" on it. There was no bigger story over the last eighteen months than the election, so we went all in.

What we found was they ended up being—especially the partisan folks—the Greek chorus, because they were having the same conversations that were going on around the country, and in many respects reflected the emotions of the viewers. That's really what it became about. On top of that, I think it was the mix of the analysts and the partisans that actually made the coverage very dynamic.

I am amazed at what CNN did throughout the course of what arguably is the nation's most historic election, ever. Thousands of our journalists spent months on the road, behind the scenes and in front of the camera, bringing these incredible stories to our audiences around the world. I am grateful for their commitment and professionalism, and immensely proud of what we accomplished.

FAITH AND
DOUBT IN THE
DIVIDED STATES
OF AMERICA

A man was dying, and a woman prayed. Daylight faded in Minnesota. Blood stained the man's white shirt. The woman kept her hands where the officer could see them. With her smartphone, she kept recording. The woman said they'd been pulled over for a broken taillight. She said a police officer shot her boyfriend as he reached for his wallet. Diamond Reynolds said all this on Facebook Live, where her video would be viewed more than 5 million times. When she turned the phone toward the car window, the picture was a grotesque distortion of the American flag. Philando Castile, his T-shirt turning red. The officer's forearm, a startling white in the setting sun. The officer's dark blue uniform. And near the center of the frame, still aimed through the window, the officer's gun.

"I TOLD HIM NOT TO REACH FOR IT," the officer shouted, apparently referring to another gun, legal, registered, that Castile had told him was in the car. The officer's voice had a desperate quality, a hint of something damaged beyond repair. Castile struggled to breathe. His girlfriend kept praying.

"Please, Jesus," she said, "don't tell me that he's gone."

Castile died a few minutes later, becoming the second African-American man in as many days to be killed by police on the streets of America. The following night at an otherwise peaceful demonstration in Dallas, a vengeful sniper killed five police officers and wounded seven others, taunting the survivors until they killed him with a remote-controlled robot and a pound of explosives. One officer had to zip up his friend's body bag. Another stood in the hospital and fought back tears. In the hours before the rampage ended, officers strained to distinguish between potential suspects and law-abiding citizens. Some pro-testers openly carried rifles. Texas law said they could.

This was America in the summer of 2016: heavily armed, filled with anger and mistrust, eyes darting from smartphone to rearview mirror. Public confidence in government approached an all-time low. Polls showed a growing perception that race relations were getting worse. Antisocial behavior proliferated on social media. Clinton, using the Internet slang of the moment, advised Trump to delete his Twitter account. Trump declined. He took a graphic that had previously appeared on a white-supremacist message board and shared it with his 9 million followers. It contained images of Clinton, a pile of money, what appeared to be the Star of David, and the caption *Most Corrupt Candidate Ever!* People stumbled along sidewalks, glued to their

This was America in the summer of 2016: heavily armed, filled with anger and mistrust, eyes darting from smartphone to rearview mirror. Public confidence in government approached an all-time low.

phones, playing a new game that promised "augmented reality." Officials in Washington asked them to stop hunting Pokémon at the Holocaust museum.

In Trump's version of reality, an American judge's Mexican heritage made him a "Mexican" whose objectivity would be compromised by Trump's plan to build a wall on the Mexican border. After Trump said this in early June, Paul Ryan called it "the textbook definition of a racist comment." But he did not rescind his endorsement, because Trump was still the presumptive Republican nominee. The laws of partisan loyalty remained intact. They made words essentially meaningless. Former Texas Gov. Rick Perry, who called Trump a "cancer on conservatism"

during his own brief run for president, now said he would do everything possible to help him win. Marco Rubio, who previously called Trump a "con artist," now said he'd be willing to attend the Republican convention and speak on Trump's behalf. (He sent a video message instead.) As for the Christian right, some of its members withheld their support. But there was Jerry Falwell Jr., president of one of the nation's largest Christian universities, posing for a picture with his new friend in front of a gold-framed cover of the *Playboy* magazine that featured Trump on the cover. Falwell had just introduced Trump at a meeting of Christian leaders. He said he was honored.

Top: **A child poses by a #SayHerName sign at the August 8, 2015, Social Security and Medicare anniversary rally in Seattle. The hashtag memorialized African-American women and girls who were killed by police.** *Opposite:* **Attendees at a Donald Trump rally in Manchester, New Hampshire, go through security.** *Following spread:* **Police at the Democratic National Convention in Philadelphia.**

WHAT MAK
AMERICA?

ES US

When an ISIS-inspired gunman murdered forty-nine people at a gay nightclub in Orlando, Trump thanked his followers on Twitter for supporting his worldview: "Appreciate the congrats for being right on radical Islamic terrorism, I don't want congrats, I want toughness & vigilance. We must be smart!" The nation's worst terrorist attack since 9/11 quickly became a merry-go-round of self-vindication. Trump said it proved him right about Muslim terrorists. Gun-control advocates said it proved them right about guns. Trump-haters said Trump's response proved them right about Trump. And when President Obama lashed out at Trump, Trump once again tried to raise ominous questions about Obama's true loyalties: "He was more angry at me than he was at the shooter."

Polls showed that Trump and Clinton were the two most-disliked presidential candidates in modern history. Many voters supported Trump purely to stop Clinton, and vice versa. No wonder, then, that both devoted multiple speeches to the same topic: *My Opponent Is Bad for America.*

"Now imagine Donald Trump sitting in the Situation Room, making life-or-death decisions on behalf of the United States," Clinton said in San Diego on June 2. "Imagine him deciding whether to send your spouses or children into battle. Imagine if he had not just his Twitter account at his disposal when he's angry, but America's entire arsenal. Do we want him making those calls—someone thin-skinned and quick to anger, who lashes out at the smallest criticism? Do we want his finger anywhere near the button?"

Bottom: **A demonstrator and a police officer square off at the March 11, 2016 Trump rally at the University of Illinois at Chicago—which ultimately was canceled because of violence.** *Opposite:* **Protestors and security at the rally.**

"I'm here to insist that we're not as divided as we seem," Obama said at a memorial service in Dallas, as if the insistence could make it true.

But if Trump kept giving Clinton fresh ammunition, Clinton and the Democrats did the same for Trump. The sequence of their actions in late June and early July did not quiet the conspiracy theorists. The way Trump spoke about Attorney General Loretta Lynch's private meeting with Bill Clinton, he could have been accepting congratulations.

"Bill Clinton didn't accidentally run into the attorney general on the airport tarmac last week in Phoenix," Trump said in a statement on July 5, the day FBI Director James Comey announced he would not recommend that Lynch prosecute Hillary Clinton in connection with her use of a private email server as secretary of state. "Hillary Clinton didn't accidentally sneak into the FBI during one of the country's biggest holiday weekends to testify on her illegal activities, something that wouldn't be afforded to others under investigation (and on a Saturday of all days). It was no accident that charges were not recommended against Hillary the exact same day as President Obama campaigns with her for the first time. Folks—the system is rigged."

That was the night Alton Sterling's life ended, and the chain of violence began. He was selling CDs outside the Triple S Food Mart in Baton Rouge, Louisiana, when two white officers responded to a call about a man with a gun. In a struggle that continued after they pinned him down, Sterling, a black man, was shot to death.

The next night in Falcon Heights, Minnesota, an officer killed Philando Castile.

The night after that in Dallas, an African-American military veteran killed Sgt. Michael Smith, Sr. Cpl. Lorne Ahrens, and Officers Brent Thompson, Patrick Zamarripa and Michael Krol. Other police officers were shot in Georgia, Missouri and Tennessee, leading authorities to suspect retaliation. As protests continued in Baton Rouge, someone hurled a rock at an officer and knocked out his teeth. A picture by Reuters photographer Jonathan Bachman showed a young black woman standing peacefully in the road, dress billowing in the wind, accosted by two officers in riot gear.

"I'm here to insist that we are not as divided as we seem," Obama said at a memorial service in Dallas, as if the insistence could make it true. In Statesboro, Georgia, a 43-year-old white man named J.J. Crawford had a moment of personal conviction. When he closed his eyes, he later said in an interview, he could see the African-Americans in his life. He saw decades of racial injustice, a series of incidents he'd done nothing to prevent, and he knew it was time to act. When black protesters organized a march through downtown Statesboro, Crawford joined them. They marched to the courthouse, and then to the police station. They wanted to talk with the chief.

Interim Chief Robert Bryan walked outside in the stifling heat. He closed his eyes and bowed his head. The protesters laid hands on his shoulders. And they prayed.

But evil persisted, and it drove a 40,000-pound truck, and it barreled down the promenade in the dark, smashing 286 people who just wanted to see the fireworks. It was Bastille Day in Nice, France, and a Tunisian man went on the vehicular killing spree. These are the horrors a president must confront. What will we do? Who will we be? What makes us America? Former House Speaker Newt Gingrich responded to the massacre by going on Fox News to say, "We should frankly test every person here who is of a Muslim background, and if they believe in sharia they should be deported." In his last-ditch effort to become Trump's running mate, it seemed he'd forgotten the Constitution.

In the days before the conventions, as the last two major-party candidates prepared for the next phase of the election, Americans were still listening. Messages got through, for good and evil.

People kept forgetting things, kept changing their minds. Confusion took hold. Trump's associates said the erstwhile football star Tim Tebow would speak at the Republican National Convention, but Tebow said that was news to him. Trump agonized over his list of potential running mates, including Gingrich, Chris Christie and Indiana Gov. Mike Pence, and even after word leaked that he'd chosen Pence, even after Pence had flown to New York for the big announcement, Trump was still questioning his decision. Yes, it was Pence, the safe choice, the social conservative, but then Trump took the stage and got so wrapped up in himself that he almost forgot to introduce Pence. Fiction could not match this strange new reality. The campaign released and then retracted a Trump-Pence logo that some people found obscene. Elsewhere in America, Facebook users claimed that a photograph showed the departing spirit of a motorcycle crash victim. A Florida woman drove her car into a house while praying with her eyes closed. Pence finally got his turn to speak, and of course

TRUMP
PENCE
MAKE AMERICA GREAT AGAIN!

Left: **The original Trump-Pence logo, which was quickly redesigned after critics lampooned it as being suggestive.** *Opposite:* **Demonstrators and Trump supporters as they leave the canceled rally in Chicago.**

he spoke about Trump. "He will rebuild the arsenal of democracy," Pence said, "stand with our ene—"

He corrected himself. "Allies." He meant Trump would stand with our allies. Down was up, up was down, and both candidates had lost the public trust. In one survey after another, both Clinton and Trump were overwhelmingly seen as dishonest. Worse for Clinton, a 56–35 majority in a Washington Post/ABC News poll disapproved of the FBI's recommendation against charging her with a crime. On July 15, Michael Folk, a Republican lawmaker from West Virginia, sent out the following message on Twitter:

> @HillaryClinton You should be tried for treason, murder, and crimes against the US Constitution... then hung on the Mall in Washington, DC.

It was just "hyperbole," he later said, as if words meant nothing, as if all politicians could be ignored. But in the days before the conventions, as the last two major-party candidates prepared for the next phase of the election, Americans were still listening. Messages got through, for good and evil. People heard Trump when he said a protester deserved to be roughed up, and more protesters got roughed up. The Islamic State told its followers to kill, and its followers killed. Black protesters carried signs that said, OINK OINK BANG-BANG. Thoughts led to words, to irreversible actions. The news came out of Baton Rouge, Louisiana on Sunday, July 17. Three more police officers were dead.

Donald Trump played the media like no other candidate in modern history. A master entertainer, he knew how to draw attention to himself. A keen observer of the public mood, he knew how to cast blame on an unpopular industry that was hardly in a position to fight back.

He simultaneously ran a savvy media-driven campaign and a vicious anti-media crusade. He was a one-person driver of ratings and readership and a serious menace to press freedom. During the course of the campaign, he both suggested that he should be paid to appear in debates and threatened to curtail the First Amendment.

Trump made the media a player in the race, creating unique challenges for journalists and media outlets, including CNN, that have long strived for balance in political coverage. We were alternately accused of building him up and of tearing him down. We alienated liberals by (they say) giving too much free airtime to Trump and his more controversial supporters, like campaign-manager-turned-CNN-commentator Corey Lewandowski. We alienated conservatives by (they say) piling on Trump and demeaning his supporters. During this long and divisive campaign, "trust in media" levels fell to record lows in

Gallup polls. Trump celebrated the results and took partial credit.

But how far would he have gotten without the media? Consider how the star of "The Celebrity Apprentice" produced his bid for the presidency: He programmed his rallies for maximum cable news effect, then attacked the very camera crews that were beaming his face into living rooms across the country. He blacklisted some of the country's best-known news outlets from his rallies, but still granted interviews to some of them. He called out media executives the way other candidates recite emotional stories about voters. He characterized reporters as "disgusting" and "scum," and at least once added, "I would never kill them." But he gave hundreds of interviews and watched cable news on a loop. Toward the end of the race, he spun conspiracy theories, accusing the media that reported and aired his every utterance of colluding to destroy him.

These contradictions show why it's so difficult to reach any single conclusion about Trump and the media. The Hillary Clinton campaign was more typical. Reporters respected the candidate, resented their lack of access to her, called her out when she made false claims or failed

STAR, MPAIGN

BY BRIAN STELTER

*Host, CNN's "Reliable Sources"
& Senior Media Correspondent*

to respond to serious questions—and generally engaged in the same kinds of battles with her campaign that they do with nominees from both parties every four years.

But the Trump campaign was different. In some ways, it was barely a real campaign at all. When I visited the Trump Tower campaign headquarters in May 2016, I was startled by how small and half-finished it felt—more like an "Apprentice" set (which it used to be) than the control room of a serious presidential campaign.

But the campaign *felt* big on TV, and that mattered a lot. For all the talk about Snapchat and Periscope and Instagram and Facebook Live, this was a television election. With a smartphone in one hand and a remote in the other, Americans reacted on social media to what they were watching on the television screen.

And what they saw really *did* have the trappings of a reality show. As a Sunday morning host on CNN, I tried to frame it as "The Trump Show." Trump, more than Clinton, benefited from the media's slavish devotion to the "story." He clearly knew a lot more about us than he let on. What do journalists really care about? What makes us tick? Contrary to Trump's public claims, it's not a desire to elect Democrats or to make more profits for the parent

> **Trump made the media a player in the race, creating unique challenges for journalists and media outlets, including CNN, that have long strived for balance in political coverage.**

company. And, at least in the mainstream press, it's not ideological. While many reporters lean to the left in their personal politics, they are by and large driven by a desire to cover a great "story," to get scoops, to beat the competition. Don Hewitt's maxim from the launch of "60 Minutes" holds true today: "Tell me a story."

And there's no denying that Trump was a great story. The best. As he might say, the story of his campaign was, indeed, yuuuuuge. The media wrote about him, aired his rallies, linked to his speeches—and the public ate it up.

Trump was clickbait. Many days, all five of the most-viewed articles on The Washington Post's website were about Trump. He was a ratings magnet, too. Why? Partly because he was entertaining to watch. But that's not the entire answer. It's also because he was channeling the views of a big chunk of America—a population that wasn't used to hearing a national politician express their views. For every Trump rally viewer who was horrified ("this is sick"), another viewer was inspired ("someone is finally saying what I'm thinking").

Most of all, Trump was a ratings and traffic magnet because he knew how to "make news." He could be entertaining, charming, shocking. Some days, he had the mind of a television producer. Other days, he had the mind of a host. His old friendships with conservative stars like Bill O'Reilly and Sean Hannity and producers like Mark Burnett surely didn't hurt.

As a creature of the media for decades, Trump had learned the sweet spots. "Trump is almost addicted to media coverage," New York Times political editor Carolyn Ryan told me on CNN's "Reliable Sources." So it's no wonder that he was his own best PR person. Decades ago, he apparently assumed a phony name to speak about himself in the third person. Variations on this behavior continued throughout the campaign. During the primaries, he spent hours in his Trump Tower office dictating tweets and ordering up press releases. Savvy reporters could tell when Trump himself had a hand in the emails coming from campaign press secretary Hope Hicks.

But it was usually the words straight from his mouth—at rallies and interviews—that spawned news. Split-second decisions in TV control rooms are determined by what just happened and what might be about to happen. So Trump's unpredictability—"what's he going to say next?"—and his accessibility worked to his particular advantage during the primaries, when he vanquished sixteen opponents.

These day-by-day factors drove media coverage during the primaries, causing disparities that spurred outrage among Trump critics and, later, some second-guessing by

newsroom leaders. CNN was singled out for giving Trump too much airtime in 2015 and early 2016. In an interview for this book, CNN president Jeff Zucker expressed pride in the network's coverage. Ignoring the Trump phenomenon would have been journalistic malpractice as well as a bad business decision. "Do I think we took a few too many of his rallies in those early days, just unedited and straight to air? Yeah, that's probably a fair criticism," Zucker said. "On the other hand, he was making news at virtually all of them, and we are in what's called the news business."

Often overlooked is how skeptical much of the early coverage of Trump was. On the morning of his announcement, anchors on CNN and elsewhere openly doubted that he would actually run for president. The event was treated more like a stunt than a serious entry into the race. And for the first few weeks, the overriding narrative was: "Should we take this man seriously? Why is he really running, to boost his businesses? When will he get out of the race?" The Huffington Post went so far as to run stories about him in the entertainment section of the website.

In retrospect, I wonder if this dismissiveness inadvertently added fuel to Trump's fire.

In any case, the writings of hard-nosed journalists and voices of anti-Trump TV guests were drummed out by the "Trump Show." The spectacle, with its big hair and even bigger rallies and angry tweets and even angrier crowds, was something to behold in the summer of 2015. And the summer seemed to extend for a full year, until the general election was well underway. Conservative media leaders like Hannity and Rush Limbaugh had primed their audiences for a Trump-like candidate. While Trump horrified serious writers like George Will, causing an extraordinary fracturing of conservative media, he excited entertainers like Limbaugh. And once the campaign began in earnest, it was hard to tell where Trump stopped and Hannity began.

Trump appealed to a subset of voters, mostly conservative, who were angry at the "system" and rejected the mainstream media. With the help of alt-right websites like Breitbart, he exploited and reinforced his supporters' distrust of more traditional news outlets with the most

Opposite: **Donald Trump walks out to a large crowd at his rally in Mobile, Alabama, on August 21, 2015.**

Some of the most insightful reports of the entire election ultimately involved interviews with fired-up, fed-up Americans who felt that their voices were no longer heard in far-off Washington. These were the people to whom Trump spoke, the ones who made him the Republican nominee.

extreme criticism we have ever heard from a presidential candidate. Day in, day out, for more than a year, he denied the very legitimacy of journalism. Consequently, his base essentially opted out of it, media critic Jay Rosen observed. They dismissed investigations into Trump and fact-checks of his statements as left-wing attacks. Exasperated journalists spoke of a "post-truth election." A verbal shrug, "nothing matters," became a popular saying among beat reporters assigned to the Trump campaign.

I saw this firsthand just a couple of weeks into the campaign, back when Trump was holding small events in early primary states. On the last day of June 2015, a couple of curious local Republicans gathered around a backyard pool in Bedford, New Hampshire, riveted by a Trump stump speech.

Snickering cameramen quietly mocked the candidate, pointing out his pompous statements and promises that they said "can't possibly come true." Trump couldn't hear them, but he gave as good as he got. He called out reporters by name. "Katy!" he said, and went on to complain about coverage by NBC's Katy Tur. "You can't believe the press," he told the crowd. "You can't believe the press."

The admonishment struck a chord with at least one voter, who could barely contain her excitement. "Oh, my gosh. I have been saying this for years," said Sharon Gannon. "I don't believe the stuff the media says."

Hicks weaved around the swimming pool. She guided Trump through hundreds of interviews with outlets big and small—a free-media strategy that won him even more airtime and attention. In those early days, Trump seemed to be everywhere—even though he was usually sitting in his office. The networks were criticized for letting Trump call in to their shows. Eventually, though, other candidates in both parties copied the strategy when it suited their purposes.

All the while, the real "story" was unfolding many miles from Trump Tower. Too many journalists were slow to recognize and respect the motivations of the voters who would become Trump's base of support. Some of the most insightful reports of the entire election ultimately involved interviews with fired-up, fed-up Americans who felt that their voices were no longer heard in far-off Washington. These were the people to whom Trump spoke, the ones

The Committee to Protect Journalists reviewed Trump's press abuse—banning news outlets from rallies, insulting individual journalists, threatening lawsuits—and concluded that he presented an unprecedented threat to press freedom in the United States.

who made him the Republican nominee. But too often, their stories were drowned out by partisan bickering or by their candidate's own outlandish or offensive (and, therefore, newsmaking) comments.

Despite Trump's attempts to discredit the Fourth Estate, reporting *did* matter. Tough coverage of both Trump and Clinton contributed to record-high unfavorable ratings for the nominees. Media critics singled out newspapers like The Washington Post for praise—pointing out that, at a time of severe turbulence for the publishing industry, old-fashioned newsrooms produced important investigations about the candidates' backgrounds.

In a nod to the changing media landscape, TV operations like CNN, nonprofit newsrooms like ProPublica and fact-checking outfits like PolitiFact all stepped up to the Trump challenge. And make no mistake—it was a challenge. As Trump was crowned the GOP nominee, media critics and many onlookers argued that the candidate had to be covered differently than Republicans from years past.

"He is the first candidate in modern times who just is absolutely, positively willing to make things up as he goes along," veteran journalist Steven Brill said.

Indeed, Trump's frequent fibs and exaggerations pushed many reporters into a more adversarial posture than they were used to. As a TV host and reporter, I wrestled with this personally, and I gradually became more blunt about describing Trump's fictions. Sources like PolitiFact showed that Clinton shaded the truth on occasion, as politicians tend to do, but Trump routinely said things that had no basis in fact, and famously never apologized for any of it. When it came to the truth, the two candidates were not equal. It was imperative to say so. Journalists who ignored this were, in effect, shading the truth from their readers and viewers.

Eventually, The New York Times used the word "lie" on the front page. CNN pointed out Trump's falsehoods in bottom-of-the-screen banners. This, in turn, pushed Trump to denounce the media even more severely. Amid verbal attacks from Trump supporters at rallies, reporters occasionally worried about their safety. With a month to go before the election, the Committee to Protect Journalists reviewed Trump's press abuse— banning news outlets from rallies, insulting individual journalists, threatening lawsuits—and concluded that he

presented an unprecedented threat to press freedom in the United States.

The rebuttal from some Trump supporters: That's just more media bias.

But others lauded the press for going beyond typical "he said, she said" reporting. When The Washington Post obtained NBC's 2005 "Access Hollywood" tape of Trump bragging about sexual assault to Billy Bush, there was saturation coverage, and reporters and anchors freely expressed shock and discomfort at his remarks. When Trump contended, with no evidence, that the election was rigged and refused to say he would accept the outcome, reporters stood up for basic democratic values.

Watching the critical coverage, a viewer or reader might have sensed that the media was a collective body trying to fight off an infection. Some conservative commentators accused the media of propping up Trump early in the race, then taking him down at the end. The Republican nominee alleged a massive media conspiracy to help Clinton get elected. But Trump himself knew better than that, even though he claimed otherwise. He had spent decades as a media star. He knew his trajectory, with all its unusual twists and turns, was simply the best "story" of the year.

Top: **Supporters pack the bleachers of a football stadium at the Trump rally in Mobile, Alabama.**

8

**ROCKING
IN CLEVELAND
WITH THE GRAND
NEW PARTY**

ecades earlier, before everyone in America knew his name, a developer tore down the iconic Bonwit Teller Building in Manhattan and replaced it with a fifty-eight-story monument to himself. Now Donald Trump went to work on the Republican Party.

He installed a new guiding principle: a steadfast and unquestioning belief in Trump. This remodeled party had no room for conscientious objectors. Good riddance to George Will, long the conscience of American conservatism. In Trump's view, he was overrated. Same for Ohio's governor, John Kasich: a relic of the past, according to Trump's campaign chairman, Paul Manafort, and if Kasich wanted to embarrass his whole state by skipping the convention, that was *his* problem. As for George W. Bush, he could stay in Texas, painting cats and dogs, wondering if he'd be the last Republican president.

Trump's long-term effect on the party could not yet be known. Would he make it bigger, or smaller? Right now it was certainly louder, more highly charged, with frequent dancing to the Rolling Stones. It could be ferocious, or joyful, sometimes both at once. "This is a movement," Trump supporter Maria Espinoza said on July 20 as she stood in Cleveland's Public Square on the third day of the Republican National Convention. Espinoza was co-founder of the Remembrance Project, a nonprofit organization for the families of Americans killed by undocumented immigrants. She said politicians had ignored her until Trump came along. This feeling was common among Trump supporters in Cleveland: the sense that he understood them in a way no other politician could. And they understood each other. During a welcome party at the Rock & Roll Hall of Fame, where several guests wore T-shirts that said: *CHINESE AMERICANS ♥ TRUMP*, dozens joined in a spontaneous chant: *BUILD THAT WALL! BUILD THAT WALL!*

He had promised a showbiz extravaganza, a celebration like they'd never seen. What he delivered was surreal and disjointed, rambling and bizarre, and, in the final analysis, another resounding victory over conventional wisdom. Never mind the lack of star power. With help from B-list actors Scott Baio and Antonio Sabato Jr., along with a midlevel country star whose cover of "Ring of Fire" caused widespread merriment among the delegates, Trump and his new party smashed the preconceptions once again.

The first Republican president visited Cleveland in 1861, en route to his inauguration, and again four years later on the way

He had promised a showbiz extravaganza, a celebration like they'd never seen. What he delivered was surreal and disjointed, rambling and bizarre.

to his grave. Rain fell on April 28, 1865, as thousands of Clevelanders walked beneath a canopy in the public square to see Abraham Lincoln in his open casket.

Today a statue of Lincoln stands inside the massive Soldiers' and Sailors' Monument at the edge of the same public square. Many statues depict Lincoln unchaining a slave, but the bronze relief in Cleveland is unusual in this regard: It also shows Lincoln giving him a rifle. Lincoln hesitated to recruit black soldiers, afraid of stirring white anger in the border states, but he finally decided the Union needed their help. Black men comprised 10 percent of Lincoln's army by the end of the Civil War, and sixteen were awarded the Medal of Honor for extraordinary courage.

For many Republicans, this remains a glorious image: black men and white men fighting together to free the slaves. But that was more than 150 years ago. By the time of Trump's convention, the party of Lincoln had been losing the African-American vote for more than five decades. With Barry Goldwater and his white lilies and his white Southern women in lily-white gowns. With Richard Nixon and his Southern Strategy. With Ronald Reagan's denunciation of welfare queens and George H.W. Bush's exploitation of Willie Horton. With voter-ID laws and the birther movement and finally the birther candidate, Donald Trump, whose support among black voters remained in single digits nationally and had recently been measured at zero percent in Ohio.

Trump delivered a spectacle, all right. And if much of it was the accidental kind, like a Ferris wheel breaking loose from its axis, one aspect went roughly as planned. Trump and his allies said they would put down the insurrection, and that is what they did.

Some visitors brought guns to Cleveland. Ohio's open-carry law made it easy. A medical doctor packed a slim nine-millimeter in his checked luggage just in case he needed to shoot his way out. A military reservist brought his twelve-gauge shotgun just in case the police needed help. A survivalist militiaman carried a black SIG Sauer with a banana clip just because he could. These men walked the blistering streets of a city that also contained a left-wing subversive intent on burning the American flag and a right-wing preacher who threatened to burn the rainbow flag. It was hot and cops were everywhere: in cars, on foot, on bicycles and horses. Nearly 3,000 were dispatched from more than a dozen states. Some carried assault rifles. One stood on the roof of the Rock & Roll Hall of Fame, a sentinel between the lake and the rising moon.

Andrew Lee did not bring a gun, because he lived in Washington, D.C., where legally acquiring one was a major hassle. Gun control was a sore subject for Lee, a 29-year-old black conservative, and part of the reason he opposed the Democrats. He thought their policies had failed in major cities such as Washington and Chicago, where the bad guys had guns and most law-abiding citizens did

not. Lee had worked in Republican politics on Capitol Hill for several years before leaving for a marketing job in the private sector. He knew the Republicans had work to do in the race-relations department, but he still saw a place for himself in a party that aligned with much of his worldview. That is, until Trump started firing up the white supremacists.

Late in June, Lee got a call from Dane Waters, a Republican strategist who had worked on five presidential campaigns. Waters invited Lee to serve as press secretary for a last-ditch effort in Cleveland to stop Trump from winning the nomination. It sounded dangerous, especially for an unarmed black man. Lee had a wife and a 2-year-old daughter. He would have to take time off work and pay his own expenses. He wanted to go, but first he had to answer one question:

"Am I willing to die for this?"

* * *

Many things went wrong at Trump's convention. Celebrities, ex-presidents and major corporations stayed away. Staff members from the California delegation were quarantined in their hotel with severe intestinal distress. Mike Pence's speech went nearly unnoticed in the uproar over Ted Cruz's theatrical non-endorsement. Melania Trump's speech contained passages plagiarized from a 2008 speech by Michelle Obama. Trump delivered a spectacle, all right. And if much of it was the accidental kind, like a Ferris wheel breaking loose from its axis, one aspect went roughly as planned. Trump and his allies said they would put down the insurrection, and that is what they did.

From the start, the rebels had almost no chance to win. Their detractors say it was a pointless exercise designed to shame the nominee or introduce rules that would help Cruz win the nomination in 2020. The rebels deny this. According to Dane Waters, one of their leaders, he and his compatriots built a spreadsheet that contained the names of 1,287 delegates—fifty more than a majority—who were willing to nominate someone other than Trump.

This claim is impossible to verify. But it explains why the rebels believed they could stop Trump from reaching a delegate majority at the convention. More than 1,400 of the 2,472 were pledged to Trump based on the primaries and caucuses, but some party elders contended that all delegates were free to vote their consciences. These issues had been mostly irrelevant since 1976, when Gerald Ford defeated Ronald Reagan at the last contested Republican convention. Now they threatened to complicate Trump's nomination, even if the outcome was not in doubt.

The rebels purchased 2,000 lime-green baseball caps, hoping delegates would

Opposite: **A man totes a gun and a Donald Trump sign in Cleveland's Public Square during the 2016 Republican National Convention.** *Bottom:* **Ohio's open-carry law allows civilians to carry guns outside the Republican National Convention.**

When a journalist discovered Melania Trump's plagiarism, Trump's campaign chairman found a way to blame Clinton.

wear them on the convention floor as glowing signals of their dissent. But the Trump team had spies in the rebel camp, and upon discovering the hat scheme they made a brilliant countermove. On the first day of the convention, Trump's own representatives on the convention floor—called "whips" in the parlance of Congress—arrived before the opening gavel wearing fluorescent caps of a similar shade: slightly more yellow than green, but close enough to make it seem as if all glowing hats were beacons for Trump. Realizing they'd been outfoxed, most of the rebels went hatless.

Eliot Cohen told a story a few days before the convention. It made him choke up. Cohen, a prominent military historian and former State Department counselor under President George W. Bush, recalled the events of September 1, 1939, on the Westerplatte promontory at the edge of the Baltic Sea. Severely outgunned by German ships and airplanes, the garrison's Polish soldiers were expected to surrender within hours. Instead they fought for seven days, giving up only when they ran out of ammunition. Decades later, at a youth rally on the same ground, Pope John Paul II said, "Each of you, my

young friends, will find in life some personal Westerplatte. Some measure of tasks that have to be undertaken and fulfilled. Some rightful cause for which one cannot avoid fighting. Some duty, or necessity, which one cannot shun."

Now Cohen wondered who in his own party would stand against Trump.

"You just have the feeling a lot of these politicians don't even know there's a Westerplatte moment, that such a thing exists," he said. "That maybe you're going to put your career in jeopardy, maybe you'll foreclose your opportunity to be reelected to the Senate or to become president, but where you just have to say, 'No, no, I have to do this.'"

Some duty or necessity which one cannot shun? Republican leaders saw one of those, although not the same one Cohen did. They would uphold the will of the voters. They would surrender to Trump.

No, not just surrender. They would help him crush the rebellion.

On the convention floor, Trump campaign and RNC officials worked together. "We control the mics," one floor official said to another about an hour before the convention began. "So we can shut down mics."

They began talking about what to do with a rebel who got out of line.

> ## What happened that Monday afternoon in the arena was fair and just, if you believe the Trump campaign and the RNC, or an exercise in fascism, if you believe the rebels. Either way, it was the convention's most turbulent day in forty years.

FLOOR OFFICIAL ONE: *You don't think he's gonna rush the microphone, do you?*

FLOOR OFFICIAL TWO: *I'll throw an elbow on 'im.*

Trump and his allies had boasted for days about a victory in the Rules Committee that would prevent the delegates from voting independently and potentially reversing the outcomes of the primaries. But now the rebels appeared to have enough signatures on a petition to bring the rules vote to the convention floor—effectively allowing the delegates to decide for themselves what rules would govern them. This was personal for Kendal Unruh, a 51-year-old schoolteacher from Castle Rock, Colorado, and a leader of

the Free the Delegates movement. She once had an autistic son named Cameron, but lost him at age 6 to a heart condition. When she saw Trump on television in 2015 mocking a disabled reporter, she vowed to stop him if she could.

What happened that Monday afternoon in the arena was fair and just, if you believe the Trump campaign and the RNC, or an exercise in fascism, if you believe the rebels. Either way, it was the convention's most turbulent day in forty years.

The rebels went looking for the secretary of the convention, hoping to deliver the signed petition for the roll-call vote, but at 2:36 p.m. Lee told supporters via text message that the secretary was "hiding behind armed guards in (an) attempt to muzzle the delegates." They

Top: **House Speaker Paul Ryan starts the roll call of states that leads to the nomination of Donald Trump.** *Opposite:* **Chairman of the New Hampshire delegation and former Trump campaign manager Corey Lewandowski announces his state's vote for Trump during the roll call.**

eventually turned in the petition, but convention officials put the rules to a voice vote instead. It is hard to accurately judge a voice vote in a large arena where anyone could be shouting, delegate or not. From the upper level, the anti-Trump "no" vote sounded louder than the pro-Trump "yes" vote. But the man with the gavel, U.S. Rep. Steve Womack of Arkansas, heard it differently. "In the opinion of the chair," he said, "the ayes have it."

This was not quite the end of the rebellion. Fifteen minutes of chaos followed, and those fifteen minutes offer a window into the mind of Trump. He had once re-tweeted a quote from Benito Mussolini. He spoke admiringly of Vladimir Putin. When Trump and his lieutenants described their victory at the convention, they did so in Trump's favorite vernacular: the language of unchecked power. Both Trump and Manafort said Trump's opponents had been "crushed." When Trump's delegate wrangler, Rick Gates spoke of the opposition, he said, "Our goal is to destroy them."

The noise persisted long after the chair made his determination, with the rebels chanting *ROLL-CALL VOTE! ROLL-CALL VOTE!* Even without microphones, they were very loud. But they were overwhelmed by another chant, the one stirred up by Trump's yellow-hatted floor whips, the same one that carried Trump through the primaries: *U-S-A! U-S-A! U-S-A!*

The rebels had enough signatures to force a roll call vote. But Womack left the stage, giving the Trump whips several minutes to circulate through the aisles and cajole the delegates into rescinding their signatures. Womack reappeared ten minutes later, called another voice vote, ruled again in favor of the ayes. The insurrection was over.

By the time the nomination became official the following night, many of the rebels had left the building. Some got drunk at a nearby microbrewery called Hofbräuhaus. Andrew Lee was sipping Macallan Scotch and watching on television when Paul Ryan, the convention chair, said he was already looking ahead to the next State of the Union address, when he planned to sit on the rostrum behind President Trump. Trump had not destroyed the Republican establishment. He had *seized* it, with the acquiescence of men like Ryan.

"Democracy is a series of choices," Ryan said. "We Republicans have made our choice."

★ ★ ★

If the primaries had fractured the Republican Party, and if it was Trump's job to reassemble the pieces, Trump and his allies did offer one

When Trump and his lieutenants described their victory at the convention, they did so in Trump's favorite vernacular: the language of unchecked power.

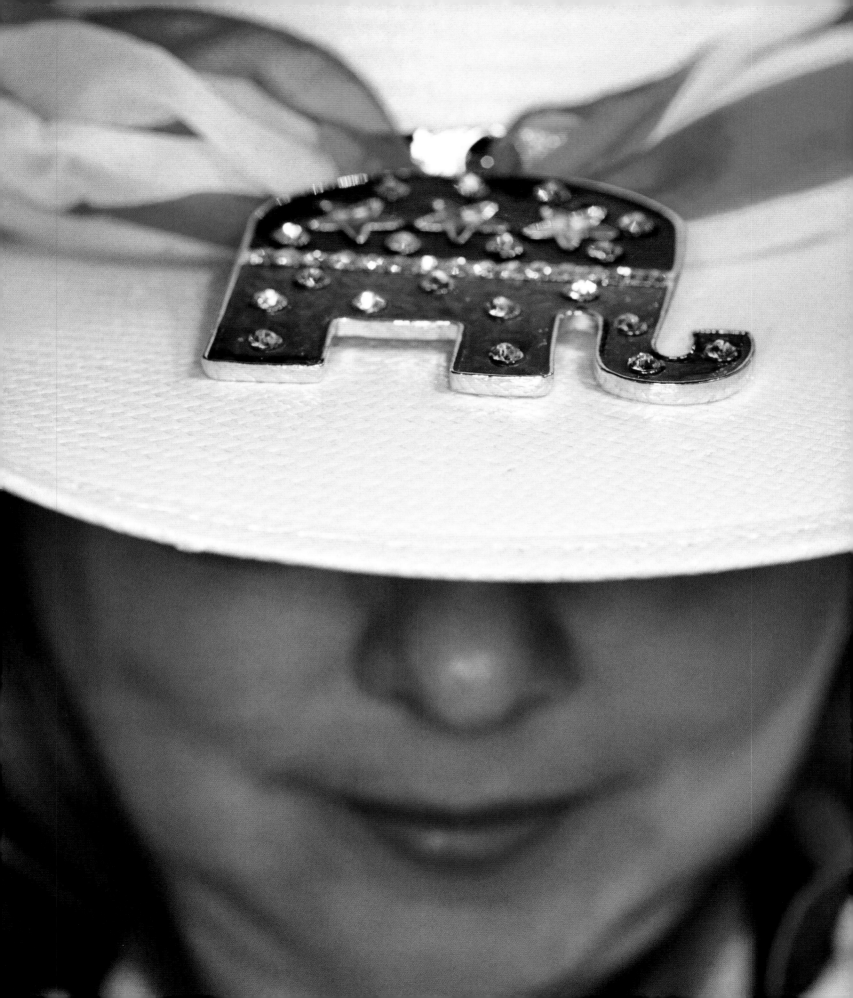

THIS WAS ONLY
THE BEGINNING
OF TRUMPISM,
AND ONLY THE'
FIRST DONALD
TRUMP.

unifying imperative. It came up more often at the convention than building the wall, revering the veterans or punishing China for unfair trade. And if you tried to guess the party's official platform by listening to the convention speakers, you might conclude this was the central plank:

"Hillary for prison," said Pat Smith, mother of Benghazi victim Sean Smith. "She deserves to be in stripes."

"We should send her an email," said Darryl Glenn, the Republican Senate candidate from Colorado, "and tell her she deserves a bright orange jumpsuit."

"Yeah, that's right!" yelled retired Lt. Gen. Michael Flynn, responding to chants from the audience. "Lock her up!"

In American politics, the winner did not imprison the loser. That happened in those other countries, where generals smashed the palace doors, where dictators fled to distant islands, where the peaceful transfer of power was only a theory in a book. But Trump had said it more than once, and he would say it again before November. If he became president, he would prosecute Hillary Clinton.

For some Republicans, this fantasy was even more thrilling than middle-class tax cuts. Which is why the former federal prosecutor Chris Christie put on a show trial for the delegates. These jurors found Clinton guilty

As described by the two daughters and two sons who spoke for him at the convention, Trump was not cruel or sexist. He was a kind and attentive father who taught them the value of ambition and hard work.

of sowing chaos in Libya, letting Boko Haram terrorists run wild in Nigeria, aiding and abetting the Castro brothers in Cuba and negotiating a very bad "nuclear arms deal" with Iran. (Among other things.) Delegates shook their fists, chanting, "Lock her up!" As time went on, Christie seemed less like a prosecutor and more like someone inciting a mob. Or a priest from the book of Leviticus, burdening his goat with the sin of humankind. This exercise continued throughout the week. When a journalist discovered Melania Trump's plagiarism, Trump's campaign chairman found a way to blame Clinton. ("This is once again an example of when a woman threatens Hillary Clinton, how she seeks out to demean her and take her down," Manafort said.) Ben Carson drew a line from Clinton to the left-wing activist Saul Alinsky to Lucifer himself. Then you had the anti-Trump Republicans who believed the entire Trump candidacy was a scheme to help the Clintons. Hatred of Trump could make a person hate Clinton all the more.

A man wandered the convention floor wearing a Clinton mask and an orange jumpsuit. A friend of Trump's went on the radio and said Clinton should be shot to death for treason. Detailed plans to create jobs, improve health care, fix Social Security? Those stayed in the background at Trump's convention. For now the party had a different priority. It involved a woman and a prison cell.

░░░░░░░░░░░░░░░ ★ ★ ★ ░░░░░░░░░░░░░░░

When they weren't denouncing Clinton, the Republicans did make an affirmative case for Trump. It sounded most convincing when it came from his children, three of whom served as vice presidents in his corporation.

"In the same office in Trump Tower where we now work together," said Ivanka, 34, "I remember playing on the floor by my father's desk, constructing miniature buildings with Legos and Erector sets while he did the same with concrete, steel and glass."

As described by the two daughters and two sons who spoke for him at the convention, Trump was not cruel or sexist. He was a kind and attentive father who taught them the value of ambition and hard work. "I still keep all of my report cards, some dating back to kindergarten," said Tiffany, a 22-year-old just out of college, "because I like to look back and see the sweet notes he wrote on each and every one of them."

For all the coverage of his tax returns and bankruptcies, it was easy to forget Trump's achievements. Eric, 32, told the story of the ice-skating rink in Central Park that his father could see from his office window. The city had bungled its renovation for six years, sinking millions into the project with no completion date in sight. Trump offered to take over. He finished it in less than five months, under budget and ahead of schedule.

Bottom: **Trump's daughter Ivanka smiles as a convention-goer takes a photo.** *Following spread:* **Trump applauds his running mate, Indiana Gov. Mike Pence, after Pence's convention speech.**

"I AM YOUR VOICE," Trump said to the nation's forgotten and abandoned workers.

"We didn't learn from MBAs—we learned from people who had doctorates in common sense," said Donald Jr., 38, whose skillful delivery caused speculation about his own future in politics. "Guys like Vinnie Stellio, who taught us how to drive heavy equipment, operate tractors and chain saws, who worked his way through the ranks to become a trusted adviser of my father. It's why we're the only children of billionaires as comfortable in a D10 Caterpillar as we are in our own cars."

Trumpism was not conservatism. As Ivanka said, "I do not consider myself categorically Republican or Democrat." Trumpism sounded more like the lunchtime conversation at a construction site, a distillation of the hopes and fears and grievances of a certain kind of blue-collar worker. Trump himself was 70 years old. He would fade away in a few years. But his philosophy had taken root. This was only the beginning of Trumpism, and only the first Donald Trump.

⋆ ⋆ ⋆

On Wednesday afternoon, the day before Trump's epic speech, the rebels vacated their temporary headquarters on the sixteenth floor of an office building downtown. A box of garbage bags sat on a chair. A blue Ethernet cable hung from the suspended ceiling. Andrew Lee carried a shoulder bag and a folding table onto the elevator. He rode down to the first floor and then walked to the parking garage and opened the hatch of his black Volkswagen GTI. He tossed in his useless lime-green hat. He put in the table and the shoulder bag. He slammed the hatch. There was no room for Lee in the party of Trump. "I can look my friends, my family, my wife, my baby in the face and say, 'I did what I could,'" he said. Then he started the engine and got out of town.

That night Cruz gave an eloquent speech about liberty and conscience. But these ideas were lost in the noise of what he would not do, which was endorse the man who insulted his wife's appearance and accused his father of conspiring to kill President John F. Kennedy. Trump's children watched Cruz from the family's box just off the convention floor. Delegates booed. One yelled, "Get off the stage!" As Trump entered the arena and

On Thursday night, as he delivered the longest and angriest convention speech in recent political history, Trump did not sound quite like himself. The freewheeling entertainer of the primaries had given way to a politician straining to meet the moment.

joined his wife and children, many delegates turned their backs on Cruz. But if Trump and his allies felt snakebitten by their fellow Republican, they had only themselves to blame. They knew full well who Cruz was before they let him in.

On Thursday night, as he delivered the longest and angriest convention speech in recent political history, Trump did not sound quite like himself. The freewheeling entertainer of the primaries had given way to a politician straining to meet the moment. He spoke slowly, tentatively and very loudly, as if volume could stand in for gravitas. "I AM YOUR VOICE," he said to the nation's forgotten and abandoned workers, following a script that capitalized the words.

A good show needed action, conflict, and through much of 2016 the anti-Trump protesters had kept Trump well-supplied. They should have asked for paychecks. "Get 'em out," Trump would say, or "Get 'em the hell out," or "Throw 'em out," and his deportation force would obey, and thus Trump would cleanse the room in the same way he wanted to cleanse the nation. But now he did his best to resemble a statesman. He barely responded when a protester interrupted his speech. Showing a new kind of self-restraint, he did not tell anyone to throw her out. He simply waited until the officers took her away. Then, in a triumphant ad-lib that could have come from a Republican focus group, he said, "How great are our police?"

Top: **Sen. Ted Cruz's failure to endorse Trump draws boos from delegates on the third night of the Republican National Convention.**

If Lincoln was the first great Republican president, many in the party believed Ronald Reagan was the last. Twenty-seven years after his second term ended, it was his name that Republican candidates most often invoked. But Trump was another creature entirely. Reagan painted a glowing picture of America as a "shining city on a hill"; Trump painted an ominous picture, saying America had been ruined from within. Reagan told Mikhail Gorbachev to tear down a wall; Trump told Mexico it should pay the United States to build one. Reagan said, "In this present crisis, government is not the solution to our problem; government is the problem." Trump said, "Nobody knows the system better than me, which is why I alone can fix it." Reagan stared down the Soviet Union, pushing it toward the ash-heap of history. Trump changed the Republican platform to make it more favorable to Russia and said he might not defend the Baltic states from Russian attack. Lincoln? Reagan? In seventy-six minutes, Trump never said either name.

"Remember," he said, near the end of the speech that closed the convention, "all of the people telling you you can't have the country you want are the same people that wouldn't stand—I mean, they said, 'Trump doesn't have a chance of being here tonight. Not a chance.' The *same people*. Oh, we love defeating those people, don't we?"

Anger, populism, disdain for the elite: Trump sounded more and more like Andrew Jackson, the first Democratic president. The Republican delegates stood and hailed their nominee. It was just past midnight. Outside the moon was waning, and a young man who called himself a gay atheist conservative wore a red hat that said *MAKE AMERICA GREAT AGAIN.* Trump had driven old Republicans away, but he'd drawn new ones in. *Oh, we love defeating those people.* Journalists and commentators called Trump's convention

> **Trump was another creature entirely. Reagan painted a glowing picture of America as a "shining city on a hill"; Trump painted an ominous picture, saying America had been ruined from within.**

a historic disaster. Voters said otherwise. A CNN/ORC poll would show an impressive 6-point convention bounce, briefly giving Trump a 5-point lead over Clinton.

In downtown Cleveland, the public square was nearly deserted. Two men stood in the moonlight, talking about Trump. A 32-year-old Bulgarian immigrant named Martin Genev had flown to Cleveland from Seattle to be near the first man for whom he'd ever cast a vote. Every political movement was a reaction to the last. Genev recounted a story from the old days under Soviet rule in Bulgaria. He said American political correctness reminded him of those days, when his grandfather was arrested for telling a joke.

The flag on the soldiers' monument stood at half-staff, commemorating one recent tragedy or another. The statue of Lincoln stood inside, along with an unfastened chain. Genev talked about politics. The conservative movement was fading, he said. Clinton was corrupt; Sanders a socialist. Genev could see only one rational choice.

"You compare Trump to the rest," he said, "he comes off as a savior."

"I remember playing on th[e] floor by my father's desk, constructing miniature buildings with Legos and Erector sets while he did the same with concrete, steel and glass."

—Ivanka Trump

Children of all ages enjoy the balloon drop at the end of the Republican National Convention.

Pastor Mark Burns delivers an impassioned speech on the first day of the Republican convention.

"Our goal is to destroy them."

—Trump's delegate wrangler Rick Gates

A reproduction of a Trump mural is erected in Cleveland for the Republican convention.

"Am I willing to die for this?"
—Andrew Lee, a conservative who worked to stop Trump from winning the nomination

"It's why we're the only children of billionaires as comfortable in a D10 Caterpillar as we are in our own cars."
—Donald Trump Jr.

'Democracy is a series of choices. We Republicans have made our choice."
—House Speaker Paul Ryan

New Jersey Gov. Chris Christie gives a rip-roaring speech in which he "prosecutes" Hillary Clinton.

"Hillary for prison."
—Patricia Smith, mother of Benghazi victim Sean Smith

BY

JEFFREY LORD

*CNN Political Commentator
and Donald Trump
Supporter*

"JEFFREY, THIS IS DONALD"

The time: 6:04 on the evening of July 21. The place: Cleveland. The scene: The CNN box overlooking the floor of the Republican National Convention.

As part of a CNN panel, I am sitting next to Anderson Cooper during a commercial break. Looking down at my cell phone—which I keep silenced on the set—I see a flash of light indicating that I have an email from Hope Hicks, the press secretary for Donald Trump. The subject line is short. It reads: "Re: Phone number? Mr. Trump wants to talk."

I nudge Anderson and move my phone over so he can read the message. He looks at me, I look at him. There is no time to talk because the break is over. Anderson looks into the camera and we are back on the air. I type in my cell number and wait as Anderson turns away from me and starts talking to the CNN analysts who always sit to his right. At this moment, they are John King, Nia-Malika Henderson, Michael Smerconish and Gloria Borger. Before the break, we had been discussing whether the new GOP nominee was having a "good convention." I said yes; several of my colleagues said no. Soon enough, Trump would take to the stage far below us to give his acceptance speech, a speech I am sure will be a home run on this last night of the convention. I look down again. The phone vibrates. As I pick it up and turn away from Anderson to muffle my voice, I look out beyond the lights, knowing the CNN producers packed into the tiny space behind the cameras have got to be wondering why I would ever take a call on air. I hit the talk button—and am connected to Donald Trump.

"Jeffrey, this is Donald. You tell Anderson Cooper..." Clearly, the nominee is miffed. There is an epithet in there. He feels—as I do—that he has had a great convention. Yes, there was the Ted Cruz kerfuffle. I like the senator from Texas. He is a conservative's

conservative. Yet Cruz was still angry at the manner of Trump's victory in the primaries. Along the primary trail Trump had tweeted an unflattering photo of Cruz's wife, Heidi, and mentioned a *National Enquirer* story that suggested Cruz's Cuban-refugee father had some shadowy connection to the pro-Castro JFK assassin Lee Harvey Oswald. Thus, in his speech to the convention one night ago—received with an angry barrage of boos from the delegates—Cruz adamantly refused to endorse his rival. Trump made it clear to me that he had seen Cruz's speech before it was delivered and thought—correctly, as it turned out—that Cruz had damaged himself. (Later, as the fall campaign progressed and Republicans criticized Cruz for reneging on a primary pledge to support the nominee, Cruz would finally come on board with an endorsement.) There is more. And then the newly minted GOP nominee says goodbye.

Anderson, knowing that something is afoot, quickly finishes his discussion with John King and swivels around to call on me. "Jeffrey?" he says. I take a deep breath and start in.

"Anderson, as a matter of fact I've just heard from Donald Trump himself," I begin. Over Anderson's shoulder I can see the faces of John, Nia, Michael and Gloria. They suddenly are realizing what I had been doing and are staring at me, waiting. I continue.

"He thinks that this convention has been a tremendous convention....He has a message for you, Anderson:

"He is not pleased. He thinks that we're not accurately representing this convention, which he feels has been a stupendous success. He knew that Ted Cruz was going to say what he said. He thinks Ted Cruz has damaged himself by doing this. He beat all of these candidates to get here. These people are totally in support of him. He feels that he's going to go out of here with an energized convention, et cetera. He specifically said to say that your ratings, our ratings at CNN, are up here because of his presence in this convention. And I think I've more or less delivered the message."

Laughter erupts. Anderson Cooper is nothing if not fast on his feet, a job requirement for television anchors. This time around he is clearly amazed. He pauses only a nanosecond before replying:

"There's no doubt about Donald Trump's impact on ratings. I mean I haven't looked at the ratings, it's amazing that Donald Trump has looked at the ratings, I haven't looked at the ratings...."

It is indeed amazing, but I have long believed one of Donald Trump's strengths as a candidate is that nothing about him is typical of the average politician. This moment—calling out of the blue to a live CNN show—was one more illustration of that fact.

"Mr. Trump wants to talk."

"He has nothing else to do," John chimes in, drawing more laughter.

"But I do think," Anderson continues, then interrupts himself. "Look, we said this last night." He gestures over his shoulder with his thumb at the crowd below. "This was an energized crowd....Beyond all the drama that we pay attention to with Ted Cruz, last night was the first night this crowd stayed until the very end, which is the first night that's happened. And it was an energized crowd. It was electric."

Now the panel of both CNN analysts and partisan commentators jump into the discussion. Behind me are my fellow commentators, Scottie Nell Hughes, Kevin Madden and Amanda Carpenter. Scottie Nell, a Trump supporter, has stopped laughing long enough to salute Trump for bringing "Baskin-Robbins" Republicans—all flavors of Republicans— together. Analyst Gloria Borger agrees that

Cruz's stout refusal to endorse Trump actually helps the nominee. Anderson jumps back in to note that Trump's mastery of stagecraft eclipsed Cruz's departure from the stage on the third night of the convention. Trump had entered his family's box in the hall before Cruz was finished speaking, and delegates—as well as TV cameras—turned their attention from the stage to the nominee. Anderson is perceptive, and indeed Trump himself confirmed to me that his arrival had been timed to take attention away from Cruz. Before we take a break, Amanda Carpenter, Cruz's former communications director who is decidedly not a Trump supporter, signals that she is not impressed.

"If he's so into micromanaging the media's interpretation of how the events have gone that he's calling in to shows at this moment in time—this convention has been bungled almost every single day," she says. "He needs to focus on his speech, his message. I'm worried, quite frankly, [that] it's not Reagan, it's going to be Nixonian, it's going to be doom and fear and gloom. That's not a uniting message."

When Amanda finishes, we are done— "clear" in TV jargon—and I make my way out of the small, crowded booth and downstairs to the concourse that circles the Quicken Loans Arena. I spot CNN President Jeff Zucker sitting in, of all things, some sort of cart (there is no seating in the concourse, beyond the stray chair) and chatting with several colleagues. I walk over and ask if he has seen what just transpired on CNN. There are no televisions in the concourse, so, of course, he has not seen it. "Donald Trump called me on air," I say. Immediately, Jeff is off the cart, pulling me aside for a private conversation. I relate the whole story, Trumpian epithet and all. His first question: Had I repeated the epithet on air? No, I assured him. He grins. "That is *great* television!" exclaims the man who knows more than a thing or two about the subject.

It was.

9

THE
DEMOCRATS
TRY TO
CAPTURE
THE FLAG

There was a woman who loved a country that had always been governed by men. She pledged allegiance to its flag and stood, hand over heart, during its national anthem. She often proclaimed its greatness—insisted it had *never stopped* being great—even as her opponent insisted it was in sharp decline. The voters had never seen such a contrast. Soon they would choose between this woman and a man who called women dogs, judged their bodies, insulted their faces, hinted crassly about their personal hygiene, and hoped to end her political career even as he became the nation's forty-fifth consecutive male president.

It was just before 9 p.m. on Thursday, July 28. In two hours Hillary Clinton would become the first American woman to accept a major party's presidential nomination. Tens of millions watched on television, including Elizabeth MacNaughton, age 98, a psychologist born before women won the right to vote. Too frail to travel from Houston to the Democratic convention in Philadelphia, she promised her daughter she would stay alive long enough to vote at least one more time.

Thousands waited inside the Wells Fargo Center, including Kim Frederick, a Democratic activist who had seen a 2014 *Time* magazine cover that depicted Clinton on the verge of crushing a man with her high heel. Frederick was so incensed by the sexist media coverage that she founded a group called HRC Super Volunteers. Frederick had traveled from Texas to Iowa to Minnesota, losing touch with her best friends, spending most of her free time to help Clinton win the nomination. Now, as she sat with the Texas delegation, she felt as if she hadn't slept in two years.

Hundreds waited in the corridors of the packed arena, held at bay by the ushers, hoping seats would open up. Ruth Ellis, a 54-year-old teacher trainer, had driven from California in an RV with her husband and a 19-year-old son with Down syndrome. She stood outside Section 210, near the lighted sign for Chickie's and Pete's Crab House and Sports Bar. Ahead of her, after ninety minutes in a line that barely moved, another woman decided to cut her losses.

"Does anybody want my sign?" she asked.

"Are you giving up?" Ellis responded. "No, no, no, no. I'm not letting you give up."

By the time Hillary Clinton was born in 1947, Americans had already invented the airplane, the atom-smasher and the general-purpose computer. In her lifetime they would put a man on the moon and a woman in space. But another thing did not happen, and its absence seemed to call for an explanation. As dozens of other nations elected their first female leaders, the United States did not even come close. Clinton was 12 when Sirimavo Bandaranaike became prime minister of Ceylon, 18 when Indira Gandhi became prime minister of India, 21 when Golda Meir became prime minister of Israel. In 1972, when Congresswoman Shirley Chisholm ran for the Democratic nomination for president, she received about 430,000 votes and finished behind six men.

"When I ran for the Congress, when I ran for president, I met more discrimination as a woman than for being black," Chisholm said later. "Men are men."

> **Before the Democrats could wrestle Trump for the flag— before they could make the case to the nation that *they* were the real patriots—they had to reckon with their own civil war.**

Thirty-six years would pass before another woman received that many votes again.

"Oh, come on," Ruth Ellis said as a man left the line outside Section 210. "Don't give up. Hillary didn't give up!"

In October 1984, the same month Indira Gandhi was assassinated, the first American woman to run on a major-party ticket took part in a vice-presidential debate.

VICE PRESIDENT GEORGE H.W. BUSH: *Let me help you with the difference, Ms. Ferraro, between Iran and the embassy in Lebanon.*

CONGRESSWOMAN GERALDINE FERRARO: *Let me first of all say that I almost resent, Vice President Bush, your patronizing attitude that you have to teach me about foreign policy.*

After the debate, Bush remarked that he had "kicked a little ass."

In 1986, Corazon Aquino of the Philippines became the first female president in Asia. In 1988, Benazir Bhutto became prime minister of Pakistan. The following summer, Arkansas First Lady Hillary Clinton and her 9-year-old daughter, Chelsea, were vacationing in London when they noticed a crowd outside the Ritz hotel. They watched Bhutto get out of her limousine and walk into the lobby. As Clinton would later write, "Bhutto was the only celebrity I had ever stood behind a rope line to see."

A few months later, 11-year-old Kim Frederick was riding in the car when she heard a radio news report about Clayton Williams, the man running for governor of Texas against State Treasurer Ann Richards.

Bottom: **An attendee at a pro–Sen. Bernie Sanders of Vermont rally during the 2016 Democratic National Convention in Philadelphia.** *Opposite:* **Sanders supporters, with signs proclaiming their opposition to the so-called Trans-Pacific Partnership trade proposal, vie with Hillary Clinton supporters for attention at the Democratic National Convention.**

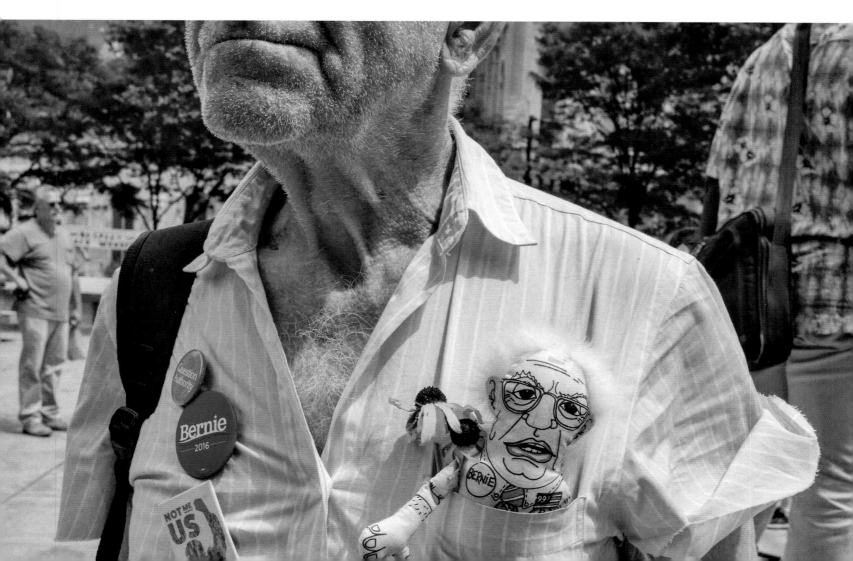

In his speech on the convention's first night, Sanders went on for a while about himself and his revolution. And then the newly minted Democrat did his part to repair the Democratic Party.

With reporters present, Williams had recently made a joke about rape: "If it's inevitable, just relax and enjoy it." The following year, 1991, Frederick watched the all-male Senate Judiciary Committee aggressively question Anita Hill about her allegations that Clarence Thomas, who was nominated to sit on the Supreme Court, had sexually harassed her. The year after that, when Bill Clinton was running for president, Frederick read Hillary Clinton's defiant quote in defense of her law career—"I suppose I could have stayed home, baked cookies and had teas"—and watched her withstand the ensuing attacks. A teenage girl was becoming a feminist.

Hope dwindled in the corridor outside Section 210. The line barely moved. Ellis strained to see beyond the curtain. She asked the usher to move aside, to make a sight line, but the usher refused.

"Seriously," Ellis said with exasperation, "this is once in a lifetime."

Or once in 227 years.

A sound came from the arena, louder and louder, a battle cry that conjured visions of a Trump rally. But these were Democrats, chanting with all their hearts:

"U-S-A! U-S-A! U-S-A!"

★ ★ ★

Before the Democrats could wrestle Trump for the flag—before they could make the case to the nation that *they* were the real patriots—they had to reckon with their own civil war.

Three days before the convention, WikiLeaks published a trove of stolen emails, some of which appeared to show Democratic National Committee officials plotting against Bernie Sanders during the primaries. In the most flagrant example, chief financial officer Brad Marshall shared an idea with chief executive officer Amy Dacey a few days before Democrats voted in Kentucky and West Virginia:

> *"It might may (sic) no difference, but for KY and WVA can we get someone to ask his belief. Does he believe in a God. He had skated on saying he has a Jewish heritage. I think I read he is an atheist. This could make several points difference with my peeps. My Southern Baptist peeps would draw a big difference between a Jew and an atheist."*

Dacey replied:

"AMEN."

The DNC did not follow Marshall's suggestion. In an interview later with CNN, Dacey said, "I got an email and I was trying to be dismissive and shut down the conversation. I chose an awkward word. There was no way we were ever going to pursue that."

But the damage was done. When Clinton announced Virginia Sen. Tim Kaine as her running mate that Friday night, July 22, #DNCLeaks was the leading hashtag on Twitter. Sanders and his revolutionaries already believed the party was biased against them. Now they had fresh evidence. On Sunday morning, his campaign manager, Jeff Weaver, appeared on CNN and said, "There's obviously a problem here. Someone should resign. It should be—Debbie Wasserman Schultz should resign."

Democrats would later complain about how Wasserman Schultz, a congresswoman from Florida, conducted herself that week— about her initial resistance to resigning as chairwoman, about the way she hung around Philadelphia, looking for hugs and sympathy. Between the furious Berniecrats and the donors who were embarrassed by some of the

emails and worried their personal information had been breached, it was hard to find Democrats willing to defend her. She was loyal to Clinton. Her five years as chairwoman had led to this moment. She wanted to gavel in the first major-party convention ever to nominate a woman for president. But that was not to be.

The day before the convention started, Clinton's campaign manager, Robby Mook, and her liaison to the DNC, Charlie Baker, met with Wasserman Schultz in her Philadelphia hotel suite. Also there was Hilary Rosen, a friend of the Florida congresswoman's and a Clinton surrogate. According to Rosen, Mook and Baker told Wasserman Schultz: "The Bernie people say this is going to be bad, that they're going to protest. We don't really want a protest. But Hillary's your friend and we'll support you whatever you decide." Wasserman Schultz asked Mook and Baker to give her a few minutes to think it over.

While the Clinton emissaries waited in the hall, Wasserman Schultz talked with her chief of staff, Tracie Pough, and Rosen. The embattled DNC chair knew what she had to do, and she would do it. But only *after* opening the convention. She and Rosen contacted the White House to let them know she'd be resigning at the end of the week. Then Rosen called Donna Brazile, the DNC's vice chair. "I said, 'You better get over here. You're about

> **When his own supporters booed him at a delegate breakfast the next morning, Sanders responded…."It is easy to boo, but it is harder to look your kids in the face if we are living under a Trump presidency."**

to be the chair of the DNC.'" Rosen recalled. "She's like, 'What the fuck?'"

But things went south the next morning, at a breakfast for the Florida delegation. Sanders supporters started yelling at Wasserman Schultz and her supporters started yelling back, and the room got very loud.

According to Rosen, "Debbie said, 'Look, this is not worth it—to have us be booed at the opening of the convention. So I'm not going to open the convention. I've already resigned. Forget it.'"

No one starts a revolution in the hope of tamping it down. But this is what Sanders did. His aides worked with Clinton's on a plan to prevent disruptions, and convention speakers were coached to ignore protests on the floor and focus on the TV audience. Sanders himself sent out a text message to the delegates. "I ask you as a personal courtesy to me to not engage in any kind of protest on the floor," he wrote. "It's of utmost importance you explain this to your delegations." When his campaign manager, Weaver, ran across the new interim

DNC chairwoman, Brazile, he pledged to help her however he could. "I love you," they both said, embracing.

In his speech on the convention's first night, Sanders went on for a while about himself and his revolution. And then the newly minted Democrat did his part to repair the Democratic Party. He said, "Hillary Clinton must become the next president of the United States."

When his own supporters booed him at a delegate breakfast the next morning, Sanders responded with his own version of an appeal to fear that Clinton had been using for months. "It is easy to boo," he said, "but it is harder to look your kids in the face if we are living under a Trump presidency."

★ ★ ★

The convention speakers—younger, more diverse, and collectively about a thousand times more famous than their Republican counterparts—had one main objective: repair the damage that Trump and the Republicans

IT WAS
CLINTON,
OR
NO WOMAN
AT ALL.

had done to Hillary Clinton's reputation. And, of course, join together in a star-studded rendition of "Fight Song," during which the pop singer Ester Dean incorporated Clinton's book titles into a set of rap lyrics. They did know how to have a good time.

"In the spring of 1971 I met a girl," Bill Clinton said on the second night, trying to personalize his wife's story while also trumpeting her decades-long work on such issues as equality, education, child welfare, health care and aid to the 9/11 first responders.

"Now," he said, "how does this square? How did this square with the things that you heard at the Republican convention? What's the difference in what I told you and what they said? How do you square it? You can't. One is real; the other is made up. You just have to decide. You just have to decide which is which, my fellow Americans."

Long ago, the Republicans had decided they would rule the territory of flags and fireworks and parades and police officers and banging the drum for America. And after they noticed something unusual about the first night of the convention, Trump went on Twitter to question the Democrats' patriotism once again: "Not one American flag on the massive stage at the Democratic National Convention until people started complaining

> # "I see Americans of every party, every background, every faith who believe that we are stronger together."
>
> —President Barack Obama

—then a small one," he wrote. "Pathetic."

But in 2016 the Republicans were losing their grip on patriotism, thanks in part to the nominee who had just called on Russia to find Clinton's missing emails. And as the Democrats methodically built an argument for Clinton as the most qualified candidate ever to run for president, some conservatives also thought the Democrats looked more like Republicans than the Republicans did. As *National Review* editor Rich Lowry tweeted, "American exceptionalism and greatness, shining city on hill, founding documents, etc—they're trying to take all our stuff."

Suddenly American flags were everywhere: on the stage, in the bleachers, atop the tall blue signs that said *HILLARY*. The Democrats held up a mirror to Trump and dared the voters to call him a patriot. "He even mocks our POWs, like John McCain," retired Rear Admiral John Hutson said on the third night of the convention. "I served in the same Navy as John McCain. I used to vote in the same party as John McCain. Donald, you're not fit to polish John McCain's boots."

Vice President Joe Biden lit up the room that night, and when he said, "It's never, never, never been a good bet to bet against America," the delegates broke into an unexpected chant. Trump didn't own those three letters, and neither did the Republicans.

Bottom left: **President Barack Obama addresses the Democratic National Convention.**

U-S-A! U-S-A! U-S-A! The feminist attorney Gloria Allred chanted vigorously, as did Kim Frederick, as did a man in a royal blue turban.

"And most of all," President Obama said a few minutes later, "I see Americans of every party, every background, every faith who believe that we are stronger together—black, white, Latino, Asian, Native American; young, old; gay, straight; men, women folks with disabilities, all pledging allegiance, under the same proud flag, to this big, bold country that we love. That's what I see. That's the America I know!"

This was another kind of patriotism, broader than the kind Trump was selling. And if it felt ambivalent about the past that Trump glorified, it viewed the present and future with unabashed optimism. In the forty years before Obama's inauguration, with Republicans dominating the White House, the Democrats drew much of their vitality from protest and dissent. Now they'd been in charge for almost eight years: jump-starting the sputtering economy, killing Osama bin Laden, passing a health care plan that drastically reduced the number of uninsured Americans. If Trump wanted to bring back the nation that existed in his mind, Obama described the nation that actually was—the one that elected a black president and might soon elect a woman president, the one where more than 50 million residents spoke Spanish, the one whose white population was expected to fall below 50 percent before 2050. In this America, the headstones at Arlington National Cemetery bore all kinds of inscriptions. Some had Muslim crescents.

The Army captain was 27-years old on the day an orange car drove up to the gates of his base. He was a good soldier, fighting Bush's war, admiring John McCain, ordering his fellow soldiers to take cover even as he walked toward the suspicious car. That car exploded on June 8, 2004, in Baquba, Iraq, killing Captain Humayun Khan, and twelve years later his mother and father took the stage together on the fourth and final night of the Democratic National Convention. Ghazala Khan said nothing. Khizr Khan said only 357 words. He could have said less. What

mattered was the physical, the indisputable, the sight of two Muslim Americans who had given their son for the country they loved.

"Hillary Clinton was right when she called my son the best of America," Khizr Khan said. "If it was up to Donald Trump, he never would have been in America."

He reached into his jacket, drew out his pocket U.S. Constitution and offered to lend it to Trump.

"You have sacrificed *nothing*, and *no one*," he said, baiting a trap that his adversary would barrel into.

★ ★ ★

More than seventy modern nations had inaugurated a female head of state by the time the Democrats nominated Clinton. Given this context, one line from First Lady Michelle Obama's convention speech stood out all the more: "And because of Hillary Clinton, my daughters—and all our sons and daughters— now take for granted that a woman can be president of the United States."

This was the paradox of Clinton, a woman who had come to seem almost ordinary in her long and lonely pursuit of the extraordinary. She was the one who finally surpassed the

mark set by Shirley Chisholm in 1972. She surpassed it by more than 17 million votes. And she still lost the nomination to a man with half her accomplishments—a man who told her, with a mixture of kindness and condescension, "You're likeable enough."

There was something people said about Clinton. Men said it. Women said it. Liberals said it. Conservatives said it. Young people said it. Old people said it. They said, with slight variations:

> I want a woman to be president. Just not that woman.

They gave all kinds of reasons. Not a woman who laughed the way she did. Not a woman who looked the way she did. Not a woman who yelled the way she did. Not a woman who stretched the truth the way she did. Not a Democratic woman. Not a moderate woman. Not a liberal woman. Not a hawkish woman. Not a woman who took large corporate donations, used a private email server, and mixed State Department priorities with those of the Clinton Foundation. Not a woman who would return the nation to the scandal-filled days of her husband's two terms in office. Not a woman whose rise to national prominence was inextricably linked

Top: **Hillary Clinton and longtime aide Huma Abedin watch from backstage as Chelsea Clinton introduces her mother at the Democratic convention.**

with her choice *not* to leave her cheating husband. Did they judge men by the same standards? One had only to look at her husband's enduring popularity to conclude that they did not.

"You can be the most admired person in the world, until you want power, girl," Rosen said. "Then all of a sudden there's a ceiling on how willing we are to let you claim it, you girl-in-a-pantsuit who doesn't smile enough for us."

Clinton's loss to Barack Obama in 2008 left her in a strange place. She had shown that a woman could *almost* win her party's nomination, could *almost* be president. But as Michelle Obama said, it meant that more voters would take her for granted next time around. They now assumed that a woman could become president, *would* be before too long. Clinton received fewer votes as the winner of the 2016 primaries than she had as the loser in 2008. As if she were running for re-election to an office she had never held.

Just not *that* woman? She had no counterpart in American history. It was Clinton, or no woman at all. That was how Kim Frederick saw it, anyway. She was only 38, but she was convinced of this: "If Hillary Clinton can't become president, I will not see a woman president in my lifetime."

✶ ✶ ✶

Ruth Ellis had come all the way from California to see Clinton accept the nomination, but now she was stuck in the corridor outside Section 210. *Maybe it's not gonna happen*, she thought. Finally, at 9:33 p.m., the usher let Ellis and three friends walk past the curtain and stand in the tunnel that led to the arena.

"WOOOOO!" Ellis said. She was on the upper level, staring far down across the vast arena toward the left corner of the stage. There was Katy Perry, singing about victory, her sequined dress glittering in the spotlights.

> ## The wall behind the stage pivoted, and Clinton walked out through the opening. "Thank you," she kept saying, and "Oh, my gosh." She paced the stage, hand over heart, apparently overwhelmed with gratitude. The standing ovation would last more than three minutes.

The fire marshal walked in, clearing the tunnel, sending Ellis and her friends back to the corridor. Two gave up and left the building. And then the fire marshal was gone, and Ellis and another friend went back inside. This time no one stopped them.

"Ladies and gentlemen," Chelsea Clinton said, "my mother, my hero and *our next president*. Hillary Clinton."

The wall behind the stage pivoted, and Clinton walked out through the opening. She hugged her daughter, waved to the cheering crowd. "Thank you," she kept saying, and "Oh, my gosh." She paced the stage, hand over heart, apparently overwhelmed with gratitude. The standing ovation would last more than three minutes. Kim Frederick had planned to hold it together, but no.

Here came the tears. Ruth Ellis turned to her friend and screamed. For a moment she felt as if she were on stage with Clinton, as if they had done this together. Ellis could remember being 7 years old, watching Neil Armstrong's televised walk on the moon. She felt then the way she felt now: overjoyed, filled with awe, proud to be an American.

"It's never, never, never been a good bet to bet against America."

—Vice President Joe Biden

A protester at the Democratic convention.

"You can be the most admired person in the world, until you want power, girl."

—Hilary Rosen, campaign surrogate for Clinton

Vermin Supreme, a performance artist and activist, outside the Democratic convention.

Clinton and her running mate, Sen. Tim Kaine, celebrate with their spouses backstage after Clinton's speech at the Democratic conventi

"Don't give up. Hillary didn't give up!"

—Ruth Ellis, Clinton supporter

"If Hillary Clinton can't become president, I will not see a woman president in my lifetime."

—Kim Frederick, Clinton supporter

zala and Khizr Khan during an emotional moment at the Democratic convention.

Pop star Katy Perry poses for a photo with Rep. John Lewis after Hillary Clinton's speech.

anders supporter outside the gates of the Democratic vention.

10

THE FALL AND RISE OF DONALD TRUMP

t was worse in 1828, when Andrew Jackson blamed political slander for the apparent heart attack that killed his wife, but by August the 2016 election had become one of the nastiest in American history. Already the negative campaigning had filtered into at least two obituaries. "In lieu of flowers, please do not vote for Hillary Clinton," said the notice for Elaine Fydrych, 63, of Runnemede, New Jersey. In Pittsburgh, 70-year-old Jeffrey Cohen made the opposite wish: "Jeffrey would ask that in lieu of flowers, please do not vote for Donald Trump."

Both candidates infuriated Bill Bryant Jr., a retired Army officer in Marietta, Georgia. He was young for 87, fond of a terrier named Jewel and the Honda Accord he still drove to the grocery store. But he wasn't sure he could take three more months of Clinton and Trump—much less whichever presidency came next.

"I'm done with it," he told his third son, Alan. "I'm ready to go. I don't even want to see what happens."

What happened from late July through the first half of August was unusual even for Trump. He had a pile of grenades and he wanted to see them explode, anywhere, everywhere, no matter the damage to others or himself. He was feeling boxed in by his campaign chairman, and he wanted the world to know that Paul Manafort was not the boss of Donald Trump. Quite the opposite. If Manafort was leaking stories about the new Trump, the old Trump had to work twice as hard to prove him wrong. Kaboom, kaboom. Did he really want to be president? Yes, if he could also hold a news conference the day after his convention and threaten to punish John Kasich and Ted Cruz by funding a super PAC to prevent their re-election. Sure, as long as everyone knew he didn't *want* Cruz's endorsement, and would reject said endorsement if offered, and oh, by the way, he still thought Cruz's father might have had something to do with the Kennedy assassination.

Trump might have moved past the Khizr Khan story by offering a few well-chosen words of gratitude and condolence. But he couldn't, or wouldn't. He once told biographer Michael D'Antonio, "When I look at myself in the first grade and I look at myself now, I'm basically the same." Khan hit him first, and Trump hit back.

"I'd like to hear his wife say something," he told Maureen Dowd of The New York Times the day after Khan's convention speech. Trump liked to drop hints, to make disturbing implications that his surrogates could recast if politically necessary. Now he made that impossible. In an interview with George

What happened from late July through the first half of August was unusual even for Trump. He had a pile of grenades and he wanted to see them explode, anywhere, everywhere, no matter the damage to others or himself.

Stephanopoulos of ABC News, he said, "If you look at his wife, she was standing there. She had nothing to say. She probably—maybe she wasn't allowed to have anything to say. You tell me."

She told him. In The Washington Post, Ghazala Khan explained her silence at the Democratic convention. Twelve years after his death, she still cried for her son every day. "I cannot walk into a room with pictures of Humayun," she wrote. "For all these years, I haven't been able to clean the closet where his things are—I had to ask my daughter-in-law to do it. Walking onto the convention stage, with a huge picture of my son behind me, I could hardly control myself. What mother could?"

Trump seemed incredulous about the growing uproar. "I was viciously attacked by Mr. Khan at the Democratic Convention," he tweeted. "Am I not allowed to respond?" He was allowed, of course, just as the Khans were allowed to respond to his responses, and their dialogue sustained a narrative that was unequivocally horrible for Trump.

Clinton operatives debated how to respond. According to Teddy Goff, her chief digital strategist, "That weekend I've got people on my team chomping at the bit to do a video, do an ad, and it was (policy adviser) Jake Sullivan who said, 'Nope. Nope. Nope. Nope.' We're just going to let him do what he's going to do." And so, Goff said in an interview, they "let him dig his own grave."

One prominent Republican after another took the Khans' side. Dozens abandoned

Trump altogether. Richard Hanna, a Republican congressman from New York, took it a step further: He said he would vote for Hillary Clinton.

Trump felt more besieged than ever, and his solution was more grenades. He blasted a fire marshal in Colorado for limiting admission to his rally. He offended Purple Heart recipients by casually saying he had always wanted one. When a baby cried at a rally in Virginia, he said, "You can get the baby out of here." Speaking on condition of anonymity to CNN's Jim Acosta, a Republican fundraiser asked, "Why doesn't he kick a puppy and call it a day?"

Not even Trump could insult a Gold Star mother without some cost to himself. Some polls from early August showed him behind Clinton by double digits, both nationally and in swing states such as Colorado and Pennsylvania. One even showed him trailing narrowly in Georgia, which had not voted Democratic in a presidential election since 1992.

Yes, it could get worse. One day Trump hinted about what "Second Amendment people" might do to stop the next President Clinton from taking their guns. The next day he called President Obama the "founder of ISIS." When reporters disputed this claim, his response defied interpretation: "Obviously I'm being sarcastic, but not so sarcastic, to be honest." Anyway, he explained, it was all the media's fault. His fans at a rally in Florida

Top: **In Phoenix, Trump is joined onstage by the relatives of people who were killed by undocumented immigrants.** *Opposite:* **Attendees at a Trump rally in Green Bay, Wisconsin, on October 17, 2016.**

agreed. They turned to reporters in the press pen and chanted, *LOCK THEM UP!*

No one did, because this was not Russia, and the media struck again on August 14. The New York Times reported that Ukrainian investigators had discovered evidence that Manafort and others might have received millions in illegal payments from Ukraine's former pro-Russia ruling party. Manafort, who worked for the former Ukrainian president as a consultant before joining the Trump campaign, denied the allegations, but the controversy gave Trump one more reason to let him go. By week's end, Manafort had resigned. Campaign adviser Kellyanne Conway had been promoted to campaign manager. And Trump had brought on a new chief executive who also liked throwing grenades: Stephen Bannon, former chairman of the pro-Trump website Breitbart. The site had recently published a headline calling Bill Kristol, editor of *The Weekly Standard*, a "renegade Jew."

Finally, Clinton and Trump agreed on something.

"There is no new Donald Trump," she said.

"I am who I am," he said.

The mudslinging continued. Around mid-August, Bill Bryant Jr. drove his Honda to the grocery store. Back at home he tried to carry too many bags up the stairs, and he fell and suffered a concussion. One bad thing led to another, the way it sometimes does when you're 87. A kidney stone, an infection, a decision to enter hospice care. Bryant kept saying he didn't want to see how it ended. He died on September 10, fifty-nine days before the election.

⁘⁘⁘⁘⁘⁘⁘⁘⁘⁘⁘ ★ ★ ★ ⁘⁘⁘⁘⁘⁘⁘⁘⁘⁘⁘

By now, Americans understood that future generations would judge them for what they did in the time of Trump. Many signed open letters, if only to memorialize their dissent. There were writers against Trump, historians against Trump, technology leaders against Trump. He drove the conversation, *demanded* a response, and those who found him hateful were tempted to respond with hate. Thus, when the pro-Trump author Ann Coulter appeared at the Comedy Central Roast of Rob Lowe, one celebrity after another turned viciously on Coulter. (Her many provocations included a call for Trump to deport Nikki Haley, the Indian-American governor of South Carolina.) The retired quarterback Peyton Manning mocked Coulter's appearance. The comedian Jimmy Carr suggested she kill herself. The comedian Nikki Glaser told her, "The only person you will ever make happy is the Mexican who digs your grave." It went on like that. When an anarchist group installed a

By now, Americans understood that future generations would judge them for what they did in the time of Trump.... He drove the conversation, *demanded* a response, and those who found him hateful were tempted to respond with hate.

statue of a naked Trump at Union Square Park in New York, assistant parks commissioner Sam Biederman made an official statement that belittled the statue's anatomy. What did people do in the time of Trump? Some accidentally followed his example.

It fell to Clinton to actually stop Trump, and on a bus tour after her convention she struck at the vulnerable heart of his candidacy.

"The only thing he makes in America are bankruptcies," she said in Hatfield, Pennsylvania, at a factory owned by the company that brought the production of Lincoln Logs from China back home to the United States. This line of attack might have stopped Trump in 2015 if the other Republicans had used it more often. The man who wanted to punish corporations for outsourcing jobs had outsourced production of his own Donald J. Trump clothing line to such places as Honduras and Bangladesh, where the average factory worker earned thirty-three cents an hour. Clinton drove home the point the next day by repeatedly advertising the American-made plaid shirt her husband wore as he sat behind her, chewing his gum and occasionally clapping.

Crossing hostile territory in rural Pennsylvania and Ohio, Clinton deftly avoided standard Democratic talking points on race,

guns and abortion. Instead she talked about football, hot peppers, jobs, jobs, jobs. It was time to widen the tent. She made her supporters wait for hours on July 30, blaming thunderstorms, not mentioning the late start she got in Harrisburg on account of a rare interview with Chris Wallace of Fox News. She made them wait so long the next afternoon in Columbus that dozens were treated for heat-related illness. What were they going to do? Vote for Trump? He could barely persuade the Republicans.

In early August, Clinton stepped aside and let Trump inflict his own wounds. No need to interfere with his self-destruction. She held fewer rallies and gave fewer public speeches. Instead she went on a fundraising blitz, headlining thirty-seven events that month and taking in close to $70 million. Her celebrity friends turned out in force. When Leonardo DiCaprio had to cancel a fundraiser because of a scheduling conflict involving his climate-change documentary, he called for backup. Yes, Justin Timberlake and his wife, Jessica Biel, would host the event at

> **"Respectfully, the public has heard for thirty years that the media, not all the media, but from a significant portion of you, that every single Republican who has run is the dumbest, least honest, most racist whatever.... So when an actual stupid, crazy, dishonest racist showed up, no one believed you."**
>
> —Undecided voter at an AARP focus group

their house in the Hollywood Hills; and yes, Jamie Foxx and Jennifer Aniston would be there. During a swing through the Hamptons later in August, Sir Paul McCartney asked Clinton to dance while Jimmy Buffett played "Cheeseburger in Paradise." McCartney also played a few, including "Can't Buy Me Love."

"This is the first time I've paid to hear myself sing," he said.

Clinton did make a notable speech on August 25 in Reno, Nevada. It was supposed to be about small business, but now something else was on her mind. "Donald Trump has built his campaign on prejudice and paranoia," she said. "He is taking hate groups mainstream." She talked about racial discrimination in previous decades at Trump apartments and casinos, the racist ideology

of the pro-Trump "alt-right" movement and the wild conspiracy theories encouraged by Trump himself. None of these charges moved the polls in her favor. In a competing speech that day, Trump called them "the oldest play in the Democratic playbook." A few weeks later, according to the Chicago Sun-Times, an undecided female voter at an AARP focus group made a similar point:

"Respectfully, the public has heard for thirty years that the media, not all the media, but from a significant portion of you, that every single Republican who has run is the dumbest, least honest, most racist whatever that has ever run for office....So when an actual stupid, crazy, dishonest racist showed up, no one believed you."

To win in November, Clinton would need to

Above and following spread: **Trump supporters convene inside an aircraft hangar at Grand Junction, Colorado, in October 2016.**

AGAIN!

His supporters filled
the silence: TRUMP!
TRUMP! TRUMP!

TRUMP
PENCE

MAKE
AMERICA
GREAT AGAIN

THE
NEW
DONALD
TRUMP

mobilize women, minorities, college-educated whites and Democrats. "Voters want to vote *for* something," Democratic pollster Celinda Lake said. "Particularly women, and particularly our base...When we're doing the negative messaging, sometimes we solidify *their* base."

Her Republican counterpart and occasional collaborator agreed. "With the exception of 1972, we as a nation voted for the most positive, optimistic, forward-looking, pleasant candidate," Kellyanne Conway said in an interview before she became Trump's campaign manager. "When you look at the polling, you will quickly find people go for the more optimistic candidate—particularly females."

The Democratic convention had made the affirmative case for Clinton. But in August, she did not press the case for herself. And in her frequent absence from the campaign trail, negative stories filled the void. On September 2, the FBI released documents from its investigation into her private email server. They indicated that Clinton told investigators at least thirty-nine times that she couldn't recall or remember something. They quoted an aide who took one of her old mobile devices and smashed it with a hammer. They said a civilian who managed her server admitted deleting her emails even after the House Benghazi

> ## He never said he was sorry. But this vague and oddly cheerful half-apology was half an apology more than he'd previously given for any of the vast array of offenses he'd committed in his 429 days as a presidential candidate. It was something like progress. And it began an improbable recovery for a campaign that many observers had already pronounced dead.

Committee issued an order for their preservation. Clinton's email scandal just kept coming back. So did the last man between her and the presidency.

* * *

The new Donald Trump first appeared in Charlotte, North Carolina, on August 18. He was a lot like the old Trump—nearly identical, in fact—but he did something the old Trump never would have done.

"Sometimes, in the heat of debate, and speaking on a multitude of issues, you don't choose the right words," he said. "Or you say the wrong thing. I have done that."

He gave a knowing smile, a long pause. Laughter came from the audience.

"And believe it or not, I regret it," he said, still looking jovial. He paused again. His supporters filled the silence: *TRUMP! TRUMP! TRUMP!* He smiled more broadly, gave a thumbs-up and finally turned somber.

"And I do regret it," he said. "Particularly

where it may have caused personal pain."

He never said he was sorry. He did not specify an offense or a victim. But this vague and oddly cheerful half-apology was half an apology more than he'd previously given for any of the vast array of offenses he'd committed in his 429 days as a presidential candidate. It was something like progress. And it began an improbable recovery for a campaign that many observers had already pronounced dead.

It happened because Trump listened to a woman.

Kellyanne Conway was a Republican pollster who had known Trump for ten years, occasionally giving him political advice. She once co-wrote a book and ran her own business the same year she gave birth to twins. "That woman is unbelievable," said her co-author, Celinda Lake. "She gets more done by noon than most of us get done all day." Conway, 49, ran a super PAC for Ted Cruz during the primaries, occasionally slashing at Trump for his

sins against conservatism, but she joined the Trump campaign as an adviser in early July. As the new campaign manager in mid-August, she could talk to Trump in a way that Manafort never could. When she made a suggestion, she had poll numbers to back it up. She tried to get him to stop insulting people not named Clinton (though her success at that was short-lived) and to start giving more Americans more reasons to vote for Trump.

The candidate who had often ridiculed opponents for using teleprompters now used them regularly. He held fewer news conferences and called in to fewer TV and radio shows, diminishing his chances to go off-message. After heavy rain in Louisiana caused the nation's worst natural disaster since Hurricane Sandy, Trump handed out supplies and thanked the National Guard. He visited Mexico and made a surprisingly cordial joint appearance with President Enrique Peña Nieto. (Only later did they publicly contradict each other on who would pay for the border

Top: **Trump is joined by his wife, Melania, and children for a town hall with CNN's Anderson Cooper on April 12, 2016, in New York.**

wall.) He visited an African-American church in Detroit and said, "The African-American faith community has been one of God's greatest gifts to America and its people."

The polls tightened. Trump kept making gaffes, or what would have been gaffes for anyone else, or what would have been gaffes in any other cycle, or what would have been gaffes if anyone could prove they actually diminished his chances of becoming president. Maybe they were not gaffes at all. Maybe enough voters were just angry enough with the status quo that they would forgive almost anything from a disrupter who temporarily refrained from denigrating Gold Star families. Or maybe he was altering standards of propriety in real time. When Nykea Aldridge, a cousin of the NBA star Dwyane Wade, was shot to death amid Chicago's most violent month since 1997, Trump tweeted, "Just what I have been saying. African-Americans will VOTE TRUMP!" When NFL quarterback Colin Kaepernick refused to stand for the national anthem, Trump said, "Maybe he should find a country that works better for him." Did he regret saying these things? Apparently not. The polls kept tightening.

In Castle Rock, Colorado, the anti-Trump activist Kendal Unruh tried to compromise with her fellow Republicans. She had been a precinct committeewoman since 1988, helping turn out as many as 98 percent of registered Republicans in previous elections, and now she offered to canvass for down-ballot candidates if she could just avoid canvassing for Trump. No deal, party leaders told her: Campaign for Trump or don't campaign at all. Which is why Unruh left the Republican Party. She had grown up in a religious cult, and Trump reminded her of a cult leader, and Trump's followers reminded her of cult members. Nothing would dissuade them. "They're in a pit," she said. "And you have to shine the light on the pit. And they have to come to the realization that they're in the pit.

> # The polls tightened. Trump kept making gaffes, or what would have been gaffes for anyone else, or what would have been gaffes in any other cycle, or what would have been gaffes if anyone could prove they actually diminished his chances of becoming president.

And they have to crawl out on their own."

If Trump said the sun was blue, someone would have believed him. At a rally in Connecticut in August, he kept telling camera operators to turn their lenses and show the crowd. And then a protester made a disruption, and Trump said, "Oh, look! The cameras are turned. Awww. Look. The cameras are turned. Wow. Oh, that's great. Those cameras never, ever turn unless there's a protester, because, see, a protester is considered a bad thing for Trump. 'Oh, he had a protester.' So I didn't think they could turn, but when there's a protester, they're like pretzels."

The cameras had not turned. Trump simply made it up, and his supporters booed accordingly. Some even turned to look, and saw that no cameras had turned, and kept booing the media, and kept cheering Trump. No legion of fact-checkers could match that kind of power. After what could have been a ruinous month, Trump still had a chance. A national CNN/ORC poll on September 6 showed him in a virtual tie with Clinton. Sometimes he seemed invincible.

Opposite: **A young attendee at the October 2016 Trump rally in Grand Junction, Colorado.**

BY
PATTI SOLIS DOYLE
*CNN Political
Commentator and
2008 Campaign Manager
for Hillary Clinton*

NO, MR. TRUMP, I DID NOT START THE BIRTHER MOVEMENT

Near the end of the first presidential debate of the general election, Donald Trump accused me of starting the birther movement. Me?!

The moment taught me how low Trump was prepared to go and how little he valued the truth. It also taught me how effective CNN can be at setting the record straight.

Let me set the scene. There I was in one of CNN's trailers, watching the debate on our monitors, scribbling in my notepad, organizing my "Hillary nailed it" facts for my post-debate panel. Suddenly, Trump was telling the moderator, NBC's Lester Holt, that Hillary Clinton and her 2008 campaign started the whole birther thing. As evidence, he cited an interview of me by Wolf Blitzer weeks earlier.

It was strange and, honestly, a bit creepy to hear my name come out of Donald Trump's mouth. By that point in the debate, Trump had taken every piece of bait that Hillary dangled in front of him and was flailing. And from where I sat, he looked like he knew it. In retrospect, he sounded an awful lot like the imitation of Trump that Alec Baldwin would do on "Saturday Night Live" that weekend.

The tactic was familiar: When he was accused of doing something sleazy, bigoted or absurd, Trump blamed Hillary. Caught avoiding taxes? Trump blamed Hillary for not fixing our tax laws. Burned for attacking the mother and father of a soldier killed in combat? Trump blamed Hillary for their son's death. Confronted with footage from one of his juvenile performances on Howard Stern? Trump argued that it was Hillary who hated women, not him.

Now facing criticism for years of promoting the birther movement, which suggested that President Obama was not born in the United States, Trump blamed Hillary for starting it.

The facts? In 2007, I was running Hillary's first presidential campaign when one of our volunteers forwarded an email to her friends claiming (falsely) that Obama was Muslim. She didn't write it, but she passed it on, so I asked her to leave the campaign. (You could say I "fired" her, but she didn't actually work for us.) I also called David Plouffe, Obama's campaign manager, to apologize. (He was gracious about it.)

In Trump's universe, my firing someone for forwarding an email about Obama's faith made me responsible for Trump's years of mischief about Obama's citizenship.

It was absurd. But that didn't make it any easier. Eighty million people were watching.

> ## For the next few minutes, I enjoyed something rare in politics: the chance to set the record straight in real time.

"We happen to have Patti Solis Doyle here on set," a smiling Anderson Cooper explained when we were back on the air, comparing the moment to a funny scene from Woody Allen's "Zelig."

For the next few minutes, I enjoyed something rare in politics: the chance to set the record straight in real time. After I made my points, the cameras switched to Trump in the spin room, where he doubled down on his charges and advised America to "watch the tape." Again, I was lucky, because Anderson had the tape, ran it and confirmed my side of the story. When Trump's surrogates tried to muddy the water, David Axelrod, who was a top adviser to Obama in the 2008 campaign, stepped in, confirmed my facts and generally lent his warmth and credibility to my defense.

By this point, the Democrats on the set

were laughing during commercial breaks. We all understood that Trump should have been trying to broaden his base of support by appealing to moderates, women and minorities. Instead he was wasting critical time, in front of the largest number of viewers of the campaign, calling me out. Meanwhile, my phone was exploding. Friends from Hillaryland were texting me emoji fistbumps and thumbs-up emojis.

Of course, plenty of the 80 million people who watched that debate were tuned in to other networks, so they never heard my real-time rebuttal. Based on the hate I have received on Twitter and Facebook, plenty of Trump supporters out there blamed me.

Was this my favorite campaign 2016 moment? Of course not. I much preferred the five minutes or so CNN spent backstage with Hillary the night she clinched the Democratic nomination. We got to watch her look out at a crowd of supporters, enjoy the moment, appreciate the history of it all. To me, that was so much more meaningful than anything Donald Trump could say or do.

MY AMERICA

This election has been long, and it's been memorable. But I'd like to forget much of it.

Donald Trump launched his campaign on June 16, 2015. That was the day he called Mexican immigrants "rapists." I was not born in Mexico. I am not of Mexican descent. But I knew he was talking about me and all those immigrants who have come from south of the border and look and sound like me. That was when this election got very personal for me: on Day One of the Trump campaign. That's when I determined that I would oppose this divisive man, who peddles racism, with every fiber of my being and every breath in my body.

Throughout the campaign, Trump went on to say many other things that I found

BY
ANA NAVARRO
CNN Political Commentator and Republican Strategist

> ## He asked me if in Trump's America, his children's ability to do their jobs would be attacked merely because their dad was born in Africa.

personally offensive. But there was one moment at which it stopped being about how I alone felt. That was when he attacked Judge Gonzalo Curiel, an American born in Indiana. Trump dismissed Judge Curiel as "Mexican" and questioned his ability to do his job impartially because he was the child of immigrants.

In the midst of that controversy, I got into a taxi in Washington, D.C. Taxi drivers there often have CNN on their radios. Sometimes they recognize me just by my voice (I suspect my accent helps). That day, the driver was from Ethiopia. He was outraged, hurt, worried by Trump's words against Judge Curiel. He told me he was the father of three U.S.-born children. He said he drove a taxi fifteen hours a day, six days a week, so his children could one day go to college and be professionals. He told me about how grateful he was for our country and how proud his family was to be American. He asked me—his voice breaking—if in Trump's America, his children's ability to do their jobs would be attacked merely because their dad was born in Africa.

I think of that man often. I don't know his name. I don't know his children's names. But I do know that in the America I know, we are not measured by where we were born or where our parents were born. In America, we are measured by our character, our actions and our love of our shared country.

11

THE SURPRISES OF OCTOBER

The final stage of the presidential race began during a hurricane, thirty-two days before the election. There was hard rain in Florida, wind lashing the palms, an exploding power line giving off showers of phosphorescent sparks. The Atlantic Ocean washed out roads and poured into living rooms. Nature imposed on everyone, even future presidents, and October held unpleasant surprises for Clinton and Trump alike. Sex, lies, video, federal agents and Russian hackers: In a campaign that defied all expectations, this would be the wildest month yet.

On Friday, October 7, the leaves were turning in New York. Clinton left her home in Chappaqua for the Doral Arrowwood hotel in Rye Brook to prepare for Sunday's debate. Trump held a roundtable meeting with Border Patrol agents at his tower in Manhattan and warned of an election swayed by undocumented criminals. The World Clown Association announced it would not endorse a presidential candidate but would favor the party with the best cream pies and bounce houses. Until late afternoon, it was a normal day by 2016 standards. Then the story broke in The Washington Post.

"You know, I'm automatically attracted to beautiful—I just start kissing them," Trump said in the accompanying video, a

Becoming president would take some restraint. Which is why Republican leaders were trying to wrestle Trump into a straitjacket. The video undid all those efforts. *You can do anything,* he had said, and eleven years later he still seemed to believe it.

conversation from 2005 with the TV personality Billy Bush on an "Access Hollywood" tour bus. "It's like a magnet. I don't even wait. Just kiss. I don't even wait. And when you're a star, they let you do it. You can do anything. Grab 'em by the pussy. You can do anything."

This election was already the greatest battle of the sexes America had ever seen. Now it became something more primitive: a study of the men in all their desperation. For Clinton, there was something familiar about this. She knew some men couldn't control themselves, or *wouldn't*, anyway, and she'd spent decades facing the consequences. For all the grief it caused her personally, male sexual misbehavior had not been entirely bad for her career. It had not been entirely good. Twenty-one days later, it would alter the race yet again.

The most important variable in the race was Trump's ability to control himself. He did not need to do this in the primaries, because his unregulated impulses appealed to the faction of Republicans who wanted political correctness destroyed at any cost. But he needed to in October, to reassure the Republicans and independents who were grasping for some reason to believe he had the judgment to be their president. The "Access Hollywood"

video, which Trump dismissed as mere "locker-room talk," showed an alpha male who'd become rich and famous by answering to no one but himself. This Trump was struggling to build a winning coalition. He was having trouble persuading the Mormons in Utah and Nevada, the suburban women outside Philadelphia, the college graduates along Interstate 4 in Florida. Becoming president would take some restraint. Which is why Republican leaders were trying to wrestle him into a straitjacket.

The video undid all those efforts. *You can do anything*, he had said, and eleven years later he still seemed to believe it. Never before had a major party's nominee been so unaccountable to the norms of his party and his country. In his latest rampage he would attack the Democrats, the Republicans, the free press and the very foundations of peaceful democracy. He would insinuate that women who accused him of sexual assault were not attractive enough to deserve

his attention. He would threaten to sue his accusers. And the Republican National Committee would stand by him through it all.

The video forced elected Republicans into excruciating contortions. Many rebuked him in public statements. Some said he should step aside and let Mike Pence lead the ticket. And then, when Trump refused to quit, several Republicans who had unendorsed him or called for his withdrawal said they would vote for him after all. In a different year, the video might have been a campaign-ender. Not this time.

"Voters really do seem to have a pretty short memory," Navin Nayak, director of opinion research for the Clinton campaign, said in an interview. He noted that the video had dominated the news and that polls showed the vast majority of Americans, initially, were aware of it and even offended by it. But, he said, less than three weeks later, they seemed to have forgotten about it. In focus groups, Nayak said, "we were

Opposite: **An attendee at a Hillary Clinton rally in Palm Beach, Florida, on October 26, 2016.** *Top:* **Donald Trump at a rally in Miami on November 2, 2016.**

testing an ad where the Republican mother is talking about how, 'When that tape came out, and he dismissed it as locker-room talk, I realized I just couldn't look at my daughters and vote for him.' And half of the people in that focus group didn't know what she was talking about."

According to chief strategist Sean Spicer, the RNC never seriously considered distancing itself from Trump. "Our job is to get people to get out and vote," he said. "You can't then say, 'By the way, when you go into the voting booth, only do the following.' It doesn't work like that."

Had Trump confessed on tape to sexual assault? Was he trying to destroy their party? Either way, the Republicans needed him to stay competitive. His fortunes on November 8 would affect the entire party. They were all in this whirlwind together.

★ ★ ★

As Clinton and Trump prepared for their first debate on September 26, eleven days before the "Access Hollywood" tape surfaced, national polls showed them in a virtual tie. This was all the more surprising given that Trump's campaign seemed to be in perpetual turmoil. Republican operative Chris Wilson called it "the worst campaign in the history of modern American politics."

Several Trump campaign employees left within weeks or even days of their hiring.

Most of the party's brightest political minds stayed away altogether. According to a senior Republican strategist with inside knowledge of the subject, "There was no thought, there was no planning, there was no actual campaign structure and there was no real leadership to make decisions. And some of the campaign leadership that would be strategically sitting in a room doing that is chasing the candidate around trying to get him to not tweet and say stupid things, and using up all of their bandwidth on it."

No one could control Trump. But those close to him on the campaign learned that some tactics worked better than others. Telling him "no" was a bad idea. You had to deliver advice as a *suggestion*, preferably accompanied by some kind of affirmation. His former aide Sam Nunberg found it effective to use flattering metaphors—comparing him to gold or marble, for instance—and then to muse about how one might sell these precious materials to the American people.

The winning formula was simple. Both candidates had consistently negative favorability ratings. Thus, if Trump could make the election a referendum on Clinton, he would win. If she made it a referendum on Trump, she would win. Too often Trump took a news cycle that could have been bad for Clinton and made it bad for himself instead. In early August, the conversation could have been about tumult at the Democratic National Committee or a claim Clinton made about her emails that received four Pinocchios from the fact-checker at The Washington Post. Instead Trump kept the negative spotlight on himself by attacking a Gold Star family.

He got smarter from mid-August to mid-September, and generally stayed out of the way during Clinton's most terrible weekend. On September 9, she insulted half of Trump's supporters by putting them in a makeshift purgatory she called the "basket of deplorables." (She quickly apologized for using the word "half.") Then she was caught on video collapsing as she left a 9/11 memorial ceremony. Her campaign offered no explanation at first, then said she was "overheated," then finally acknowledged she had pneumonia. The incident made it look as if she were hiding something again—as if she and her aides didn't trust the voters enough to tell them the whole truth. And it emboldened the conspiracy theorists who'd been saying without evidence that she was too sick to be president. How would Trump handle it? Would he act gleeful, or presidential?

"I hope she gets well soon," he said the next morning on Fox News, and Republican leaders sighed with relief.

Clinton had the opposite problem: She was too predictable, too controlled. Her speeches were average at best. Her forums on opioids or child care didn't generate many headlines, because hyperbole often drowned out serious issues in 2016. This neutralized what might have been an advantage for Clinton. Her command of policy extended to such arcane topics as the allocation of radio spectrum, but this was never going to break through in a campaign against Trump. "Our policy team, bless their hearts, are like, 'Okay, but this is what's wrong with this policy and this policy,'" Clinton spokeswoman Christina Reynolds said. "And we're like, 'Nope. Nobody cares. Nobody cares about the policy.'"

As Clinton and Trump prepared for their first debate on September 26, eleven days before the "Access Hollywood" tape surfaced, national polls showed them in a virtual tie.

Every day Trump didn't make a major error, he seemed to gain support. But Clinton's aides thought she could reverse that trend at the upcoming debate. "When the American people have seen her unfiltered, even in very high-stress situations, high-wire acts in many ways, she has always been her best advocate," her adviser Mandy Grunwald said. "Each of those moments have been more important than advertising. If you look at the critical turning points of the campaign, they have been these big moments where the American people have been able to see her, not commentators' views of her, not what Donald Trump says, or Bernie Sanders, or what anyone else says about her. Just Hillary Clinton, herself, answering questions or speaking to the American people. Those have been the most critical moments of the campaign."

At campaign headquarters as the first debate approached, Clinton's aides filled a suggestion box with ideas for handling Trump. They said Clinton should wear American-made clothes and mention his company's Chinese ties, her friend Hilary Rosen recalled. Drop the names of foreign leaders and challenge him to identify their countries. Fight back if he brought up her husband's womanizing by reminding him of his own. Clinton's

aides saw a pattern in Trump's behavior, an inability to let a slight go unreturned, and they thought Clinton could use this trait against him. If she played it just right, provoked him just enough, he might prove her case about his unpresidential temperament.

"Do you have your strategy?" Rosen asked.

"Oh, yeah, I've got my strategy," Clinton replied, according to Rosen. "I have to be warm enough that people like me, tough enough to be commander in chief, deep enough on policy that people know I have an agenda, direct on his faults. Oh, and by the way, I have to be his fact-checker, too."

Their meeting at Hofstra University on Long Island would be the most-watched debate in American history. Trump kept his preparations light. He didn't recruit a Clinton stand-in for mock debates. "He's not rehearsing canned thirty-second sound bites or spending hours in the film room like an NFL player," his spokesman Jason Miller wrote in a memo. "He will be prepared, but most importantly, he will be himself."

What that meant was anyone's guess. In Clinton's mock debates, her former aide Philippe Reines could wear a red tie like Trump, make serpentine hand gestures

> **Trump kept his preparations light. He didn't recruit a Clinton stand-in for mock debates. "He's not rehearsing canned thirty-second sound bites or spending hours in the film room like an NFL player," his spokesman Jason Miller wrote in a memo.**

like Trump, lean toward the microphone and interrupt like Trump, sending the Clinton team into fits of laughter. Reines' outbursts gave Clinton the opportunity to practice keeping her own demeanor in check—which advisers said was important since she had called his temperament into question.

"You're running against someone who is erratic, wild, over-the-top," Clinton's chief strategist, Joel Benenson, said in an interview. "He's unsettling because of his being temperamentally unfit through his divisiveness, through his recklessness on foreign policy, his wild ideas on the economy. You want to in all ways be the counter to that. You want to embody the antithesis of that. Her strength is her steadiness. Her toughness, her strength under fire. You want to show that, not just tell it."

But until the debate actually started at 9 p.m. on September 26, no one knew which Trump would show up.

"Now, in all fairness to Secretary Clinton—yes, is that OK?" the disciplined Trump said at the outset, making sure to address her correctly. "Good. I want you to be very happy. It's very important to me."

When her aides poll-tested attacks against Trump, they found that voters responded most intensely to Trump's own words. Paraphrasing didn't work as well, advisers said. Clinton needed to quote Trump directly. And she did. "In fact, Donald was one of the people who rooted for the housing crisis," she said.

Top: **Clinton backstage with personal aide Connolly Keigher before appearing at a rally in Cedar Rapids, Iowa, on October 28, 2016.**
Following spread: **The candidates at the Presidential debate in Las Vegas on October 19, 2016.**

Until the debate actually started at 9 p.m., no one knew which Trump would show up.

"He said, back in 2006, 'Gee, I hope it does collapse, because then I can go in and buy some and make some money.' Well, it did collapse."

He tried to hold it together, to keep pressing the case against Clinton, but she kept throwing the bait. She said he was rich because he borrowed $14 million from his father. He called it a "small loan." She said he called climate change a Chinese hoax. "I did not. I did not," he replied, growing more defensive as the night went on. He kept leaning into the microphone and interjecting one word—"Wrong"—even when she was right, such as the time she said he supported the invasion of Iraq, which sent him into a rambling discourse about what he supposedly told his friend Sean Hannity of Fox News. He was no longer making it about Clinton, much less the American worker for whom he claimed to speak. Clinton let him waste his time. Then, after he questioned her stamina, she *really* set him off.

CLINTON: *And one of the worst things he said was about a woman in a beauty contest. He loves beauty contests, supporting them and hanging around them. And he called this woman "Miss Piggy." Then he called her "Miss Housekeeping," because she was Latina. Donald, she has a name.*

TRUMP: *Where did you find this? Where did you find this?*

CLINTON: *Her name is Alicia Machado.*

TRUMP: *Where did you find this?*

Bottom: **Clinton arrives for a fundraiser in Seattle on October 10, 2016.**

It was there in plain sight. In his 1997 book "The Art of the Comeback," Trump had written, "I could just see Alicia Machado, the current Miss Universe, sitting there plumply."

Clinton took control of the race by taking control of Trump—by provoking the same destructive impulses that his handlers worked to conceal. The voters ignored her when she told them who he was. They paid attention when she *showed* them. Alicia Machado would haunt Trump for the rest of the week. He would go on "Fox & Friends" and call her "the worst, the absolute worst"—even though the hosts never asked him about her. He would think about her in the middle of the night, open Twitter before dawn, call her "disgusting," invoke a phantom "sex tape" and generally do all he could to keep the controversy alive, just as he'd done with Khizr and Ghazala Khan after the Democratic convention. Advisers kept telling Trump to leave Machado alone and return to his message, the RNC's Sean Spicer said. But Trump couldn't let it go. The polls turned in Clinton's favor once again. The "Access Hollywood" tape emerged. The Republican Party shuddered. Trump whirled toward November, his fury intensifying.

⁙⁙⁙⁙⁙⁙⁙⁙⁙⁙⁙⁙⁙⁙ ★ ★ ★ ⁙⁙⁙⁙⁙⁙⁙⁙⁙⁙⁙⁙⁙⁙

It is worth mentioning that the sun rose and set as usual that fall. Dogs were still loyal, cats unknowable, and children eventually fell asleep. Five o'clock still rolled around every Friday, and a good beverage was easy to find. In short, the presidential race was a distortion of American life, with the wholesome parts largely forgotten and the salacious ones blasting at full volume.

October 9 was the most salacious day yet. Anyone who thought Trump would be chastened by the "Access Hollywood" clip had not watched his so-called apology video,

> ## He would think about her in the middle of the night, open Twitter before dawn, call her "disgusting," invoke a phantom "sex tape" and generally do all he could to keep the controversy alive. Advisers kept telling Trump to leave Machado alone and return to his message, the RNC's Sean Spicer said.

during which he said, "Bill Clinton has actually abused women, and Hillary has bullied, attacked, shamed and intimidated his victims. We will discuss this more in the coming days." He was not bluffing.

"Perhaps we'll start with Paula," he said, about ninety minutes before the second debate, in a surprise appearance with four women who had accused the Clintons of transgressions against decency. Paula, of course, was Paula Jones, who claimed in a 1994 lawsuit that Bill Clinton had lured her into a hotel room, lowered his pants and asked for oral sex. (Clinton eventually settled the suit for $850,000 without any acknowledgement of wrongdoing.)

"Well, I'm here to support Mr. Trump because he's going to make America great again," Jones said.

This brazen act of political warfare also included brief statements by Kathy Shelton, whose alleged rapist Hillary Clinton represented as a criminal-defense attorney assigned to the case in 1975 (he was convicted of a lesser charge); Kathleen Willey, who alleged that Bill Clinton sexually assaulted her in 1993; and Juanita Broaddrick, who alleged that Bill Clinton raped her in 1978.

"I tweeted recently, and Mr. Trump retweeted it, that actions speak louder than words," said Broaddrick, who had changed her story over the years about the alleged rape and was not deemed credible enough by congressional Republicans to testify at Clinton's impeachment trial. "Mr. Trump may have said some bad words, but Bill Clinton raped me, and Hillary Clinton threatened me. I don't think there's any comparison."

Afterward, a reporter shouted, "Why'd you say you touch women without consent, Mr. Trump?"

"Why don't y'all go ask Bill Clinton that?" Jones replied. "Go ahead and ask Hillary as well."

Here was a spectacle worthy of Jerry Springer. ("Lots of people ask where I get the guests for my show," the TV ringmaster tweeted the day before. "The answer is Trump Tower.") It continued in the debate hall at Washington University in St. Louis, where the accusers sat as close to Bill Clinton as possible. They remained seated when others stood to applaud the former president. Would Trump and Hillary Clinton shake hands when they walked onstage? No. That small civility was gone, too. His talk about her happiness gave way to threats of a special prosecutor.

"It's just awfully good that someone with the temperament of Donald Trump is not in charge of the law in our country," she said.

"Because you'd be in jail," he said.

His second performance was both more effective and more ominous than his first, although he did have to answer for the "Access Hollywood" tape.

ANDERSON COOPER, DEBATE MODERATOR: *Just for the record, though, are you saying that what you said on that bus eleven years ago—that you did not actually kiss women*

without consent or grope women without consent?

TRUMP: *I have great respect for women. Nobody has more respect for women than I do.*

COOPER: *So, for the record, you're saying you never did that?*

TRUMP: *I've said things that, frankly, you hear these things I said. And I was embarrassed by it. But I have tremendous respect for women.*

COOPER: *Have you ever done those things?*

TRUMP: *And women have respect for me. And I will tell you: No, I have not.*

Yes, he did, said Jessica Leeds, Rachel Crooks, Mindy McGillivray, Natasha Stoynoff, Temple Taggart, Kristin Anderson, Summer Zervos, Cathy Heller, Jill Harth, Jessica Drake and one woman who kept her identity from the public. Following the debate, the women came forward to say Trump had indeed touched or kissed them without their consent. Trump denied it all, but his recorded boasting did him no favors. When former contestants accused Trump of barging into their dressing rooms at the beauty pageants he owned, their statements confirmed what Trump proudly told Howard Stern in a radio interview in 2005: "I'll go backstage and everyone's getting

> **His second performance was both more effective and more ominous than his first, although he did have to answer for the "Access Hollywood" tape.**

Top: **Trump's family meets him onstage following the Las Vegas debate.**

dressed....You know, they're standing there with no clothes. 'Is everybody OK?' And you see these incredible looking women, and so, I sort of get away with things like that."

The Bed of Nails Theory, advanced in an interview with the Democratic strategist and CNN contributor Paul Begala, held that Trump won the primaries and remained viable through the summer partly because of the sheer volume and variety of his transgressions. No single offense stood above the others. They were approximately equal, like a thousand nails arranged in a grid on which someone can lie down without getting hurt.

Now one nail began to lengthen. Some Republicans would never leave Trump, if only because they agreed with him on certain issues, but others had lost their patience. The day after the second debate, House Speaker Paul Ryan told colleagues on a conference call that he would not campaign with Trump and could no longer defend him. Trump erupted. "Disloyal R's are far more difficult than Crooked Hillary," he tweeted. "They come at you from all sides. They don't know how to win - I will teach them!" And then: "It is so nice that the shackles have been taken off me and I can now fight for America the way I want to."

That meant accusing Ryan of sabotaging his own party. Accusing the media of conspiring with Clinton. Threatening to sue The New York Times for a story about two women who said he touched them inappropriately. And with his repeated warnings about voter fraud and a rigged system, it meant becoming the first major presidential candidate since 1860 to cast doubt on the legitimacy of the electoral process.

The sun still rose every morning, but something was changing in America. The pro-Trump conspiracy theorist Alex Jones said on the radio that Hillary Clinton and President Obama were actual demons. A woman at a Mike Pence rally said that if Clinton won, "I'm ready for a revolution because we can't have her in." In Grimes, Iowa, a staunch Republican named Betty Odgaard examined her options. She and her husband had lost their wedding chapel after refusing to host a ceremony for two men, which is to say she had never been afraid to proclaim unpopular beliefs. But this was different. Trump had left her speechless. When asked how she'd vote in November, she said, "I want to keep that between me and me."

★ ★ ★

His handlers knew the question would come. *If you lose, will you accept the election results?* And as they prepared him for the third debate, they told him what to say. According to a senior Republican official with direct knowledge of the conversations, Gov. Chris Christie and RNC Chairman Reince Priebus both told Trump he could not afford to equivocate. Just give a simple, direct answer, they said: "Yes, I'm going to accept it." But Trump was Trump. They never knew what he would say.

He saw the signs of rigging wherever he looked. Saw them in Iowa and Colorado, when he lost Republican contests to Ted Cruz. Saw them in Clinton's win over Sanders in the primaries, and in the FBI investigation

Bottom: **The candidates shake hands after their first debate at Hofstra University in Hempstead, New York, on September 26, 2016.** *Opposite:* **Trump walks through the spin room with his wife, Melania, following the first presidential debate.**

At the second debate he said it was three-on-one, him against Clinton *and* the two moderators, which of course fit his larger narrative of a battle against both Crooked Hillary and her friends in the Crooked Media.

of her email server and at the first debate, when he blamed his rough night on a temperamental microphone. People laughed, said he was making excuses, but then the presidential debate commission released a statement saying "there were issues regarding Donald Trump's audio." So there. At the second debate he said it was three-on-one, him against Clinton *and* the two moderators, which of course fit his larger narrative of a battle against both Crooked Hillary and her friends in the Crooked Media.

On October 7, WikiLeaks began releasing hacked emails from the private account of Clinton's campaign chairman, John Podesta. The Clinton campaign and intelligence officials blamed the Russian government for the hack, but Trump seized on the emails as more evidence that everything was rigged. Many were interesting merely for the Democrat-on-Democrat insults they contained, or for Podesta's advice on making creamy risotto, but some contained real substance. In one email to Podesta, Clinton said ISIS was receiving clandestine support from the Saudi Arabian government—the same government that had given between $10 million and $25 million to the Clinton Foundation. Another email chain showed Clinton aides debating

whether lobbyists for foreign companies and governments should be allowed to bundle for the campaign. "Take the money!!" her communications director, Jennifer Palmieri, wrote. (They did.) Trump said the media should cover the WikiLeaks story much more and his female accusers much less, but he wasn't surprised, because, as he put it, "their agenda is to elect Crooked Hillary Clinton at any cost—at any price—no matter how many lives they destroy."

But going into the third debate in Las Vegas on October 19, the notion of media bias came from the other side. For the first time ever in a general election, the conservative-leaning Fox News would supply the moderator. Although Chris Wallace had a reputation for objectivity, some of Clinton's allies were skeptical—especially since Wallace's former boss, the recently departed Fox News chairman Roger Ailes, had been helping Trump with debate preparation.

"We hope that he takes a balanced approach," a Clinton aide said of Wallace that night, "but we will definitely be closely watching."

"Secretary Clinton," Wallace said about twenty minutes in, "I want to clear up your position on this issue, because in a speech

you gave to a Brazilian bank, for which you were paid $225,000, we've learned from the WikiLeaks, that you said this, and I want to quote: 'My dream is a hemispheric common market with open trade and open borders.' So that's the question—"

"Thank you," Trump said.

Wallace chuckled. "That's the question. Please, quiet, everybody. Is that your dream, open borders?"

After saying she'd been talking about a cross-border energy system, Clinton quickly pivoted to complain about WikiLeaks and the Russian government. Trump called her on the evasion. Until then he was giving his best and most disciplined performance. But she had mentioned Russian President Vladimir Putin, a sore subject for Trump, and Trump couldn't let it go.

TRUMP: *He has no respect for her. He has no respect for our president. And I'll tell you what: We're in very serious trouble, because we have a country with tremendous numbers of nuclear warheads—1,800, by the way— where they expanded and we didn't, 1,800 nuclear warheads. And she's playing chicken. Look, Putin—*

WALLACE: *Wait, but—*

TRUMP: *—from everything I see, has no respect for this person.*

CLINTON: *Well, that's because he'd rather have a puppet as president of the United States.*

TRUMP: *No puppet. No puppet.*

CLINTON: *And it's pretty clear—*

TRUMP: *You're the puppet!*

CLINTON: *It's pretty clear you won't admit—*

TRUMP: *No, you're the puppet.*

If the playing field was tilted in Clinton's favor, Clinton herself had done the tilting— with twice-daily prep sessions, decades of policy study and enough political combat to make her almost impervious to personal attacks. The Vast Right-Wing Conspiracy had prepared her well. Here was the most basic asymmetry of all three debates: Trump could not provoke Clinton, but Clinton could and did provoke Trump. She did it strategically, methodically, relentlessly. He tried to control himself, to resist all her bait, but the temptation was too much. He was so angry by the end of the night that an unmemorable insult during Clinton's answer about Social Security provoked his most memorable interruption yet:

"Such a *nasty* woman."

Then, as expected, Wallace asked Trump if he would accept the election results. Contravening 227 years of American protocol, Trump refused to commit.

"But sir," Wallace said, "there is a tradition in this country—in fact, one of the prides of this country is the peaceful transition of power and that no matter how hard-fought a campaign is, that at the end of the campaign that the loser concedes to the winner."

Trump was behind in the polls, and his support was slipping further. Many in both parties believed the race was already over. Trump was 70, old enough to think about his legacy. He had said it again and again: He could do whatever he wanted with women. Now, if current trends held, he would be remembered most for *losing* to one.

"Not saying that you're necessarily going to be the loser or the winner, but that the loser concedes to the winner and that the country comes together in part for the good of the country," Wallace said. "Are you saying you're not prepared now to commit to that principle?"

"What I'm saying is that I will tell you at the time," Trump said, shaking the political firmament once again. "I'll keep you in suspense."

★ ★ ★

Clinton entered the last days of October with victory in sight. Then a government report said Obamacare premiums would rise sharply in 2017. A hacked email from WikiLeaks raised more questions about the connection between her husband's paid speeches and her decisions as secretary of state. Finally, eleven days before the election, FBI Director James Comey dropped his bombshell.

In a cryptic three-paragraph letter to congressional leaders on October 28, Comey said the bureau had learned of more emails that appeared pertinent to its investigation of Clinton's private email server. Investigators would review those emails to find out whether they contained classified information. The emails had come to light through "an unrelated case," which turned out to be the FBI's investigation of former Congressman Anthony Weiner, the estranged husband of Huma Abedin, one of Clinton's closest advisers.

What were the most important issues facing the country? Jobs, immigration, national security? Maybe. But the presidential race seemed to revolve increasingly around sex and email.

Abedin and Weiner had separated in August 2016, during his third sexting scandal, when Weiner texted a lewd photo of himself while lying next to the couple's 4-year-old son. Soon after that, the FBI opened an investigation into allegations that he had traded explicit messages with a 15-year-old girl.

Weiner's first sexting scandal forced him to resign his seat in Congress. His second might have cost him the New York mayoralty. But the third now threatened to upend the presidential race and, possibly, keep a woman from finally ascending to the most powerful job in the world.

All through the campaign, Trump's own misbehavior accrued to Clinton's benefit. She wasn't just running to become the first woman president. She was running to defeat someone she and her supporters considered a vulgar, womanizing misogynist. He said Megyn Kelly had blood coming out of her wherever. He mocked Carly Fiorina's appearance. He said Clinton "got schlonged" by Obama in 2008. He reassured the nation about the size of his penis. He disgusted Republican women, and mobilized Democratic ones. But when Trump learned of Comey's letter, he gleefully turned the spotlight back toward Clinton.

He had said it again and again: He could do whatever he wanted with women. Now, if current trends held, he would be remembered most for *losing* to one.

"This is bigger than Watergate," he exclaimed at a rally in New Hampshire.

Clinton's campaign manager, Robby Mook, recalled learning about the Comey letter from traveling press secretary Nick Merrill while they were on a campaign plane between New York and Cedar Rapids, Iowa. Merrill had been informed by a Los Angeles Times reporter, apparently the only person on the plane who could get a Wi-Fi signal. "He said, 'Have you seen this? The investigation was reopened.'" Mook said.

Mook and communications director Palmieri went to tell Clinton the news. Her response, he said, was striking. "There have been moments on this campaign where I am a lot in awe of her. You can see how she's ready to be president," Mook said. "The incredible steadiness and stoic manner she had—she listened to us, she took our counsel, we made a decision to get out a statement. She was confounded the way we all were. Like, why in the world would he do this this far into the election? She wanted to respond and put our point of view out there. She was steady about the whole thing. I think anyone else would have just lost their cool."

The presidential race was scrambled again. Clinton walked off the plane in Cedar Rapids. Reporters yelled questions. She waved, and kept walking.

BY
SCOTTIE NELL HUGHES

CNN Political Commentator and Donald Trump Supporter

"STOP SAYING THAT WORD!"

As Donald Trump's surrogate, I never wanted the news to be about me. I hoped any headlines would be about Trump and his message.

Unfortunately, I wasn't always successful at staying out of the spotlight. Some of my biggest splashes came as I was flying solo in breaking news situations and I had to rely on my own wit and wisdom to survive the hard line of questions coming my way.

In April 2016, I did a segment with CNN's Kate Bolduan on "At This Hour." Like always, there were five or six separate issues regarding Mr. Trump and I had an explanation or answer for all of them. Once we were done, Kate looked at me with a half-smile and said something along the lines of "Really, Scottie?"

I will admit, some of my answers were as strong as a bridge made of toothpicks.

My mother used to criticize me for always justifying my actions, so I recognized that same "I'm not buying it" look in Kate's eyes. I guess that glimmer was more like a bright spotlight the writers of "Saturday Night Live" could not ignore.

The following weekend, my neighbor called. "Turn on 'SNL'!" he screamed.

The opening skit was a parody of the segment Kate and I had done earlier in the week. "Oh, my gosh....Is that me?" I cried out. "They gave me roots and a gosh-awful tacky necklace!"

I spent the next few days trying to downplay the entire situation. I did not want to become the cartoon character of the 2016 election cycle.

Months later, on Friday October 7, 2016, I was planning to spend some much-needed time with my family. Unfortunately, a ghost from eleven years ago, in the form of a recorded conversation between Trump and NBC's Billy Bush, put an end to those plans.

"Honey, it's bad...really bad," I remember telling my husband as I called him to cancel our dinner plans.

I spent much of that night and the next morning on CNN. By the sixth straight hour of being on air, I must admit that my patience was running thin. The same arguments against Trump were being repeated, and there were only so many ways I could say something to the effect of, "I don't defend Trump's comments, but the fact they were released within one month of the election shows this was politically motivated."

In the end, I would be remembered for asking others on the set not to repeat on air the vulgar term that Trump used on the tape.

> ## I probably would have said the exact same thing again. I believe two wrongs never make a right—even in politics.

I had just spoken on the phone with my husband. Although it was 11 p.m. in Nashville, where we live, my 8-year-old daughter was still awake. I knew CNN was on in almost every room in our house.

Earlier in the evening, the "p-word" had been said on air and I bit my tongue. But by midnight, when the word was repeated not once but twice, my mama-bear instinct could not take it anymore. "Will you please stop saying that word?" I interrupted. "My daughter is watching!"

I didn't expect the reaction I received. I was accused of hypocrisy for supporting the man who said the word originally—even though I repeatedly condemned Mr. Trump for saying it—and was the brunt of crude comments and memes on social media.

Oftentimes, I have looked back and realized I could have phrased something better or made my case differently to avoid controversy. However, in this particular situation, I probably would have said the exact same thing again. I believe two wrongs never make a right—even in politics.

BY
VAN JONES
CNN Political Commentator and Former Adviser to President Obama

RACE IN AMERICA: LIVE AND UNSCRIPTED

I wasn't supposed to say anything at all.

Through my earpiece, CNN superproducer Rebecca Kutler had just whispered to me that the next discussion would be for Republicans only. Donald Trump was winning Super Tuesday in a blowout. Kutler wanted to give our GOP voices some airtime to process this stunning outcome.

Therefore, as a Democrat, I just had to listen to my conservative colleagues debate. At the commercial break, I would be free to go home.

I didn't mind. I had been on TV for several tough hours. As they fretted about the fate of their party, my own thoughts drifted toward pizza.

Then it happened.

Trump supporter Jeffrey Lord blurted out: "I hate to say this about the Republican establishment: Their view of civil rights is to tip the black waiter five bucks at the country club." He went on to say that Trump is "not going to patronize people."

My jaw dropped at the tone-deaf offensiveness of such a remark.

Suddenly, I heard Kutler's voice in my earpiece: "Van, get in there!"

But I had nothing to say. My mind went completely blank.

Here's a secret: Guests on live news shows are not "scripted," but we are "directed." In other words, nobody puts words into the mouths of on-air contributors. But producers do give us a heads-up about upcoming topics.

For example, during a break, a producer might say, "When we come back, let's really dig into Trump's vote totals in Florida." Or the host might say, "I want to get into women's responses to Clinton's new ad."

Therefore, our minds are already thinking up relevant things to say, long before the cameras start rolling.

But in this case, I had zero warning. I was told to plunge into a live, on-air discussion of the most explosive topic of all—American racism—with no time to prepare. I had no prerehearsed lines. No zingers. No statistics. Nothing. Seated before a global audience, I had only one thought: "My kids are watching."

That thought saved me. I turned my body to face Lord, a move we rarely make in cable news. And I spoke to him as authentically as I could. I tried to model the respect that my wife and I are trying to instill in our boys.

Lord responded in kind. As a result, we had that rarest of rare things: a raw, unscripted, heart-to-heart on race. I said Trump had crossed a dangerous line by, among other things, failing to condemn the Ku Klux Klan and other white supremacists who supported him. Lord tried to suggest it

> **I was told to plunge into a live, on-air discussion of the most explosive topic of all—American racism—with no time to prepare.**

was Democrats—and me—who were dividing the nation.

Clips of our conversation went viral. The moment became a touchstone of the 2016 political season. It may be one of the only times in the history of U.S. election coverage in which a total lack of preparation paid off so beautifully.

A MIND CONSERVATIVE AND A HEART LIBERAL

BY
CARL BERNSTEIN
CNN Political Analyst

While writing "A Woman in Charge," I was particularly struck by a question Hillary Clinton asked her youth minister while she was a freshman at Wellesley College during the political upheavals of the 1960s: "Can one be a mind conservative and a heart liberal?"

"No description of the adult Hillary Clinton—*a mind conservative and a heart liberal*—has so succinctly defined her as this premonitory observation at age 18. She believed it was possible, though difficult, to be both," I wrote.

Yet, throughout the 2016 campaign, as she retreated deeper and deeper into her worst instincts for secrecy, obfuscation and expedient political posturing—especially as Bernie Sanders threatened her nomination—I kept looking for signs of this essential dichotomy in her.

Sadly, it was at last found in the WikiLeaks transcripts archive of her hacked emails, which contained the overpriced speeches she had given for Goldman Sachs and had refused to release—the secrecy again—when Sanders had challenged her.

Here, in her words, *was* the real Hillary Clinton—mind conservative/heart liberal— speaking with candor about the "sausage-making" of politics, schmoozing and flattering her plutocratic audience. But she was also talking about real-life economics and the real obligations of the privileged and influential, injecting real nuance into the political discussion, advocating a fact-based course to social, political and economic progress, all while showing throughout her instinctively "conservative" principles and "liberal" sensibilities. Here were flashes of the idealism and grit and faith of her earlier life and commitment to public service.

In 2007, as Hillary embarked on her first presidential campaign, I had written the closing paragraphs of "A Woman in Charge," which now seem even more premonitory in 2016:

Since her Arkansas years, Hillary Rodham Clinton has always had a difficult relationship with the truth. She is hardly different from most conventional politicians in this regard. But she has always aspired to be better than conventional: Her memoir, *Living History* was meant to demonstrate that. But judged against the facts, it underlines how she has often chosen to obfuscate, omit, and avoid. It is an understatement by now that she has been known to apprehend truths about herself and the events of her life that others do not exactly share.

In her artfully crafted public utterances and written sentences there has almost always been an effort at baseline truthfulness. Yet almost always, something holds her back from telling the whole story, as if she doesn't trust the reader, listener, friend, interviewer, constituent—or perhaps herself—to understand the true significance of events...

Three pillars have held her up through one crisis after another in a life creased by personal difficulties and public and private battles: her religious faith; her powerful urge

toward both service and its accompanying sense (for good or ill) of self-importance: and a fierce desire for privacy and secrecy. It is the last of these that seems to cast a larger and larger shadow over who she really is…

Hillary is neither the demon of the right's perception, nor a feminist Saint, nor is she particularly emblematic of her time—perhaps more old-fashioned than modern. Hers is a story of strength and vulnerability, a woman's story. She is an intelligent woman endowed with energy, enthusiasm, humor, tempestuousness, inner strength, spontaneity in private, lethal (almost) powers of retribution, real-life lines that come from deep wounds, and the language skills of a sailor (and of a minister), all evidence of her passion—which, down deep, is perhaps her most enduring and even endearing trait.

As Hillary has continued to speak from the protective shell of her own making, and packaged herself for the widest possible consumption, she has misrepresented not just facts but often her essential self.

Great politicians have always been marked by the consistency of their core beliefs, their strength of character in advocacy, and the self-knowledge that informs bold leadership. Almost always, Hillary has stood for good things. Yet there is often a disconnect between her convictions and words, and her actions. This is where Hillary disappoints. But the jury remains out. She still has time to prove her case, to effectuate those things that make her special, not fear them or camouflage them. We would all be the better for it, because what lies within may have the potential to change the world, if only a little.

No description of the adult Hillary Clinton—*a mind conservative and a heart liberal*—has so succinctly defined her as this premonitory observation at age 18. She believed it was possible, though difficult, to be both.

> "The forgotten men and women of our country will be forgotten no longer."
>
> —Donald Trump, in his victory speech, just before 3 a.m, November 9, 2016

12

TRUMP'S AMERICA

Almost everyone thought he would lose. Clinton did. Her vaunted political operatives did. The pollsters did. The #NeverTrump Republicans did. For all his bluster and bold predictions of victory, Trump himself had been worrying all day. He kept pressing aides for information, but they were worried, too. Even his internal models showed him falling short of the 270 electoral votes needed to win.

But as the night went on, strange and unexpected numbers flashed across the television screens of America. Early returns put Trump ahead by 3 points in Florida, 10 in Ohio and North Carolina. Virginia was not supposed to be competitive, but Trump had an early lead there, too.

"There isn't panic," a Clinton aide said around 8 p.m. Then it was 9, and 10, and the numbers held in Florida and Ohio, and now Trump was leading in Michigan and Wisconsin. Could he crack the Democrats' so-called Blue Wall in the industrial Midwest? Clinton's aides doubted it. They thought he'd missed his chance in Michigan by not campaigning much there until the end. Clinton was so confident about Wisconsin that she never campaigned there at all. She was not so sure about Pennsylvania, which is why she'd hit Philadelphia three times in three days and

visited Pittsburgh the previous morning. But now, even in Pennsylvania, her lead narrowed as the night went on. Five points, 4, 3. Something was happening out there, a seismic disruption whose foreshocks nearly all the experts had ignored. By 10:04 p.m., Dow futures had plunged by nearly 500 points. And the wildest campaign in modern history appeared to have one more astonishing twist.

As it turned out, the experts' combined wisdom was no match for that of Dave Calabro, also known as Jersey Dave, a 57-year-old South Philadelphian and Trump supporter who thought America had lost its way. He'd acquired his nickname by selling Eagles jerseys in sports bars to provide for his family. He did not always drink beer, but when he did, he usually drank Coors Light. He yelled *BLUE LIVES MATTER* to cops on Broad Street. He used to love Bruce Springsteen, but now he thought the Boss had disgraced himself by supporting Clinton. Jersey Dave Calabro said it that summer, and kept saying it until Election Day: Trump would carry Pennsylvania, which no Republican had done since 1988, and he would be the next American president.

"The guy never loses," Calabro said.

There were two Americas in 2016. One had been advancing for a long time. One had been retreating. And on November 8, Trump

For all his bluster and bold predictions of victory, Trump himself had been worrying all day. He kept pressing aides for information, but they were worried, too.

and his army of Jersey Dave Calabros found a
way to reverse the trend.

The two Americas were nearly a century in
the making. They resulted from women's suf-
frage, the civil rights movement, the women's
rights movement, the gay rights movement
and a Hispanic population that increased
by roughly 50 million in the last fifty years.
These changes had two things in common:
They gave power to those who previously
had little or none. And they diminished the
supremacy of straight white men.

Clinton's America was a coalition of these
historically disadvantaged groups, along
with their white male allies. Year by year, it
seemed to align more closely with large corporations and the global elite. It was urban,
ascendant, seemingly unstoppable.

Its inhabitants saw the last hundred years
as a good start, an unfinished march of
societal progress. Yes, the nation had same-
sex marriage, an African-American president
and a number of female chief executives, but
this America still felt itself chafing against
systemic inequality. Did racism, sexism and
homophobia still exist? Of course they did.
Clinton's America wanted them eradicated.

Trump's America drew in some women
and minorities. But much of its energy came
from white male grievance. Factories had
been closing for decades. Many manufactur-
ing jobs had moved overseas or given way to
automation. As wages stagnated, more and
more blue-collar men felt themselves working
hard and going nowhere. They felt abandoned
by the new information economy, swindled

by Washington politicians, stifled by the new cultural orthodoxy. Certain men of Trump's America were thrilled when he said, "Frankly, if Hillary Clinton were a man, I don't think she'd get 5 percent of the vote." These men were tired of being blamed for the sins of their fathers, sick of hearing the phrase *white guy* thrown around like an insult. Wasn't *that* racism, too? Couldn't there be sexism *against* men? They felt as if the people of Clinton's America had overtaken them somehow, probably by cheating.

"I know I'm the projection for many of those wounded men," Clinton once said, as quoted in "Hillary's Choice," a 1999 book by Gail Sheehy. "I'm the boss they never wanted to have. I'm the wife they never—the wife who went back to school and got an extra degree and a job as good as theirs….It's not me, personally, they hate—it's the changes I represent."

A year before Clinton's campaign officially began, two allies were emailing about strategy. "In fact, I think running on her gender would be the SAME mistake as 2008, ie having a message at odds with what voters ultimately want," Robby Mook, her eventual campaign manager, wrote in a message later hacked and released by WikiLeaks. "She ran on experience when voters wanted change….It's also risky because injecting gender makes her candidacy about HER and not the voters and making their lives better."

But Clinton's America wanted to rally behind the woman who could bring societal progress to its next logical step. If she won, they would *all* win, at least symbolically, and so the campaign adopted the slogan *I'm With*

Bottom: **Clinton speaks in Pittsburgh at the first of four rallies the day before the election.** *Opposite:* **Trump held his final election rally in Grand Rapids, Michigan, just hours before voters went to the polls on Election Day.**

marveled at the reams of negative stories about Trump that had no effect. Decorated generals and establishment Republicans joined forces with Clinton to tell the men of Trump's America they were making a huge mistake. But the men ignored the message, because they distrusted the messengers, and because, like Trump, they hated being told no. These rugged individualists who felt their country being stolen were not about to "listen to reason" from those they suspected of committing the theft. No, you *can't* elect someone like Trump? Their campaign slogan might as well have been *Yes I Can.*

You *can't* vote for a man who insults women and immigrants and Muslims and people with disabilities.

Yes I can.

You *can't* vote for a man who boasts about sexually assaulting women.

Yes I can.

You *can't* give the nuclear codes to a man who might blow up the world because someone looked at him sideways.

Yes I—

Her. On the day she testified before the House Select Committee on Benghazi in October 2015, online appeals using this slogan helped her raise $133,000 in a single hour.

"I don't want you to vote for me because I'm a woman; I want you to vote for me on the merits," she said that year. "But one of my merits is that I'm a woman."

Early in 2016, her campaign chairman, John Podesta, received an email that was later released by WikiLeaks. "I'm a dinosaur to the Democratic Party...white, southern, veteran, male senior," wrote Dana Folsom of Augusta, Georgia. "...I would like to have my ilk shown a tiny bit of respect by the leaders of the Hillary campaign."

"You've earned that respect and we'll try to show it," Podesta replied.

Was Clinton's America big enough for men like Dana Folsom? He did vote for her in the Georgia primary. She added other slogans, such as *Fighting for Us* and *Stronger Together.* Still, many blue-collar men were suspicious. *Fighting for Us* sounded like fighting for the people who were *not* them, rallying those people *against* them, and *Stronger Together* still evoked the progressive union against the way things used to be.

"I'm with *you*," Trump said, and they liked that more than *I'm With Her.* Her aides

---

★ ★ ★

These men were tired of being blamed for the sins of their fathers, sick of hearing the phrase *white guy* thrown around like an insult....They felt as if the people of Clinton's America had overtaken them somehow, probably by cheating.

Trump's campaign had been declared dead in August, and again in October. Now, if he could somehow control himself, he had a chance to win. "Stay on point, Donald," he said aloud at a rally on November 2. "Stay on point."

In the last week of the campaign, he was narrowing the gap. Polls showed him leading in some battleground states, drawing closer in others. Regardless of his intentions, James Comey's letter had given Trump a gift. It had helped unite Republicans against Clinton.

Senate Minority Leader Harry Reid of Nevada said Comey may have violated the Hatch Act barring political activity by federal employees. Three former U.S. attorneys general, including two who served under George W. Bush, lashed out at Comey for writing the letter so close to the election. Thirty-six former state attorneys general signed a statement saying Comey's letter contained "unfair speculation and innuendo." His letter infuriated and terrified Clinton supporters, some of whom believed it would cost her the election. When it was over, a top Clinton aide would say it had.

Two days before the election, on Sunday, November 6, Comey sent Congress another letter saying the Clinton email investigation was closed again, meaning that she was once again in the clear.

Analysts thought he was wrong, and that was fine with him.... Even some operatives in his party thought he was running a terrible campaign: no organization, no ground game, no clue.

★ ★ ★

The sky was clear in Florida the final weekend of the race. Inside a warehouse at the state fairgrounds in Tampa, Trump convened his first of four rallies. A sign in the crowd said *DOWN WITH THE SWAMP WITCH*.

"If she were to win, it would create an unprecedented constitutional crisis," he said, raising the legally impossible specter of a criminal indictment against a sitting president.

He went on to an airport hangar in Wilmington, North Carolina, where two small boys wore rubber Trump masks. "As you know," he said, "the FBI has reopened its criminal investigation of Hillary Clinton." This hyperbole led to chants of *LOCK HER UP, LOCK HER UP*, and a woman near the press riser said, "Put Obama in there with her." A pale crescent moon hung behind the stage. "We're winning," Trump said. "We're winning *everywhere*."

Analysts thought he was wrong, and that was fine with him. (The polls had also failed to predict Brexit, the United Kingdom's surprising choice that year to leave the European Union, and Trump liked to call himself "Mr. Brexit.") Even some operatives in his party thought he was running a terrible campaign: no organization, no ground game, no clue.

"We made a conscious decision to let that narrative continue," his deputy campaign manager, Michael Glassner, said in an interview, "because we believed that it was in our interest for them to underestimate us."

After Mitt Romney fell short in 2012, Republican National Committee Chairman Reince Priebus vowed not to let the Republicans get out-hustled again. The RNC spent more than $175 million to improve its ground game. They had a file of 197 million voters, each scored on a hundred-point scale for their likelihood to vote Republican. And the RNC deployed all these weapons in the service of Trump. Five days before Election Day, the RNC's models showed Trump winning Michigan by two-tenths of a point.

He left Wilmington and went on to Nevada.

Inside the Reno-Sparks Convention Center, where a young woman wore a pink hat that said *DEPLORABLE*, he continued his assault on Clinton.

"We didn't bring any so-called stars along—we didn't need them," he said, referring to the bevy of celebrities, from Jay-Z to Lady Gaga, who campaigned for Clinton in the final days. Her dazzling cast of surrogates included both Obamas, her ex-president husband, Vice President Biden and her former opponent, Bernie Sanders. In 2016 Trump ran against the Democrats, the Republicans, two political dynasties and the last three presidents. Through the force of his personality, he would defeat them all.

Trump would not win by mobilizing an unprecedented coalition of Republicans.

Opposite: **Trump supporters at a rally on November 2, 2016, in Miami.** *Top:* **Trump addresses a rally on November 4, 2016, in Wilmington, Ohio.**

(Indeed, at the time of publication, Clinton held a lead in the nationwide popular vote.) He would win because Clinton underperformed Obama's showing in 2008 and 2012.

There were chants of *U-S-A* and *LOCK HER UP*, and it seemed like a normal Trump rally until someone yelled something about a gun.

The sequence began when Trump noticed a protester in the crowd. "Oh, we have one of those guys from—from the Hillary Clinton campaign," he said. "How much are you being paid? Fifteen hundred dollars?"

He paused, shielding his eyes, looking back into the crowd. Two Secret Service agents ran onto the stage. "Go, go," one of them said, hustling him behind the curtain. People ran for the exits. Officers in tactical gear ran toward the stage. The officers led a man out of the room. The crowd went wild, chanting *U-S-A* again. The stage was empty for almost four minutes. Then Dan Scavino, Trump's director of social media, took the microphone.

"NOBODY IS GONNA STOP THIS MOVEMENT!" he shouted.

Trump swaggered back out. He let the applause wash over him.

"Nobody said it was going to be easy for us," he said. "But we will never be stopped. Never, ever be stopped."

The authorities never found a weapon. No arrests were made. Nevertheless, both Scavino and Donald Trump Jr. retweeted a Trump supporter who said, referring to Clinton's rain-shortened rally in Florida, "Hillary ran away from rain today. Trump is back on stage minutes after assassination attempt."

The violence that attended the 2016 campaign was unlike anything the nation had seen since the 1960s. There were victims and perpetrators on both sides, although markedly more on the Trump side. Left-wing protesters attacked Trump supporters, stealing their *MAKE AMERICA GREAT AGAIN* hats and setting them ablaze. Someone fire-bombed a Republican Party office in North Carolina. In Mississippi, someone torched

Top: **Trump steps to the side as his wife, Melania, speaks at a rally on November 4, 2016, in Wilmington, North Carolina.** *Opposite:* **Police close a men's room to question a man suspected of having a gun at a Trump rally November 5, 2016, in Reno, Nevada. They would find no gun.**

an African-American church, leaving the words *VOTE TRUMP* on the side. And some Trump supporters hinted at further violence if Clinton was elected.

"On November 8th, I'm voting for Trump," former Congressman Joe Walsh tweeted. "On November 9th, if Trump loses, I'm grabbing my musket. You in?"

It was an unsettling question, contrary to all protocols of American democracy. But it would be left unanswered.

✷ ✷ ✷

In late July, Clinton visited Johnstown, Pennsylvania, a desolate city of 20,000 whose welcoming committee included the bearer of a sign that said *KILLARY KILLED COAL*. Inside Johnstown Wire Technologies, where fine gray dust covered the surfaces, Adam Wisniewski said Johnstown had been so poor for so long that it barely felt the effects of the 2008 recession. He was 38 years old, delivering caskets part-time, and he knew people who sold food stamps to buy sports equipment for their children.

Bill Clinton's America once included Johnstown. When he ran for re-election in 1996, the Man from Hope won almost every state in Coal Country and the upper Midwest. Labor unions were stronger then, factory jobs

more plentiful, blue-collar white workers more inclined to vote Democratic. Johnstown is in Cambria County, which Bill Clinton won with 51 percent of the vote that year. Twenty years later, this county would help give the presidency to Trump.

Hillary Clinton knew she had to reach some of these white working-class voters, but she went about it awkwardly. During a CNN town hall in Ohio on March 13, she was talking about renewable energy and said:

"...We're going to put a lot of coal miners and coal companies out of business, right? And we're going to make it clear that we don't want to forget those people....Now we've got to move away from coal and all the other fossil fuels, but I don't want to move away from the people who did the best they could to produce the energy that we relied on."

What did people remember from that statement? *We're going to put a lot of coal miners out of business.*

"Her point was, 'I have a plan to help coal miners transition to a new economy,'" Clinton's director of speechwriting, Dan Schwerin, said in an interview. "More than anyone else in the campaign, she has cared and thought about how we can get to working-class white voters in places like Appalachia. It's just a cruel irony that her passion for this subject led to that; it came

The violence that attended the 2016 campaign was unlike anything the nation had seen since the 1960s. There were victims and perpetrators on both sides, although markedly more on the Trump side.

out in the wrong way with that comment."

Trump kept it simple. Signs at his convention said *TRUMP DIGS COAL*. He ran against *both* Clintons, blaming them for the free-trade agreements that he said were responsible for massive job losses. Their overall effect was closer to neutral, but *KILLARY KILLED COAL* had a nice ring. When Clinton visited Johnstown, the Trump campaign released a statement comparing it to a "robber visiting their victim." Could Trump actually bring jobs back to Johnstown? Adam Wisniewski didn't think so. To him, Trump's promise was just another drug, like the opioids that killed fifty-three people in Cambria County the previous year.

"People feel so lost today," he said. "They would rather just take the magic pill and go back to sleep."

All across the industrial Midwest, Hillary Clinton lost counties that had previously voted for Bill Clinton and Barack Obama. She lost Cambria County by 38 points, and she lost Pennsylvania.

★ ★ ★

She had two speeches written, just in case, and as the first results came in she was reviewing them at the hotel suite in Manhattan. Her top aides were there, along

> # The experts had been talking all year about chaos in the Republican Party, but it was the Democrats who had fallen apart.

with Bill and Chelsea and the grandkids. There was salmon with roasted carrots on the buffet in the hallway, vegan créme brûlée for dessert. The concession speech was a precaution from a woman who liked to be prepared. A mile and a half away at the Jacob K. Javits Convention Center, other staffers prepared for a victory party. The building had an actual glass ceiling. Cannons would fire green-tinted confetti that resembled shattered glass.

"Thinking about my daughter right now," a confident Tim Kaine tweeted at 8:30. "No little girl will ever again have to wonder whether she, too, can be president."

Clinton's own mother had been unwanted by her parents. Left to roam the streets of Chicago at age 4. Sent to live with her cruel grandmother at age 8. Turned out on her own at age 14. Her name was Dorothy. She got married, had children, spent her life giving them the home she never had. She took a break from hanging up the clothes to lie in the grass with her daughter and look up at the clouds. Dorothy Rodham died in 2011 at age 92, five years too early to witness this night. Her daughter was running for president a second time, and once again she would come up short.

At 11:07 p.m., CNN projected the battleground of North Carolina for Trump.

Around 11:20, a young Clinton staffer wiped away tears.

Around midnight, with Clinton still sequestered in the hotel, people began leaving the

Javits Center. At a bar nearby, a man lay on the floor and wept.

The returns kept coming in. Experts had expected Trump to lose, and to drag other Republicans down with him, costing them the Senate and drastically reducing their majority in the House. Instead, his long coattails helped them keep control of both chambers. The experts had been talking all year about chaos in the Republican Party, but it was the Democrats who had fallen apart. Obama's legacy was now in jeopardy, his many executive orders subject to nullification by President Trump, his signature health-care law in danger of being scaled back if not repealed altogether. The new president might choose as many as three or four Supreme Court justices, thus shaping the high court for decades to come and putting Roe v. Wade in question.

The Democrats had a candidate who connected with the angry white worker. Some of his rallies were even larger than Trump's. In the primaries he defeated Clinton in both Wisconsin and Michigan, hinting at the vulnerability of her Blue Wall. Head-to-head polls in May showed him leading Trump by as many as 15 points. But the Democrats nominated a status quo candidate when many voters desperately wanted change. And the Clinton campaign ignored the lessons of the primaries, essentially deciding to ignore Wisconsin and avoid Michigan as long as Trump did.

Opposite: **CNN, Instagram and CA Technologies projected results onto the Empire State Building on election night.** *Top:* **Clinton concedes the morning after the election, saying, "I know we have still not shattered that highest and hardest glass ceiling, but someday someone will, and hopefully sooner than we might think right now."**

CNN called the race at 2:48 a.m.

Opposite: Trump gives a victory speech in the wee hours of November 9, 2016. *Top:* Trump and his family pose for a portrait at a CNN town hall in April 2016. Top row, from left: Tiffany Trump, Vanessa Trump, Donald Trump Jr., Jared Kushner, Ivanka Trump, Melania Trump, Eric Trump and Lara Yunaska. Front row: Kai Madison Trump and Donald Trump.

Midnight turned to 1 and 2, with Clinton nowhere to be seen. The race had not been officially called, but it was clearly over. Her campaign chairman, John Podesta, addressed the weary faithful at the Javits Center.

"Several states are too close to call," he said on live television, provoking chants of *LOCK HER UP* at the Trump victory party about twenty blocks away. "...You should get some sleep."

Shortly after 2:30 a.m., Clinton called Trump to concede and offer congratulations. CNN called the race at 2:48. Trump took the microphone at 2:49 to chants of *U-S-A.* Despite his many previous threats, he said nothing about locking her up.

"Hillary has worked very long and very hard over a long period of time, and we owe her a major debt of gratitude for her service to our country," he said. "I mean that very sincerely. Now it's time for America to bind the wounds of division; have to get together. To all Republicans and Democrats and independents across this nation, I say it is time for us to come together as one united people."

For all the uproar over the racial tension he stirred, exit polls showed that Trump captured 8 percent of the black and 29 percent of the Latino vote, slightly better than Romney had in 2012. Clinton could not quite re-create the Obama coalition. She fell short among both minorities and young voters, as well as white-working-class voters in the Midwest.

And while she won women overall by 12 points, she lost white women by 10 points.

Later, Clinton's allies would blame Comey for lower-than-expected turnout—and for her

Bottom: **A Trump supporter celebrates at his victory party.** *Opposite:* **Clinton supporters watch electoral results during what they had hoped would be a victory party.**

Obama's legacy was now in jeopardy, his many executive orders subject to nullification by President Trump.

loss. They had seen encouraging trends in early voting before October 28, particularly among minorities. But on Election Day itself, Clinton did not hit her targets.

"If you were on the fence, and you were repelled by Trump and open to her, and the Comey letter happens, and you were reminded of the emails, a lot of people decided, 'Never mind,'" a senior adviser told CNN, speaking on condition of anonymity. "And it killed the mood among minority voters."

Next morning she had to face the cameras. At a ballroom in the New Yorker hotel, nearly all her top aides teared up. Her husband worked the rope line, wiping away tears. This would be one of the hardest things she had ever done.

A concession speech can be more important than a victory speech, and this concession speech was more important than any in recent memory. Clinton had just lost to a man she considered temperamentally unfit for the presidency. Her political career was probably over. The hopes of tens of millions of women were dashed. "A piece of me died last night," her supporter Ruth Ellis wrote in an email. Clinton had come so far, gotten so close, and it might be a long time before voters gave a woman another chance. Her own mother had died waiting for the first woman president,

and no one knew how many others would do the same. She said the glass ceiling would shatter one day, a reference to her concession speech from eight years earlier. She told her followers not to lose heart. And she told them to give Trump a chance.

"Last night, I congratulated Donald Trump and offered to work with him on behalf of our country," Clinton said. "I hope that he will be a successful president for *all* Americans."

She lingered on the word *all*, making the emphasis unmistakable. It sounded like a challenge, and maybe a prayer.

Protests broke out that night in several major cities. In Los Angeles, young Latinos kindled a piñata in the shape of Trump's head and chanted, *NOT MY PRESIDENT! NOT MY PRESIDENT!* But he was, or would be soon. He would not just preside over the roughly 60 million people who voted for him. He would preside over the slightly larger number who did not. He would preside over the flag-wavers on the plains of Iowa and the flag-burners on the streets of New York. He would preside over Jersey Dave Calabro, Khizr Khan, the young men and women in Los Angeles who gave his effigy a crown of fire. Now he had the power he wanted. It was time to bring together the nation he had helped to drive apart.

An optimistic sign points the way to Trump's election night party.

The empty podium at the Clinton election night party. Clinton did not appear.

"Thinking about my daughter right now."
—tweet from Tim Kaine before the election results were known

A chocolate cake created for Trump's election night party.

"Nobody said it was going to be easy for us. But we will never be stopped. Never, ever be stopped."
—Donald Trump

A campaign worker steams wrinkles out of the flags that will serve as the backdrop for Trump's victory speech.

The Clintons vote in Chappaqua, New York.

"On November 9th, if Trump loses, I'm grabbing my musket. You in?"

—tweet from former Congressman Joe Walsh

...dent-elect Trump kisses his wife, Melania, at his election night celebration.

"A piece of me died last night."

—Clinton supporter Ruth Ellis

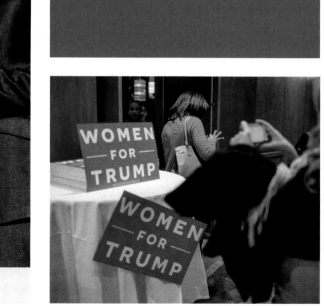

"Several states are too close to call.... You should get some sleep."

—Clinton campaign chairman John Podesta

A Clinton supporter at what was supposed to have been her victory party.

"People feel so lost today."

—Adam Wisniewski of Johnstown, Pennsylvania

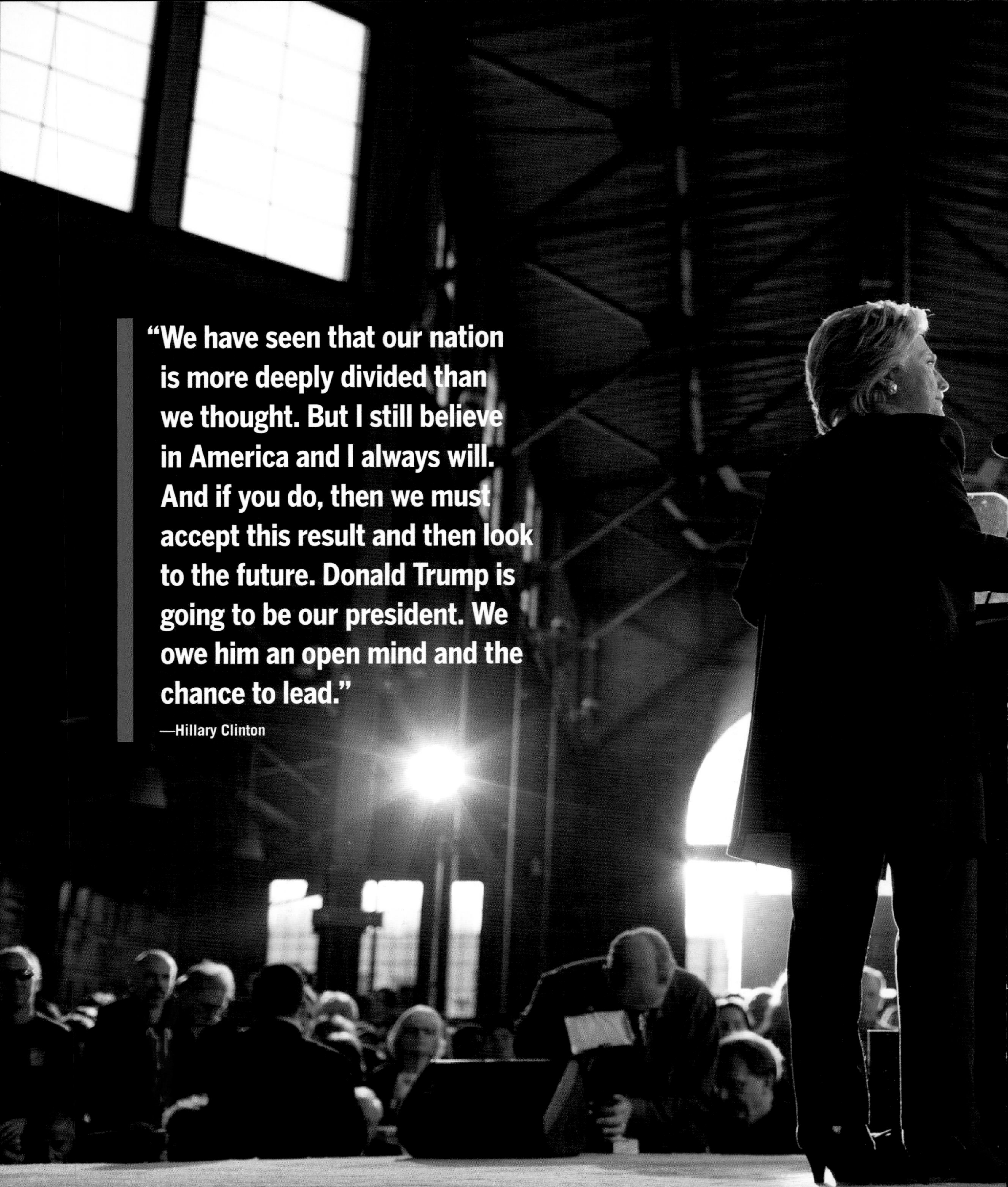

"We have seen that our nation is more deeply divided than we thought. But I still believe in America and I always will. And if you do, then we must accept this result and then look to the future. Donald Trump is going to be our president. We owe him an open mind and the chance to lead."

—Hillary Clinton

"Now it's time for America to bind the wounds of division.... To all Republicans and Democrats and independents across this nation, I say it is time for us to come together as one united people."

—Donald Trump

MAY 20TH 1775

N★C

APRIL 12TH 1776

"Ours was not a campaign but rather an incredible and great movement, made up of millions of hardworking men and women who love their country and want a better, brighter future for themselves and for their family."

—Donald Trump

"I hope that he will be a successful president for *all* Americans."

—Hillary Clinton

WA
CLINTON 54.3%
TRUMP 38.1%

OR
CLINTON 50.1%
TRUMP 39.1%

MT
TRUMP 56.5%
CLINTON 35.9%

ID
TRUMP 59.3%
CLINTON 27.5%

ND
TRUMP 63.0%
CLINTON 27.2%

MN
CLINTON 46.4%
TRUMP 44.9%

TRUMP
CLI

SD
TRUMP 61.5%
CLINTON 31.7%

WY
TRUMP 68.2%
CLINTON 21.9%

IA
TRUMP 51.2%
CLINTON 41.7%

NV
CLINTON 47.9%
TRUMP 45.5%

NE
TRUMP 60.2%
CLINTON 34.1%

UT
TRUMP 45.4%
CLINTON 27.8%

CO
CLINTON 48.2%
TRUMP 43.3%

CA
CLINTON 61.7%
TRUMP 32.7%

KS
TRUMP 57.2%
CLINTON 36.2%

MO
TRUMP
CLINTON

AZ
TRUMP 49.0%
CLINTON 45.5%

NM
CLINTON 48.3%
TRUMP 40.0%

OK
TRUMP 65.3%
CLINTON 28.9%

AR
TRUMP
60.6%
CLINTON
33.6%

TX
TRUMP 52.4%
CLINTON 43.3%

L
TRU
58
CLIN
38.

AK
TRUMP 51.6%
CLINTON 36.4%

HI
CLINTON 62.2%
TRUMP 30.0%

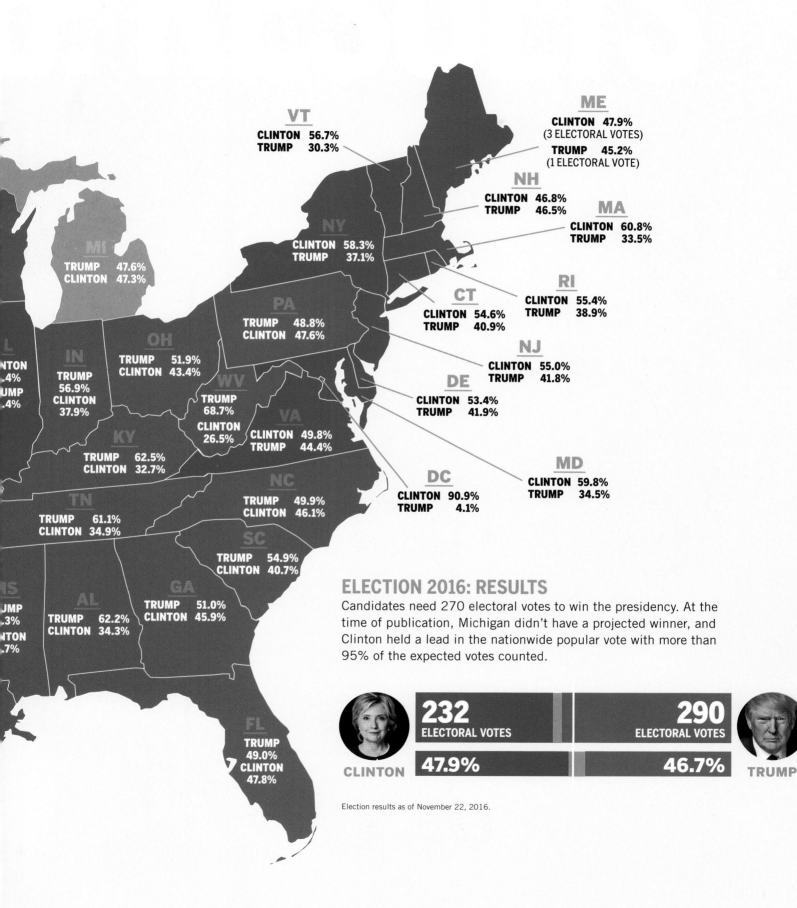

VT
CLINTON 56.7%
TRUMP 30.3%

ME
CLINTON 47.9%
(3 ELECTORAL VOTES)
TRUMP 45.2%
(1 ELECTORAL VOTE)

NH
CLINTON 46.8%
TRUMP 46.5%

MA
CLINTON 60.8%
TRUMP 33.5%

NY
CLINTON 58.3%
TRUMP 37.1%

RI
CLINTON 55.4%
TRUMP 38.9%

MI
TRUMP 47.6%
CLINTON 47.3%

CT
CLINTON 54.6%
TRUMP 40.9%

PA
TRUMP 48.8%
CLINTON 47.6%

NJ
CLINTON 55.0%
TRUMP 41.8%

OH
TRUMP 51.9%
CLINTON 43.4%

IN
TRUMP 56.9%
CLINTON 37.9%

DE
CLINTON 53.4%
TRUMP 41.9%

L
NTON
.4%
UMP
.4%

WV
TRUMP 68.7%
CLINTON 26.5%

VA
CLINTON 49.8%
TRUMP 44.4%

KY
TRUMP 62.5%
CLINTON 32.7%

MD
CLINTON 59.8%
TRUMP 34.5%

NC
TRUMP 49.9%
CLINTON 46.1%

DC
CLINTON 90.9%
TRUMP 4.1%

TN
TRUMP 61.1%
CLINTON 34.9%

SC
TRUMP 54.9%
CLINTON 40.7%

GA
TRUMP 51.0%
CLINTON 45.9%

AL
TRUMP 62.2%
CLINTON 34.3%

S
JMP
.3%
NTON
.7%

ELECTION 2016: RESULTS

Candidates need 270 electoral votes to win the presidency. At the time of publication, Michigan didn't have a projected winner, and Clinton held a lead in the nationwide popular vote with more than 95% of the expected votes counted.

FL
TRUMP 49.0%
CLINTON 47.8%

232
ELECTORAL VOTES

290
ELECTORAL VOTES

CLINTON

47.9%

46.7%

TRUMP

Election results as of November 22, 2016.

CREDITS AND ACKNOWLEDGMENTS

PHOTOGRAPHY

Ralph Alswang
230

Philip Scott Andrews for CNN
22–23 (bottom), 120, 121, 123 and 128

Nancy Borowick for CNN
74, 100, 214–215, 225, 227 and 271

Gabriella Demczuk for CNN
273 and 278–279

Hossein Fatemi/Panos
117, 130, 158, 159 and 161

Taylor Glascock for CNN
70–71, 73, 80 and 85

Melissa Golden for CNN
22–23 (top), 25, 42, 43, 164 and 167

Melissa Golden/Redux for CNN
82, 84, 99, 101, 102, 104 and 270

Nate Gowdy
36, 38, 39, 40, 41 and 155

Nate Gowdy for CNN
50–51 and 67

Michelle Gustafson
57

David S. Holloway/CNN
52, 94, 105, 118, 140–141, 144, 145 and 200

David Hume Kennerly for CNN
2, 19, 20, 63, 114–115, 116, 122, 127, 132, 134–135
(bottom), 151, 168–169, 170, 174–175, 178, 179,
184–185, 194–195, 197, 209, 210, 216, 217, 218,
219, 220, 221, 222–223, 226, 228, 232, 233, 234,
235, 236, 238, 239, 240–241, 242, 245, 246, 248,
250, 251, 256–257, 259, 261, 262, 263, 264, 265,
272, 280–281 and 282–283

Vincent Laforet for CNN
109

Vincent Laforet & Mike Isler for CNN
266 and 268–269

Wayne Lawrence for CNN
95, 108 and 137

Philip Montgomery for CNN
86

Landon Nordeman for CNN
26–27, 29, 30, 31, 32–33, 34, 35 and 46–47 (all)

John Nowak/CNN
15, 58, 62, 97, 129, 149, 173, 183, 186, 187 and 204

Martin Parr/Magnum Photos for CNN
72, 176, 177 and 180

Nigel Parry for CNN
44, 64, 75, 134–135 (top two rows) and 285

Edward M. Pio Roda/CNN
55

Jonno Rattman
89 and 154

Molly Riley
69

Adam Rose/CNN
53, 54, 60, 78, 81, 96, 138, 171, 182 and 199

Callie Shell for CNN
13, 61, 68, 76, 90–91, 93, 103, 106, 124–125, 131, 139, 142, 143, 201, 202, 206, 207, 208, 247, 258, 260, 267 and 276–277

CNN's "State of the Union"
10

Peter van Agtmael/Magnum Photos for CNN
152–153, 156–157, 172, 188, 198 and 205

COLLAGE PAGE PHOTOGRAPHY CREDITS

190, clockwise from top left: David Hume Kennerly for CNN; Peter van Agtmael/Magnum Photos for CNN; Peter van Agtmael/Magnum Photos for CNN; John Nowak/CNN.

191, clockwise from top left: Martin Parr/Magnum Photos for CNN; Adam Rose/CNN; Martin Parr/Magnum Photos for CNN; John Nowak/CNN; Adam Rose/CNN.

212, clockwise from top left: Adam Rose/CNN; Martin Parr/Magnum Photos for CNN; Callie Shell for CNN; Adam Rose/CNN; Peter van Agtmael/Magnum Photos for CNN.

213, clockwise from top left: Adam Rose/CNN; Callie Shell for CNN; John Nowak/CNN; Peter van Agtmael/Magnum Photos for CNN.

274, clockwise from top left: Melissa Golden/Redux for CNN; Callie Shell for CNN; Melissa Golden/Redux for CNN; Melissa Golden/Redux for CNN.

275, clockwise from top left: Gabriella Demczuk for CNN, Callie Shell for CNN, Melissa Golden/Redux for CNN, Gabriella Demczuk for CNN, David Hume Kennerly for CNN.

Special thanks to Elizabeth I. Johnson and Brett Roegiers for their photo editing, and Greg Chen for his help with photos and design.

Special thanks to Susan Baer for her countless contributions to this book.

This book was reported by Thomas Lake, Jodi Enda and Susan Baer.

CNN would like to thank the following for their contributions to this project:

Jim Acosta, Jennifer Agiesta, Meredith Artley, Ted Barrett, Samantha Barry, Dana Bash, Eve Bauer, Eric Bradner, Pamela Brown, Steve Brusk, Dylan Byers, Stephany Cardet, David Chalian, Nitya Chambers, Ashley Codianni, Marshall Cohen, Cullen Daly, Rick Davis, Jeremy Diamond, Matt Dornic, Sam Feist, Jamie Gangel, Allison Gollust, Noah Gray, Richard Griffiths, Nia-Malika Henderson, Katie Hinman, Steve Holmes, Brianna Keilar, Ashley Killough, Betsy Klein, Allie Kleva, Tal Kopan, Emily Kuhn, Rebecca Kutler, Elizabeth Landers, MJ Lee, Adam Levy, Tom LoBianco, Phil Mattingly, Dan Merica, Chris Moody, Andrew Morse, Virginia Moseley, Sara Murray, Ed O'Keefe, Lauren Pratapas, Mark Preston, Manu Raju, Gabe Ramirez, Maeve Reston, Nicole Ridgway, Meshach Rojas, Arielle Sacks, Theodore Schleifer, Eugene Scott, Sunlen Serfaty, Drew Shenkman, Rachel Smolkin, Cassie Spodak, Manav Tanneeru, Gregory Wallace, Deirdre Walsh, Tal Yellin, Robert Yoon, Jeff Zeleny and Jeff Zucker.

MELCHER MEDIA

President, CEO: Charles Melcher
VP, COO: Bonnie Eldon
Senior Producer: John Morgan
Production Manager: Susan Lynch
Editorial Assistant: Karl Daum
Design by Chika Azuma

Melcher Media would like to thank Callie Barlow, Jess Bass, Emma Blackwood, Shannon Fanuko, Patty Gloeckler, Barbara Gogan, Luke Jarvis, Aaron Kenedi, Kaarina Mackenzie, Karolina Manko, Sarah Melton, Lauren Nathan, Laura Roumanos, Rachel Schlotfeldt, William Shinker, Elizabeth Shreve, Victoria Spencer, Megan Worman and Katy Yudin.

"IT'S PRETTY STRANGE TO PUT SOMETHING LIKE THAT OUT WITH

NOT JUST STRANGE; IT'S UNPRECEDENTED, AND IT IS DEEPLY TROU

DO KNOW IS WHEN HILLARY CLINTON SAYS, 'THIS IS UNPRECEDENT

AND INDEED UNNECESSARY IS HER HAVING THAT PRIVATE SERVER I

▶ "THERE ARE SOME FOLKS OUT THERE WHO ARE COMMENTING T

ENGAGED IN A PRESIDENTIAL CAMPAIGN, AND THAT MAY BE TRUE

ELECTION, AND THAT'S WHY I'M OUT HERE."—MICHELLE OBAMA, F

FLORIDA; THEY'RE OUTVOTING DEMOCRATS IN PENNSYLVANIA. THAT

STATES HOUSE OF REPRESENTATIVES ▶ "THIS EVENT IS UNPRECED

TIME IT IS AN OPEN SEAT, AND THERE IS NO HEIR APPARENT."—ST